D1766551

Books should be returned or renewed by the last date above. Renew by phone **03000 41 31 31** or online *www.kent.gov.uk/libs*

C334740397

Sir Andras Schiff was born in Budapest in 1953. He has made a huge impact with his cyclical performances of Bach, Haydn, Mozart, Beethoven, Schubert, Chopin, Schumann and Bartók, and he has been awarded many international prizes.

Martin Meyer was editor-in-chief of the Swiss daily newspaper, *NZZ*. In addition to his journalism and essays, he has published several books, including *Conversations* with Alfred Brendel.

Music Comes
Out of Silence

András Schiff

Translated by Misha Donat

W&N
WEIDENFELD & NICOLSON

First published in Great Britain in 2020 by Weidenfeld & Nicolson
This paperback edition published in 2021 by Weidenfeld & Nicolson
an imprint of The Orion Publishing Group Ltd
Carmelite House, 50 Victoria Embankment
London EC4Y 0DZ

An Hachette UK Company

10 9 8 7 6 5 4 3 2 1

A CIP catalogue record for this book is
available from the British Library.

ISBN (Mass Market Paperback) 978 1 4746 1528 0
ISBN (eBook) 978 1 4746 1529 7

Typeset by Input Data Services Ltd, Somerset

Printed and bound in Great Britain by Clays Ltd, Elcograf S.p.A.

MIX
Paper from
responsible sources
FSC® C104740

www.weidenfeldandnicolson.co.uk
www.orionbooks.co.uk

Contents

A Note on the Text

All music is interpretation. Each musical text offers its readers guidance and direction on how to bring that music into existence. But behind every command or notation lies the imagination, and it is this that brings the music out of its silence, out of mere possibility, into performance in the here and now. Few musicians have thought about this process, as music moves from idea to reality, as intensely and precisely as András Schiff. Pianist, conductor, scientist and commentator, he is the product of numerous qualities and experiences. And in the end, music is about the performance, expressed as a statement that can be understood in the present day – and beyond.

Schiff did not become a virtuoso in order to further his own ends. Even in his youth he had a deep awareness of the responsibilities for one's own actions. Indeed, he views music as a combination of not only work and research but also spirituality and conscience, and all this is expressed through the masters, from Bach to Haydn, Mozart to Beethoven, Schubert and Schumann to Brahms.

Schiff's ability to combine intellectual tension with the sensual qualities of playing is singular. In other words, when we hear Schiff perform, we cannot help but recognize that a truly attentive musical mind must not only read the music, but consider it, guide it, even argue with it in order to produce truly great sound. For nothing would be gained if the many insights, research, knowledge and reflections involved did not lead to sound.

This book is all-encompassing, in the same sense as a *tour d'horizon*, addressing the essential points of biography, while exploring the secrets and adventures of music with a view to its design. Schiff proves to be a generous partner in conversation, discussing a multitude of topics with verve and passion, as well as his well-known – and often self-deprecating – sense of humour. Above all else, one thing is clear: the vocation of a musician does not come about by itself or because of some latent ability or talent. It requires patience and a great deal of hard work. No example is more illustrative of this than the fact that Schiff did not dive into the cosmos of Beethoven's sonatas as a talented young man, but instead, did so only relatively recently, having invested a lifetime of preparatory work.

This book is comprised of two parts. The second part contains a rich series of essays, analyses and portraits. Schiff writes about his favourite works and composers in a precise and inspired way and many of them will be familiar to you. This doesn't make an essayist's job any easier! On the contrary, the whole world seems to know what Bach, Schubert, Mozart or Mendelssohn should sound like. Sometimes it seems as if we've heard it all – until we listen to Schiff, who brings something newer, more exciting, more profound, and clearer to the table. These writings stand as testaments to Schiff's talent for the written word.

The first part shows conversations that András and I had at regular intervals over the course of two years. These conversations always seemed to me to be like music, just waiting to be launched from silence.

Martin Meyer
Zurich, January 2020

Part 1

MAKING MUSIC
OUT OF SILENCE

Conversations with Martin Meyer

Music and interpretation

Let's begin with a fundamental question: what for you is the meaning of music, what is its essence?

To begin with there is silence, and music comes out of silence. Then comes the miracle of highly varied, progressive forms growing out of sounds and structures. After that, the silence returns. And so, silence is actually a prerequisite for music. But going on from that, music of course means much more to me personally, because it's my life. It can never be reduced to mere material standpoints, even though repeated attempts to do that have been, and still are being made. Music essentially has to do with the spirit and the spiritual.

And, of course, with the soul, with emotions.

You could say that music essentially comes from the soul. That, by the way, differentiates people from animals. Some birds make wonderful music – just think, for example, how Olivier Messiaen reacted to that in composing. But the difference can perhaps be understood through a comparison. When swallows build a nest it's something we certainly admire, but at the same time we wouldn't call it high art or architecture. What differentiates Florence Cathedral from a swallow's nest? The deliberate intent to create a work of spirit and soul. And so there's also a fundamental difference between the song of the nightingale and Bach's *The Art of Fugue*.

To what extent does music affect you in a religious sense?

Quite a lot. When I occupy myself intensively with the works of Bach or the string quartets of Beethoven, I hear and feel things which can't be explained in purely rational terms. And so I hope that the music doesn't simply become extinct, but that each note somehow remains stored in the cosmos, perhaps transformed, but in any case doesn't become lost.

What happens when you perform the music yourself?
What considerations come into play?

I try to listen very attentively. Essentially, it's a question of following the sounds I produce with a third ear. The better developed this third ear is, the better the musician is, too. I had already developed this 'gift' as a student and was encouraged by my teachers to listen inwardly. That's why it's dangerous and even disastrous to sing out aloud while playing the piano. People think they can hear well at the same time, but that's a mistake. It's the piano that has to sing, not the pianist.

Music differs from other arts in being organised in time
and having fixed points between its appearance and
disappearance. On top of that, it's the least representational
of all the arts in its high level of abstraction. For practising
musicians, that's another immense challenge.

In addition, there's the fact that – as a rule, unlike literature – music is multilayered. Disregarding Gregorian chant and other related monodies, and concentrating in particular on the piano, music is almost always polyphonic. You have to

4

play several voices – as though several theatrical actors were enouncing their texts simultaneously. That virtually never happens on the stage. That's why music demands the highest concentration – particularly with Bach, in a four-part fugue, for instance, where all the voices are equal.

We've talked about disappearance. Again, in comparison with other arts, but also taken in isolation, the classical music we know and are considering has had a very short existence, barely six centuries up to now, so we don't know how it's going to develop further.

That's interesting, and perhaps worrying, too. Mind you, there have been certain cycles in the other arts, if we think, for instance, of Italian or Dutch painting. High points are followed by declines and barren periods. In music, I look at it like this: Western music reaches an absolute peak with Bach; then it experiences a second golden age in the Viennese classics up to the death of Schubert, in 1828. There are further productive periods with the romantics and late romantics, as well as the music of the early twentieth century. After that there's a comparatively long period of static development. Or to put it more provocatively, if we wanted to compile a list of musical masterpieces composed since the Second World War, it would be terribly short.

With art and literature, things would certainly look rather different.

That's true. Music is comparatively alone in that way. On the other hand, we shouldn't forget that there were a large number of relatively untalented minor composers in the days of Haydn, Mozart and Beethoven. But to go back to structural principles, and to the reason I love this period so much, the Viennese classical style is a 'language' in sonata form – exposition, development, recapitulation. And in addition, tonic, dominant, subdominant, mediant and so on. To put it another way, you always know where you are. These days, with contemporary music, you often feel as though you're in an airless space.

Is there a development in music in the sense of a history of progress? Of one thing emerging from another and taking it forward in an evolutionary way?

I don't see it like that. You can't seriously argue that Brahms is more progressive than Bach. Though, of course, there's the consciousness of the period to which they belong, which makes composers dissociate themselves, on the whole respectfully, from their predecessors. Then figures who dare to do something new suddenly appear, and over-turn everything. And there are giant figures such as Bach or Beethoven.

Bach certainly wasn't an artist who wanted to be particularly original.

He wasn't, but among many other things he was a genius at assimilating – for instance, Italian and French baroque music from Vivaldi, Corelli and Domenico Scarlatti to Lully, Rameau and Couperin. In some respects, Bach's son Carl Philipp Emanuel was more original and revolutionary. All the same, he never achieved the stature of his father. On the other hand, he built the bridge that leads from Johann Sebastian Bach to Haydn, Mozart and Beethoven, and we have to value him highly for that.

Why haven't you engaged with Carl Philipp Emanuel as a performer? That way, two rather original minds would have met head-on.

It's hard to say. Perhaps I'll still get round to it. But Carl Philipp Emanuel is really another world which demands intensive work and meticulous study. For me, his *Essay on the True Art of Playing the Keyboard* is the most important book on music of all time. I used to read it like a Bible, and still do.

So, in sum, one can hardly demand that the new must always become newer.

Even Mozart isn't particularly original: Haydn and Beethoven are far more so. And yet, in other ways, Mozart is incomparable.

The themes, the melodies, the cantabile, the proportions . . .

Exactly. Mozart is a fantastic melodist, perhaps the greatest of all, alongside Schubert. On top of that he is a marvellous magician in the realm of tone colour. But when we look at the piano sonatas, for instance, they are often quite schematically designed and in no way revolutionary.

So, 500 years of Western music, a pinnacle? Then plateaus again?

There is music elsewhere. I'm very fascinated by Indian classical music, for instance, which is an art music built out of different scales, with quarter- and eighth-tones, and extremely complex rhythms. On the other hand, it's significant that European classical music has aroused so much interest and response in the Far East (Japan, China, South Korea), and yet much less so in India. Why? Because India has its own very rich musical culture.

Can Indian classical music be compared to Western in the spiritual sense?

I'm no specialist. But I feel it as very pure and spiritual. In the West, the roots of this spirituality come from church music, Gregorian chant.

But why is there such enthusiasm for Western music in Japan and China?

That's hard to answer, because China's folklore is very interesting and Japan also has its own musical culture. But it functions mostly as court music – it accompanies ritual ceremonies. On the other hand, Beethoven's Ninth, for instance, is played in Japan hundreds of times every December.

So, is there something universal about Western classical music that speaks directly to people?

Presumably. This is music that's always made to be heard anew. If we take literature, there's not such a strong impulse for repetition, even though as I grow older – and despite my continual interest in new literature – I return with increasing frequency to my 'old friends'. With the passing of the years, and the richer experiences that accrue, one reads them differently. That goes for paintings, too: the same picture suddenly appears in a new light.

To what extent is it possible to 'universalise' musical knowledge and experience?

I think we simply don't know enough about that, even from a scientific point of view. Take the emotional demands. I know precisely where in a Schubert sonata I get the proverbial goose-pimples. But then I notice that other people, including practising musicians, are affected and stirred by other moments.

Let's take the transition into the recapitulation in the first movement of Schubert's C minor Sonata, where there's a swirling and murmuring which makes one's hair stand on end.

Absolutely! That passage is terrifying in the true sense of the word. As a performer, I naturally want the audience to react to it sufficiently. But that's often wishful thinking: success is by no means guaranteed.

It's all a question of contrasts and textures, too. So goose-pimples are rather exceptional.

As a drama unfolding in time, the trajectory of music is complex, even in its emotional content. For example, when a friend comes to me and asks me to play him the 25th variation from the 'Goldberg' Variations, I say to him: 'If you like. But you're misunderstanding something fundamental: without doubt, the 25th variation is absolutely wonderful. But should it be taken away from its context?' The placing of this variation is crucial. In a concert, it needs a 'run-in' of nearly an hour. To put it another way, a culmination of this kind relies on its preparation – it has to be built-up and can't be 'summoned forth' in a single second.

Music lovers should be made to experience such things first hand, and that's become much more difficult since fewer and fewer children, at least in Europe, are learning to play an instrument.

Education and experience are important, of course. On the other hand, there are so-called simple people without any previous experience who are suddenly deeply moved by music and those magical moments we're talking about. Sometimes too much thought can be a hindrance. Admittedly, it's not a disadvantage for people who treasure the C minor Sonata to know that Schubert also composed *Winterreise*. Equally, it's useful to have read Goethe's *Erlkönig*, and to know Schubert's setting of the ballad, when one listens to the sonata's fourth movement.

That's equally true for musicians, and their task of interpreting it.

Certainly, and an acquaintance with the musical text is important. If we compare a page of Bach with one of Chopin, even a layman can immediately see that Bach hardly provides any instructions, whereas Chopin prescribes extremely detailed performance directions. Bach told his pupils how his music should go. They passed his indications on, and so, to a certain extent, they became common knowledge among both connoisseurs and amateurs of the time. Chopin was himself an outstanding pianist, but he lived in different times. He wrote for publication, and so he wanted to provide more detailed information to purchasers and performers of the editions of his works.

In the romantic period, subjectivity plays a much larger role: moods, ideas and associations proliferate in the piece, and need to be taken into account as interpretive indications. The composers of the romantic generation give far more precise instructions and directions than their predecessors. Nevertheless, performers do not all play the same way: there is still sufficient flexibility. To put it another way, the details of the notation are not such as to lead to any greater uniformity of interpretation.

Fortunately! Otherwise it would be terribly boring. You have to take into consideration in any case that the indications, however precise they may be, have no more than limited meaningfulness. Take Bartók. He was a fabulous interpreter of his own music. His scores give quite precise indications of tempo, and not only in the form of metronome markings. Yet, when we listen to his recordings, we notice wonderful liberties which don't reflect what he wrote. In this respect, Bartók is a great model for me: freedom and exactitude, but in addition *rubato* and *parlando* – just as one speaks.

But you don't set out to imitate Bartók – deliberately to play him in the way that he did.

No. Some people may do that. But in any interpretation worth taking seriously, the personality of the performer plays a part. At the same time, of course, I know how Bartók played his works; and I even know that when – as in the case of his Sonata – we have no recordings. Besides being familiar with the language of music, I'm familiar with the Hungarian language: the stresses, the accents, the strong and weak syllables and so on. All of that provides a way in for the performance. I've noticed that pianists who don't speak a word of German make huge mistakes in accentuation and phrasing, etc. with Bach or Beethoven. They don't realise that the composer may write music that's universal, but at the same time he thinks in German. Debussy thinks in French, Verdi in Italian. With operas, that's immediately apparent; in instrumental music, much less so. Mozart thinks half in German, half in Italian. Janáček was obsessed with the Czech language. Occasionally, I hear English singers in Bartók's *Bluebeard's Castle*. A critic attests to their impeccable Hungarian. But the same critic doesn't know a word of Hungarian . . . It's not so simple. The great Cecilia Bartoli is so scrupulous that she doesn't sing any German Lieder, because she doesn't feel sufficiently comfortable with the language. Others do everything, willy-nilly, without the slightest self-criticism.

Repertoire

Let's get on to repertoire. You came around to performing Beethoven's piano sonatas relatively late.

That was a very conscious decision. I really wanted to have accumulated experiences. Beethoven was the hardest nut to crack. Especially the middle period, with the 'Waldstein' and 'Appassionata' sonatas. I needed a lot of time to find the right tone of voice for the 'Appassionata'. For years I was influenced by Richter's recordings. These days I have a more distant relationship to them, and there are many things about them that don't appeal to me at all any more. But in those days! That 'presto impossibile' in the coda of the finale of the 'Appassionata' is unbelievable.

From a purely technical point of view the sonata isn't tremendously difficult.

Yes, it is. And how! You can play the cascade of semi-quavers near the start of the first movement accurately a hundred times in your living room, and yet in the concert they suddenly go awry. Why? Because you're nervous. But nerves are psychological. Some youngsters already play everything, even the most musically difficult things, without having the slightest idea about their contents. To me, that attitude smacks of impudence and a lack of reverence. Young people aren't scared of anything anymore – they have no respect.

Where does that attitude come from?

From teachers, parents, managers. I recently had a 14-year-old who wanted to play me Liszt's 'Dante Sonata'. I refused to listen to it, because he didn't know anything about the *Divine Comedy*. On the other hand, there are pieces that are very suitable for youngsters and youthful technical wizards. I've experienced that for myself.

What about modern classics? And contemporary music? You've never played Schoenberg's Piano Concerto.

To be honest, that's a piece that doesn't particularly appeal to me. My relationship with Schoenberg is altogether somewhat problematical. Certainly, I respect him. But Alban Berg means much more to me. I played all of Schoenberg's piano works up to Op.33. I experimented, in order to find out how I felt about them. After that, I bade farewell to Schoenberg. As far as contemporary music is concerned, much of it is simply incompatible with the way I play the piano, and with what tonal refinement means to me. When a composer requires the instrument to be treated with brute force I have to pass. Only a few performers can master both classical and contemporary styles. The oboist Heinz Holliger, for instance, is a great example. I'm conscious of the fact that it's easy to garner the enthusiasm of critics with new music.

Has your repertoire fundamentally changed in the last 40 years?

It has developed and filled out. Bach as the father figure and the Viennese classics remain the main pillars. Mendelssohn, Chopin, Schumann and Brahms have always been essential, too. Later I added Janáček, who wrote wonderful music. Bartók has always been present. Bohemian music – Dvořák, Smetana – came into my repertoire somewhat later, encouraged by Rafael Kubelík. And so I got to know Dvořák's Piano Concerto, and also solo pieces by Smetana and Janáček. When I really love and cherish a composer, I always want to perform his complete works. But that's mostly beyond the realms of possibility.

To go back to the ideas of difficulties, maturity, nerves, aren't the 'Goldberg' Variations much harder than the 'Appassionata'?

You can't compare the two. A great Beethoven sonata is laid out unambiguously and has a definite character. On top of that, Beethoven's notation is extremely precise. And yet we so often hear poor performances of these works. Why is that?

Because pianists aren't sufficiently intelligent.

Sometimes, like certain conductors of period-instrument performances, they stick doggedly to metronome markings. But it's not as simple as that. Rubato and the large-scale structure, the transitions – all those have to be taken into account with a work such as the 'Appassionata' so that the music can impart its spirit accordingly.

Musical transitions: but that goes for everything – for Chopin, for instance.

Certainly. From that point of view Chopin's B flat minor Sonata is an extremely difficult work, and the same is true of the Ballades.

Let's take another composer, such as Busoni. What is your attitude towards him?

A very interesting figure! I could mention the Toccata, which I've studied even if I haven't performed it; or the Sonatinas and the Elegies. Wonderful. On the other hand, I can't summon up much enthusiasm for the gargantuan Piano Concerto. It's imbalanced, with the Tarantella followed by the choral 'Cantico': was that necessary? There are specialists who may know their way around it better, but it's their territory. However, I do play the Second Violin Sonata and the 'Fantasia contrappuntistica' for two pianos with passionate enthusiasm.

Have you ever composed yourself?

I've tried. But I've never completed anything other than

cadenzas. Obviously, nothing occurs to me. But I believe I have a precise and definite idea of what constitutes great music.

The work – and the composer

The paths towards the work are many, but preparation is necessary. On the other hand, the composer would not or should not want to be the only authority when it comes to performing a piece. If Bartók, for instance, had not laid down the law as to how a piece of his should sound, then you could say that there would be more justification to play it differently from the way in which the composer himself did.

Those are very interesting but difficult points to answer. Certainly, Bartók would have been the first to say that there are several ways of approaching things. As a counter example, we could take my former teacher, György Kurtág, whom I consider to be the greatest living composer. Kurtág is much less flexible than Bartók. He goes further than Bartók in his notation, inasmuch as he invents additional markings – for example, intermediate durations within individual crotchets or quavers. But what can never be accurately notated is speech-melody: declamation, rhetoric, how we speak. We all speak differently – lengthen a syllable, accentuate here or there, raise or lower our voice, and so on. Bartók attempted to be as precise as possible, though at times it becomes utopian. He once said to the violinist Sándor Végh, 'I notate for people who are not as musical as you. You don't need these immensely detailed directions. You feel intuitively what I have written.'

Briefly, back to Kurtág – would it be possible for him to correct your playing when you perform one of his pieces?

Of course. When I play something to him he has a comment to make about every single note. He's basically unhappy about each note, but he can sing all of them wonderfully or reproduce them on the piano. It's almost like a psychological state of mind. Kurtág is an extremely intense person, and it's difficult or even impossible to empathise with that intensity. It would inevitably lead to stress. If anyone wants to play to Kurtág, he is always prepared to work for hours, and sometimes days, with the performer. Sometimes I say to myself, 'God preserve the 92-year-old Kurtág until he's 120. What would happen to this work if it was still here, and he wasn't?'

It will be played, and it will be played in different ways, because, as we've said, it is 'more' than the composer intended to express with it.

To me, it's incredibly important to study manuscripts and facsimiles. That way, I understand much more of the composer's creative process and mental state. The printed music is already a completely cleansed and sanitised version. Recordings in which a composer conducts or plays his music are also interesting to me, especially when they're made by such outstanding pianists as Bartók or Rachmaninov. They set benchmarks. Or, in another field, when Thomas Mann reads one of his stories himself it's very instructive – even when compared to a recording by an actor. Actors often tend towards pathos when reading. Is that really necessary?

Kurtág was above all your teacher in your dealings with other composers. How did that work?

In dealing with Bach, Beethoven or Schubert, he was again concerned with detail, yet on the whole much more free. He explored and sought solutions and sounds. The same goes for my friend Heinz Holliger with his own pieces. Unlike Kurtág, Heinz is quite relaxed about dealing with different interpretations. For all the absurd difficulty of his pieces, there's no imperative from him that dictates: 'It must go thus.' That certainly stems from the fact that Heinz is also a practical musician.

There's no harm in being pragmatic, not least because interpretation is accompanied by so many imponderables, so many chance elements, which aren't directly related to musical understanding.

Let's suppose I have to, or want to, perform a work by a specific date. Then there's a firm deadline, and you have to get by as well as you can. With Kurtág's demands you will never meet your goal. Kurtág has been composing his opera *Endgame*, based on Samuel Beckett's play, for many years. Maybe he'll never finish it. The opera might just as well be called 'Waiting for Kurtág'.*

What procedure do you adopt yourself?

I don't give myself any deadlines. But, at the same time, I know that one day an interpretation has to be at hand and

---

* Meanwhile, against all odds, Kurtág did complete his opera, which was premiered at La Scala Milan on 15 November 2018.

ready for performance. There's no way around that. It's a question of compromising between what's ideal, and practical experience. I would never say: 'I have to learn Brahms's B flat Concerto in two weeks.' That would be appalling, even if some pianists do go down that path.

Going back to composers and the development of musical history. From Bach's objectification of the spirit to Beethoven's subjectivity of expressive manner and personality – or, to put it another way, from a religiously and theologically firm ordering and location in God, to a space inhabited by human experiences – what does that signify to you?

What probably moves me most with Bach is his simple, artless devoutness – a complete selflessness far removed from all egocentricity. Bach is a person rooted in belief, writing for God and for his parish. At the same time, that was his duty. Bach was fully aware of who he was and what he was capable of. But he didn't compose with his sights on posterity or eternal fame. He did what was required of him: to get a new cantata ready every other Sunday. His selflessness reminds me of the Florentine Renaissance or the Middle Ages with its great cathedrals. Who knows who their architects were? Or their stonemasons and sculptors? Haydn and Mozart, and then more fully Beethoven, already cultivated a different relationship both to themselves and to their vocation. With them, the process of subjectivity begins, which, of course, goes hand in hand with radical social changes.

But Bach's legacy was already a presence in the Viennese classical period, and in many ways a benchmark.

That's true. It shouldn't be forgotten that church music also played a special role for the Viennese classical composers. They all wanted to write music for the church, and to become church musicians. Schubert tried hard – and was turned down. To Mozart, his C minor Mass and the Requiem meant a huge amount. Beethoven's *Missa solemnis*, Haydn's late Masses or the oratorios, *The Creation* and *The Seasons* – all these were of fundamental importance, and would have been unthinkable without the legacy of Bach and Handel. In this context, I sometimes reflect that the crisis in church music today probably arises out of the fact that the church no longer plays a central role in society.

How do you see the relationship between Bach's church music and his instrumental pieces?

You can't separate them. The sacred music encompasses a great many 'worldly' elements: dance movements such as minuets and bourrées, etc. Conversely, the instrumental music – the *Well-Tempered Clavier*, the unaccompanied sonatas and partitas for violin, the cello suites, the 'Goldberg' Variations – all contain movements which could have come out of the Passions or the cantatas. For example, the B minor fugue from the first book of the *Well-Tempered Clavier* is related to the Kyrie from the B minor Mass; the 'Echo' movement which concludes the *French Overture* quotes the choral movement 'Sein Blut komme über uns und unsre Kinder' from the *St. Matthew Passion*. If you play one of Bach's keyboard concertos, you know that one or other of its movements comes from a cantata – for instance, in the case of the F minor Concerto, from '*Ich steh' mit einem Fuß im Grab*' (No.156). The piece in question has to be played and shaped against this background.

Isn't it rather unusual that the young András Schiff already began to concentrate on Bach above all, and deliberately bypassed the 'Sturm und Drang' period of Chopin, Schumann or Liszt?

I've always felt Bach as liberating. His so-called rigour often proves to be an illusion. The fact that Bach prescribes so little – hardly any tempi, no dynamic markings, no phrasing, no articulation – is very interesting to young people: it allows you to express yourself through him. My teacher George Malcolm encouraged this kind of freedom. To put it in a nutshell, you can play a Bach fugue in ten different tempi and the result is usually impressive. If you take Chopin, he allows much less freedom. People are mistaken if they think that just because Chopin is a romantic composer, they can handle him in any way they like. That's a real mistake: the slightest exaggeration can degenerate into tastelessness. With Bach, I felt more in my element, and still do.

How should we imagine the way you prepare, when you practise?

I begin every day with Bach – usually for about an hour. I used to torture myself with Czerny, which of course wasn't exactly stimulating for the mind. On the other hand, it teaches you the fingering for a B flat major scale, chromatic thirds, and so on. The daily grind of learning. Later, I discovered that I could get my 'training' under way better with Bach – a refreshment for the body, soul and spirit. One's flexibility and fluidity benefit enormously, for instance in the 'Goldberg' Variations, where the hands cross over each other. To me, it's pure physical pleasure, so long as one doesn't suffer from arthritis.

George Malcolm could have made you swear allegiance to the harpsichord.

It was in fact that great harpsichordist who told me it was absolutely unimportant which instrument Bach was played on. Of course, stylistic awareness is a prerequisite for a good interpretation, and it's precisely in the case of baroque music that improvisation and freedom play an important role.

At what point do improvisatory freedom and ornamentation end?

I find the limit is more or less reached with Beethoven. Even in early Beethoven sonatas, with the exception of the Op.49 pair, I don't add any ornaments. On the other hand, with Haydn or Mozart I do, because we know from the sources that it's an integral part of the style. Bach provides this freedom himself. If we look at the sarabandes from the English Suites, we find that Bach writes out some of the ornamentation in the *doubles*, or quasi-variations, giving us a template for their use as repeats. The repeats have to be shaded and phrased differently. Old-fashioned, dyed in the wool musicologists don't understand that. Until recently, you were taught to give notes the exact duration they had on the page. Added trills, mordents and cadenzas were strictly forbidden. If those teachers had read the books by Carl Philipp Emmanuel Bach or Leopold Mozart, they would have noticed that musicology, fantasy and taste go hand in hand. Unfortunately, in some institutions music teaching is still like the agenda of a police state. Dreadful!

Is it especially difficult to play Bach from memory?

That's what people usually say. I've never found it to be so, since I'm lucky enough to have a good memory which works ideally for Bach. To me, contemporary pieces are much harder. That probably has something to do with a lack of motivation. As someone over the age of 60, I'd rather still learn and play *The Art of Fugue*, probably from the music. I'm too old to play the whole thing from memory. One's brain has a certain capacity, and I've probably reached mine, since I'd like to be able to keep the things that I already have in my head.

What's wrong with playing from the music? Richter, for instance, regularly did that in his later years.

There's nothing wrong with it, really, apart from the imponderables of looking up at the music, and the page-turning.

It's important, too, for the contrapuntal structures to be made audible without straining. That's a matter of articulation in particular, which has to carry the flow of the discourse.

On top of that there's the music's liveliness, which is expressed through its dance-like character. I like to allow music to speak, to sing, but also to dance.

There are many movements in the suites that are quite appropiate for that.

In the suites and also in the *Well-Tempered Clavier*. Many musicians forget to bear the dance elements in mind. In a piece in ¾ time, for instance, not all the steps or all the crotchets are alike. Detached, unphrased notes should be held for a little longer than half their notated value. That produces the music's breathing and pulsation which are so important. The first beat isn't always stressed. Which are the 'strong' and the 'weak' parts of the bar? There's a lot of thought to be given to that. In Bach, Haydn or Mozart, the notated text doesn't tell us how long the notes actually are. CPE Bach and Leopold Mozart describe quite precisely what needs to be done.

Are there any other Bach interpretations that you can accept?

Why not? I'm very open-minded. In my youth I was strongly influenced by Glenn Gould; later, increasingly less so. Then, Edwin Fischer became very important, and that's still true: his stance, his inner focus are to my taste. Gould, the technology-freak, broke the pieces down in his recordings into dozens of takes, and then assembled the snippets into a whole. That's something quite alien to me. I play the piece three times and that's it – even if I don't achieve absolute perfection. Gould, on the other hand, made music like a film director: studio work was of absolutely central importance to him.

Did you ever meet?

Once I was playing the 'Goldberg' Variations in Toronto and

it was broadcast over the radio. Gould heard it. We got to know each other, and he made quite precise comments and was extremely friendly. In addition to pianists, musicians like Casals have influenced me a great deal.

How do you prepare for your concerts? There's not only a lot of effort that goes into them, but on top of that there's hard work virtually from day to day.

That's true. Just read biographies of Rubinstein, Menuhin, Casals, Cortot: they all gave more than 200 concerts a year. Of course, travel was different then: you travelled by train or ship, didn't have any jetlag and didn't suffer hours of agony at airports. All the same, hats off! As far as I'm concerned, no concert on a day of travel: so much can go wrong. In addition, my ears and my spirit aren't completely 'with it' in the new place. Physical alertness and precision are very important, which means no alcohol before a concert (afterwards, certainly), but a good lunch and a siesta – which is increasingly difficult these days because even the best hotels are not immune to noise. I go to the concert hall early, prepare myself inwardly. The first note is hugely significant.

What does that mean in concrete terms?

I live through the concert already, even before the first note is sounded. The music has to come out of silence, out of peacefulness. Physical presence comes into it, of course, if you want to play the 'Goldberg' Variations or the *Well-Tempered Clavier* well. When I was young, I didn't understand much about all that, but I was already aware that I had the ability to focus myself and concentrate. By the way, you can train yourself to do that. Goethe described Beethoven as compact, resolute and collected. The same goes for practising, which doesn't have to be for eight hours. As soon as I feel fatigue, I stop. I don't force myself: I'd rather make myself an espresso or read a few pages of a good book.

Where does your fabulous memory come from?

Well, it's not so fabulous. It's probably more a stroke of luck. It's not inbred, and it's not much use for new music. Playing from memory has its advantages. You don't have to look at the music, which can be tiring; you can close your eyes and concentrate better. How do I learn? To begin with I read, study and analyse a work exclusively from the score. Only once I've gone through this process do I go to the piano, and in the end I no longer need the score.

How is your inner hearing?

Rather good. I can already hear a piece when I read it. When playing a Schubert sonata, for instance, I don't visualise the score with my inner eye, with page numbers at the top and bottom – I don't have a photographic memory. Everything is auditory. I hear sounds, structures, harmonies, modulations – the whole itinerary. With Bach, I hear the individual voices in particular. His music isn't simply linear, so I hear perhaps between three and six 'texts' together.

How do you practise?

Very deliberately. I practise efficiently and economically. That's something I learned from my teacher Ferenc Rados: no time-wasting! Concentration and intelligence! Nothing mechanical, nothing motoric! In a conservatoire, you can often hear dreadful things. A difficult passage in Chopin played 250 times *fortissimo prestissimo*, with the result that it gets progressively worse. At first you should practise slowly. Only an idiot would begin practising Chopin's Etudes Op.25 No.6 and Op.10 No.2, or the fugue from Beethoven's 'Hammerklavier' Sonata, up to speed. Dynamics should initially be restrained. Musical details and phrasing have to be correctly formed together. Together with phrasing and articulation, attention must always be paid to the quality of sound. When you practise scales, fingering is important, but even then the sound has to be heeded. On the piano this is especially tricky, because you're generally playing more than just a single note. The art of playing the piano consists of achieving the best possible distribution or balance of the voices. In a six- or eight-part chord no two notes are equal. That makes it very difficult, but hearing polyphonically is the First Commandment. The determining of these relationships begins with practising.

The in-depth analysis of the piece comes before this technical process.

Of course. Take the beginning of Beethoven's Fourth Piano Concerto. The first chord has eight notes. It has to be balanced: which of the notes – G, B and D – has to predominate in the various registers, and in what way? If the chord is simply struck it sounds terrible. In principle, you have to build up the sounds from below, from the bass. For that reason, it's also justifiable to play the left hand a fraction of a second ahead of the right, as great pianists used to do. These days that's regarded as sacrilegious, but it's perfectly reasonable for the whole thing to have a constructional aspect – like a pyramid stretching upwards.

On Haydn and Beethoven

How should Haydn be played?

Haydn is not so far off from Bach, but his long life allowed him to follow the development of the instrument closely and he showed a lively interest in its evolution. His early pieces are for harpsichord, but after that he gradually began writing for various kinds of fortepianos – first, for Viennese models, and later for English instruments, which had a much more powerful sound as well as a wider keyboard compass. Haydn got to know them in London, where he enjoyed his greatest successes. In the comparatively early Sonata in C minor, we find, for the first time, directions such as *crescendo*, *diminuendo*, *forte*, *piano*, so it's clear that this work was already conceived not for the harpsichord, on which such dynamics would be unthinkable, but for the piano. So already with this sonata you have to articulate and phrase very precisely and clearly. Mind you, that goes for the symphonies and Masses, too, which I conduct with great pleasure. The many semiquaver passages for the first violins should not simply be run through: they have to be shaped. The same applies to the piano. Sometimes three notes have to be slurred, and the next three separated; sometimes it's the other way around. Of course, attention has to be paid to the harmonic development, too.

Ornaments are allowed – indeed, desirable?

You could put it this way: take fermatas – Haydn doesn't mean the performer to grind to a halt, a standstill, he expects him to play a short improvisation. That leads us to Haydn as the great master of rhetoric. His music speaks much more than it sings. Rather than produce broad melodies and big melodic arches, he tends to work with concentrated motifs and cells. That had a profound influence above all on Beethoven, who built up his music with similar architectural means.

What significance does Beethoven have for you?

It would be hard to overestimate it. These days, I place Beethoven above Mozart, because he stirs me more from an existential point of view. With his very greatest works I feel, in a similar way as I do with Bach, something metaphysical and cosmic. The late sonatas, the 'Diabelli' Variations, the string quartets and the *Missa solemnis* – these works open up incredible vistas. Of course, this assessment might seem subjective. A marginal comment: when I was young, I had absolutely no affinity for the 'Waldstein' sonata.

Why not?

Hard to say. I stupidly thought that nothing interesting could come out of the key of C major. Then I realised the opposite – also in connection with the First Piano Concerto. The fact that I had to grapple for so long with Beethoven is due to the many sided nature of his persona, the unprecedented multiplicity of richness. There's the heroic Beethoven, but also the dramatic; then the comic, witty and humorous; and the lyrical, tender Beethoven, as, for instance, in the F sharp major Sonata. And everywhere, human warmth. No one is more human than Beethoven.

There's something else, too. No other composer created a cycle, as Beethoven did with his 32 piano sonatas, which convey virtually his entire creative biography. For that reason, it's vital to perform the sonatas in chronological order.

We spoke about that at length in the Beethoven book we did together.* 'Vital' is perhaps putting it too strongly. But chronological performance is probably the best solution. In any case, it's a mistake for a pianist to play only with an eye on the box-office – that's to say to play at least one 'famous' sonata in each programme. I could add a small, and not terribly pleasant, story. When, between 2004 and 2008, I played the complete cycle over the course of four nights at each location, the schedule included the Theater an der Wien – where, incidentally, the premiere of Beethoven's *Fidelio* took place. The first two concerts went without a hitch. For the third, all of a sudden, there wasn't enough rehearsal time available to me. The theatre intendant explained to me at length that the hall wasn't free because tourists were being shown around backstage. We seemed to agree that the concert should be cancelled and that I should continue the cycle with the third concert at the scheduled date of the fourth. But when the intendant noticed that the 'Moonlight' Sonata had already been announced for the fourth concert, he didn't want to allow me to play the previous programme which contained, among other things, the two Op.14 sonatas instead. Things went so far that the entire remainder of the cycle fell by the wayside. That's Vienna for you.

---

* *Beethovens Klaviersonaten und ihre Deutung* (Beethoven's Piano Sonatas and their Interpretation) (2007).

In other words, it makes no sense to differentiate between the well-known and the lesser-known sonatas in terms of quality.

And furthermore it would be a mistake to underestimate the public. On the contrary, the public is generally very discerning and cultured. The yardstick isn't the lowest common denominator, but the aware listener.

Can Beethoven change your life?

For me, that definitely holds true. My range of sound on the piano has become richer, more full and more differentiated through Beethoven. After I had played Beethoven extensively, my Schubert playing also changed: it became more focused and more concentrated in terms of sound. Beethoven writes very full-bloodedly. Sometimes you're playing two fistfuls. Unlike with Mozart or Schubert, you frequently find six- or eight-voiced chords. However, with sound clusters of that kind it's very important to differentiate the sound. It's a question of 'voicing'.

Is Beethoven harder than other composers for women pianists?

Masculinity isn't necessarily a prerequisite for great Beethoven playing. There have been some marvellous female Beethoven players: Myra Hess, for instance, or Annie Fischer. It's true that Beethoven is very masculine, but that shouldn't tempt one to force. Beyond any qualities of 'masculinity' or 'femininity' there's the question of humour, which prompts me to add this: many pianists are wary of playing short notes. Already in their piano lessons they learn that short notes are forbidden. But there are places where short notes produce a very witty effect: when I begin Haydn's late C major sonata by using just one finger, for instance, or when I play the displaced chords in Beethoven's G major sonata from Op.31. To me, that's plainly a part of the music's character.

That also goes against the false ideal of 'beautiful sound'.

Absolutely. Short notes aren't beautiful, but so what? It always depends on their context and function. On top of that, Beethoven is the first composer to have prescribed extraordinary pedal markings in a quite revolutionary way. In the 'Waldstein' Sonata, or in the recitative-like passages of the 'Tempest', Op.31 No.2, and of Op.110, Beethoven writes enormously long pedal indications so that the sounds are blurred together. He clearly wants a quite special effect. But again, that's something that's frowned upon in orthodox teaching: 'if you wouldn't mind, please change the pedal with each new harmony'. Beethoven deliberately writes against rules like that, and his wish has to be respected. Questions of taste don't come into it, it's just conscientious interpretation.

Schubert has always been especially close to you.

I never had any fights or frights with him. Work, certainly, but no conflicts as with Beethoven. On the other hand, there are terrifying passages in Schubert, too, which seem designed to torment you. I'm thinking of the C minor Sonata, or the slow movement of the late A major.

Song-like moments in Schubert are very much to the fore.

I would go so far as to say that Lieder are almost omni-present. That's why it's been such a fine and important experience for me to have worked with great singers of both sexes – with Peter Schreier, Dietrich Fischer-Dieskau, Robert Holl and Cecilia Bartoli, for example. Among singers, Schreier was my most important partner.

You have also been one of the few pianists to have played Schubert's sonatas in cycles.

That was in the late eighties and early nineties. The reason behind it was purely love and interest. There had hardly been any Schubert cycles before. I had already played the sonatas at the Schubertiads in Hohenems and Feldkirch and had gradually built up the complete repertoire there. What's also fascinating about Schubert is that, unlike with Beethoven, there isn't a long history of interpretation attached to every piece. With Beethoven we think of Schnabel, Backhaus, Gulda, Annie Fischer, Serkin or Brendel. For young pianists, that can be a real burden, because you can't simply ignore those masters – and even less imitate them. Only Schubert's B flat Sonata has a comparable interpretative tradition. So I could assimilate most of Schubert's works above all by way of my own experiences and my feeling for the style. That was absolutely liberating. It was much the same with Haydn.

What does one have to look out for in particular when playing Schubert?

His forms are looser than Beethoven's. The 'problem' is

that many of the works can often disintegrate into separate sections if the performer doesn't hold them together. The binding force is rhythm. If the underlying rhythm is right, you can be freer with the details. The melody with Schubert is a given, anyway, and is self-evident; the harmony, with its amazing modulations, is a miracle that is *sui generis*. The rhythm provides the vertical element, the structure. It's a prejudice to think that rhythm isn't so important for romantic music. The opposite is true: Chopin is the best proof of that. When the rhythm is right in Schubert, the 'heavenly lengths' which Schumann spoke of aren't felt as longueurs.

Can you give an example of particular difficulties in terms of holding a work together?

It's very hard to hold the first movement of the B flat Sonata together. That's partly because of the many fermatas, which you have to situate carefully somewhere between flowing peacefulness and eerie silence; or, with regard to the rhythm, between duple and triplet motion. Then you don't need much rubato – it's written-in.

And the sound?

That's also not easy, but very natural. Schubert composed much more transparently than Beethoven. On the other hand, Schubert's sound world is very vulnerable, which brings it close to Mozart's. Strangely enough, I think it's much less easy to destroy Beethoven's works, because their form holds them together in any case. Schubert's works, on the contrary, can fall to pieces, or can lose their tension.

Has Alfred Brendel's playing influenced you?

Yes, indirectly. Brendel is an outstanding Schubert player.

He believes you have to have a central European character in your blood in order to play Schubert properly.

Like all truly great musicians, Schubert is universal. On the other hand, there's a great deal that's Viennese about him, which is where the central European sphere of culture shows itself – certainly not German or even northern German. If I try to imagine how Schubert talked – and that brings us back to speech-like articulation – I hear German with Austrian inflections.

Secrets of the instrument

Schubert's sound is also dependent, and even more so, on having the right instrument.

Schubert was no virtuoso, but he played very beautifully and sensitively, just as he had a beautiful and melodic singing voice. As far as the instrument is concerned, we have precise information about Schubert's pianos. At that time in Vienna there was a whole host of excellent piano makers: we only have to think of Conrad Graf, or the brothers Franz and Joseph Brodmann who, in turn, influenced Bösendorfer. I own a grand piano by Franz Brodmann which the harpsichordist Jörg Ewald Dähler offered to sell to me. I was immediately fascinated by it. The instrument dates from 1820 and is particularly suited to Schubert and Beethoven. It features a 'moderator' pedal which stretches a thin layer of cloth between the strings and hammers, so that the sound becomes unbelievably gentle, delicate and quiet. It's only on an instrument of that kind that you can fully experience what Schubert has in mind when he writes a triple *pianissimo*. It's for the quiet moments in Schubert that a modern Steinway can become very problematic. In any case, I play differently on a Steinway or Bösendorfer since I got to know the Brodmann piano.

Can you point to an example?

Let's take the famous trill in the bass in the opening movement of the late B flat Sonata. The aim is for us to hear not so much music, as ominous noises before the storm. In any case, it has to sound as if it comes from afar. On the Brodmann, it sounds very transparent and extremely quiet, and that taught me how I could produce the same effect on a modern concert grand.

Older instruments alter one's playing technique, too.

The keys are somewhat narrower, smaller, closer together. One immediately notices that unlike with modern pianos there's no heavy work to be carried out. With the lighter touch, however, any unevenness is more noticeable: you can't cheat, or cover anything up.

Fundamentally, in this context the question also arises as to whether such intimate sound worlds as we find in Schubert are at all suited to large modern concert halls.

The Brodmann only works in a small hall with very good acoustics. The hall in Schwarzenberg, which is actually not very large, already turned out to be too big for it. The Wigmore Hall in London is ideal. On the other hand, an instrument like that demands intensive listening. The audience, which to begin with is perhaps not altogether 'with it', only begins to concentrate later.

Let's talk a little more about instruments. In your youth, you couldn't be choosy. But you've since come to own a whole series of first-rate pianos: Steinway, Bösendorfer, Blüthner, the Brodmann we've already mentioned; and for the past few years, you've performed on a Bechstein which Wilhelm Backhaus often played. As a result, you're almost always giving concerts on your own instruments.

Early on, I wasn't exactly spoiled. These days I can be. But let's not forget that not all Steinways sound great. Almost more important than the piano is the technician, who not only tunes the instrument, but maintains it and makes sure the tone is even. That's extremely sensitive precision work. When I first heard the Steinways at the Italian firm of Fabbrini in Pescara, I was thrilled. Angelo Fabbrini used to work for Arturo Benedetti Michelangeli, then for Maurizio Pollini and other fellow-pianists. Later there was the Bösendorfer, which was particularly suited to the worlds of Schubert; and finally, I found the 1920 Bechstein. As a general rule, I tell myself: the right piano for the right piece – or, *Vive la différence!* Meanwhile, I have a handsome collection in which there's also a fortepiano and a harpsichord: I have at my disposal every imaginable instrument that's suitable for music from the early eighteenth century to the present day. As far as actual piano manufacture is concerned, there's been nothing new in the past 100 years.

What's the reason for that?

I suppose a lack of curiosity. People accept what's there, so everything often sounds much the same.

Let's come to Schumann, whom you've performed very intensively from time to time, and still play and record.

Schumann is the romantic *par excellence*. To me, Chopin isn't really a romantic and Brahms is actually a classicist. Schumann brought to music a great deal that was new: he developed the traditional forms and genres, such as sonata, variations and rondo forms, into new and fascinating things – into vignettes which break up into kaleidoscopic colours and moods and are often over in a flash. The classic example is *Papillons* Op.2. In addition, Schumann assimilated his very rich cultural and literary passions. We only have to think of writers such as Friedrich Schlegel, ETA Hoffmann or Jean Paul, all of whom find a meeting point in some way or other in Schumann. Then there's Schumann's split personality which was so fruitfully assigned in his works to the central figures of the stormy Florestan and the intimate Eusebius. It's important, too, for anyone who wants to play Schumann satisfactorily to have some knowledge of his life, about which we learn a great deal from the diaries, the household books and Clara Schumann's reminiscences.

You've also involved yourself with Schumann's late works.

His late works are beautiful and need to be defended against the view that they are of lesser value. Unfortunately, both Clara Schumann and Brahms fostered this prejudice, and barred some of his works (such as the Violin Concerto) from performance, and even burned manuscripts. So, alas, there's the label of a madman hanging around Schumann's neck. But what does that mean? His early work is 'mad' enough, if we think of the F sharp minor Sonata, for instance, or *Kreisleriana*. Some of it is much 'madder' than the late pieces. Among those, there's probably none more touching and moving than the so-called 'Ghost' Variations, especially if one knows about the circumstances in which they arose.[*] I also very much enjoy playing Schumann's chamber music, and I conduct the symphonies, too. Schumann composed wonderfully in all genres.

What does a good Schumann performer have to be able to do? How can the rich associations of his world be revealed?

One has to think, feel and play poetically – and avoid false objectivity. If, with Schubert, as we've already mentioned, there's a fundamental rhythm, that's something which is much harder to establish in Schumann. Rubato is vitally important. It's true that it has to be controlled, but at the same time it needs an appropriate degree of freedom and imagination to produce the right expressive effect.

Schumann himself wanted it that way, if we look more closely at his markings.

On top of that, he wanted the enjoyment of taking risks.

---

[*] The *Geistervariationen* ('Ghost' Variations) were the last music that Schumann composed. In writing them, he was convinced that their theme had been dictated to him in a dream by the spirits of Schubert and Mendelssohn. The very last variation was composed in the aftermath of Schumann's thwarted suicide bid by throwing himself into the Rhine. (Translator's note)

Schumann shouldn't be played too carefully. Take the notoriously difficult ending of the middle movement in the C major Fantasy. Many pianists tremble with fear and think only of getting through the thing. The whole piece is tricky, and the ending needs panache, impetus and risk-taking. Sometimes all the leaps come off, sometimes only half of them. I experienced that with both Annie Fischer and Richter: there were evenings full of wrong notes and yet the whole sweep was superb – better than mere right notes. The mottos and 'literary' instructions should inspire us to bring our imagination into play in a piece by Schumann, even when they're sometimes hard to understand.

At the same time, one has to ration one's feelings. Bathos and sentimentality are out of place in Schumann, too.

We have only to think of the first movement of the Piano Concerto. Many performers play it too slowly. Schumann prescribes a lively, or even quick tempo, with a metronome marking of 84 for the minim. That also applies to the famous oboe solo. Had Schumann wanted it slower – and his notation was always very precise – he would have made that clear. The first movement is headed 'Allegro affettuoso', and that's how it should be understood.

What do you think of as his most important works?

The C major Fantasy and *Kreisleriana* are very special. But I also think the *Davidsbündlertänze* and the F sharp minor Sonata are wonderful, and even the F minor Sonata. I'm less attracted to the G minor Sonata; and I don't play *Carnaval*, because everyone else does – although it's a phenomenal piece. I'm also a passionate enthusiast of the *Etudes symphoniques*. Finally, a word of advice: when young pianists build up a repertoire that's not completely focused on mainstream works, they should take up the late pieces such as the *Gesänge der Frühe* or the 'Ghost' Variations.

When you were a child, did you look into the Album **for the Young?**

Yes, I love it just as much today, and would gladly take it up again – perhaps on a Conrad Graf piano. But that's extremely intimate music, suited to a salon or a large room, and certainly not to a large concert hall.

Brahms, the classicist. You were drawn to the Piano Concerto No.1 early on. Will you go back to Brahms more intensively?

The label of classicism doesn't really fit the absolutely wonderful D minor Concerto, especially the first movement and the slow movement, which in terms of expression is like a Benedictus, and reflects Schumann's suicide attempt in the Rhine. The B flat Concerto, which I now play more often, fits in much more with the world of classical forms. To me, it shows strong similarities to Beethoven's E flat Concerto. The second movement, with its four-bar phrases, is modelled on Chopin's scherzos, while the slow movement and finale lead us into more intimate worlds and have a flavour of chamber music throughout. The fourth movement, like the finale of Beethoven's G major Concerto, begins not on the tonic, but on the subdominant.

How do you rate his piano pieces, and particularly the late Intermezzi?

Here, I think Brahms discovered a great deal that was new. On the other hand, we shouldn't forget that the path to the genre was already paved by Beethoven in his Bagatelles, or Schubert in his Impromptus. But Brahms introduces a very specific autumnal mood of melancholy and resignation. I don't fall in with the view that Schoenberg's piano pieces had their forerunners in Brahms. The director of the Kassel 'Musiktage' once asked me to play a programme which alternated Brahms and Schoenberg. It was fascinating. And yet I said to myself, 'Never again!' For me it didn't work in the end, because, as I said, I can't find the way in to Schoenberg's piano pieces, particularly the late ones.

If you wanted to talk about Brahms's influence, you would find it much more in Berg.

Absolutely. But on the subject of constructing programmes, which is one of my favourite occupations, it's like the art of cookery (in fact I would happily cook if I had more time). As a pianist, one is spoiled by the richness of the repertoire. All the same, not many composers are suited to monothematic recitals: Bach, Haydn, Mozart, Beethoven, Schubert, Schumann. That's it. For my taste, even Brahms isn't suitable.

Why not?

I once described it this way: when you look at the Tintorettos in the Scuola di San Rocco in Venice, you are, of course, deeply impressed. But everything is very dark, gloomy and even sinister: you long for a bit of light and a bit of sunshine. That's the way it is with Brahms. We used to play entire cycles consisting exclusively of Brahms's chamber music in five evenings. I soon noticed that it wasn't a good idea. If I play the late Brahms pieces, I alternate them with Bach, Mozart, Beethoven, Mendelssohn.

Chopin, and exclusively Chopin?

Many pianists give Chopin-only evenings. That's a tradition that stretches back to Alfred Cortot, for instance, or Arthur Rubinstein. All the same, I find it too much of a good thing. He's a wonderful composer who drains our life blood almost mercilessly.

That's a medico-musical metaphor I've not come across before.

But it's true: Chopin is really merciless. Freedom is very restricted: tempo, dynamics, pedal – everything is prescribed down to the last detail, and very well prescribed, too. Unfortunately, those directions are all too seldom followed. Chopin is more often sinned against than most other composers. A particular horror is the 'salon' rubato in practically every bar. Chopin always provides a strict tempo which applies to the left hand, while the right should articulate more freely. Liszt was very well aware of that. If I go back to Chopin again, it will be for the mazurkas. I treasure them above all else.

The magic of chamber music

Let's turn to chamber music, which you've been nurturing and performing since your youth. What does it mean to you? Also in relation to the solo repertoire?

To me, chamber music is an affair of the heart – and I think I can say not only to me. Because many great composers, from Haydn up to our own time, have confided their most precious and most profound thoughts to chamber music. The string quartet, my favourite genre, occupies a special place, but of course there is also some wonderful chamber music with piano. Just think of Haydn, and then Beethoven, Schubert, Schumann, Mendelssohn and Brahms. Here the pianist is no longer functioning alone, but has to accommodate himself, and sometimes subordinate himself, to others. It's true that for the most part he's *primus inter pares*, but he has to listen, and adapt himself to others – which is very good training for musical understanding.

When did you start playing chamber music? Which pieces were you able to choose from?

I began when I was about eight, with children of my own age. Sometimes we played at my house, sometimes at the home of the others. And, of course, we began with things that we could manage from a technical point of view – that's to say, trios by Haydn and Mozart. That way, I learned to improve my sight-reading.

A prerequisite for that was that you had to be particularly gifted and have basic aptitude.

Of course. But in Budapest that was somehow in the air. My first teacher already taught us that chamber music was an essential part of musical education. Somewhat later, that found its continuation and counterpart in performing piano concertos. There's a constant give and take with those, too, above all in the ones that are closest to my heart – Mozart, Beethoven, Schumann, Brahms and Bartók. They're not like the concertos by Paganini, for instance, where there's a main protagonist towering above the orchestra, which has to content itself with taking a back seat.

One could also mention Chopin's concertos.

Inasmuch as the orchestra has more or less the role of an accompanist. The piano part is in any case wonderful. While we're on the subject: with Liszt, on the other hand, the orchestral part is very important, and also with Tchaikovsky it shouldn't be underestimated. In short, the notion of dialogue, which was developed into its first full expression in the concertos of Mozart, is grounded in the principle of chamber music. It very quickly becomes apparent whether or not a pianist who involves himself in piano concertos of this kind is a chamber musician.

What qualifications are desirable for a pianist who takes on this role?

He has to be able not only to listen to the others very well, but also to himself. He must have, or develop, a strong sense of sound and must find a piano tone which where necessary can blend well with strings and winds, and even with the human voice. As far as Lieder are concerned, they are also based on an evenly matched partnership between the singer and the pianist. Here, too, it's a question of chamber music. Let's just remember earlier habits: in those days the pianist played more often than not with the lid closed, or on the half-stick. 'Above all, not too loud!' was the maxim. But if a pianist really knows his job, he understands that a fully opened piano offers him a rich palette of sounds and colours which plays a vital part in moulding an artistic whole. If he is unable to shade his playing with sensitivity, and has no feeling for sound and touch, he'll sound too loud and coarse even if the piano is completely closed.

How well is the modern concert grand suited to such complex tasks?

That's a very pertinent question. The bass strings on modern instruments are very powerful and thick. That can become highly problematical. Probably the best way of learning to acquire the correct balance is by playing chamber music on period instruments. With those, the reverse is sometimes true: you have to tell the violinist or viola player: 'You are too loud in relation to the fortepiano.' So, with regard to the sound balance, you always have to think about how things stood at the time the music was composed. Haydn's trios, incidentally, which I particularly love, are rather 'piano-centric'.

That goes just as much for Beethoven's.

But in Beethoven the cello has considerably more to play. In Haydn, it almost always plays in parallel with the left-hand part of the piano – and yet it's a subtle and rewarding task for the cellist to fulfil this bass function, and to produce the right intonation and phrasing. What should not be forgotten is that the violin sonatas of Mozart and Beethoven are actually sonatas for piano and violin, and that's how they're described on the title page. With those, too, an evenly matched partnership is essential.

How do you see the compositional development in Beethoven's piano trios?

It's an unprecedented evolution, if we think of the first trios, Op.1, then the Op.70 pair and finally the 'Archduke', which is the crowning glory of the series. That last work is still chamber music, of course, but it has absolutely symphonic breadth and character.

The string quartets reach out appreciably further.

Yes. Like the 32 piano sonatas, they lead us into the realms of the metaphysical. After Beethoven had completed his piano sonatas with Op.111, he went on writing quartets, up to his last work, the F major Quartet Op.135. The 'true' continuation of the Beethoven quartets is found not in Schubert, Schumann or Brahms, but in the six quartets of Bartók.

A bold conclusion!

Not at all. One can – indeed, one must – see it that way. Bartók was himself aware of it, even if his modesty would never have allowed him to say so. But his models were Beethoven for structure, Bach for polyphony, and, interestingly, Debussy in the realm of sounds and colours.

Do you work with chamber ensembles as a coach?

Yes, often. When I do, I can draw profit from my studies with Kurtág and Végh. I wouldn't be able to go so far as to suggest fingerings to string players, but as far as bowings are concerned, I can offer help. What's important is to know the works thoroughly. With Beethoven, the piano sonatas and string quartets are stylistically very closely related. As far as the quartets are concerned, it takes a lot of time before four people can work meaningfully together and develop together in a lasting way.

Which ensembles have left a formative impression on you?

From recordings, the Busch Quartet remains a shining example – unsurpassed and perhaps unsurpassable. Sándor Végh's quartet, which I was able to get to know at first hand, was also masterly. Then the Amadeus Quartet, with its splendid leader Norbert Brainin. By the way, people always talk about democracy and equal rights, but a string quartet without a superb first violinist isn't a string quartet. That's the problem with many of the ensembles of today: there's a lack of outstanding personalities. A good solution to this precondition was found by the Quatuor Mosaïques, with its first violinist Erich Höbarth.

No less important for performance practice is the right 'chemistry', a certain psychology of fitting together, of mutual understanding. That doesn't accord well with the role of the pianist as a lonely hero, as developed later by the romantic generation.

Perhaps the word 'accompaniment' used in such contexts

should in any case be banned from the musical vocabulary. In a Chopin nocturne, where the right hand for the most part has the cantabile melody, that description could be justified for the left hand. And even in some piano concertos, when, for instance, the oboe or clarinet has the theme and the piano actually does accompany, or rather provides a backcloth.

As in Schumann's Piano Concerto.

That's actually a piece of chamber music *par excellence*.

Back to performers. How do people fit together? What does one have to look out for?

Besides musical questions, very personal things come into play. You can't force true compatibility. Some concert promoters try to put famous names together, for purely box office reasons. But that can go seriously wrong. For examples of successful combinations, I could cite Fritz Kreisler with Rachmaninov or Bartók with Joseph Szigeti.

How do you know when it works?

An infallible sign is that with a good partnership you hardly have to talk. There are some music festivals – Marlboro, for example – which make it possible for musicians to rehearse in depth. That certainly has its advantages. On the other hand, it often degenerates into endless discussions in which each and every person long-windedly insists on expressing their own point of view. Yet for chamber music a certain degree of selflessness is essential. You have to play in a non-egotistical manner. In the case of chamber music with piano, the pianist has the advantage of having the score with all the parts in front of him, so that he can, and should, sensitise the others. Theoretically, that could apply to the strings if they played from the score. In my experience, good string and wind players always have the score at hand during rehearsals.

Are there any key chamber works that you would like to record again, or for the first time?

When my wife, Yuuko, and I got to know each other in Marlboro, we practised and played Mozart's violin sonatas for hours on end. With a few exceptions, I find them distinctly more interesting than the piano sonatas. We hardly needed to speak: it all happened mostly by itself. For the rest, I'm lucky enough to have played most of the important works in the repertoire. A great experience, and one which I hope will be repeated, was to have performed the Beethoven cello sonatas and variations with Miklós Perényi.

Are you loyal in terms of your ensembles?

When a good partnership has come into being and has become used to playing together, I wouldn't want to change its make-up. For instance, I've been playing Dvořák's Piano Quintet with the Panocha Quartet from Prague for decades. I would have a hard time of it to perform it with another ensemble.

How did things go with the music festival in Ittingen?

Heinz Holliger and I worked together very productively for decades and, in all modesty, the thematic programming could really be seen and heard. Fortunately, Swiss Radio was often there to record the concerts. In addition to the box that has already appeared, we'll probably be able to issue a few more recordings.

Teaching

Let's talk a little more about your activities as a teacher. When did they begin, and what experience have you gained from them?

If I'm to be honest about it, when I began to teach chamber music at the Academy at the age of 19 in Budapest it was much too early, because I wasn't sufficiently prepared for such an important task. So, after two years, I stopped. What I was still learning at that time myself, and still had to learn, was more important. When you reach the age of 50, on the other hand, you have garnered many experiences, and are happy to pass them on. From then on there's no age limit, so long as you're healthy and have your wits about you.

What are your feelings about masterclasses?

They've been very fashionable for a long time now. As a student I took part in classes of that kind, and already then I was aware that they're not ideal learning platforms, though they're obviously much better than nothing. In the end, what's best is face-to-face tuition – on one side the teacher, on the other the pupil. Instruction is an extremely private matter.

Why haven't you taken your own teaching that far?

It was simply a question of not having the time, and I've always loathed all forms of bureaucracy and administration. And if you teach at a college or an academy, you have to have be present at exams and discuss them with other teachers, and perhaps give notes or marks. Not for me, thank you very much.

But you do occasionally give masterclasses yourself.

I'm interested in gifted young people, in what preoccupies them and how they can be influenced in a good way. And time and time again I find musicians of both sexes who are not only obsessed with their careers, but who want to make music – indeed, have to make music – out of inner necessity. Sometimes I teach youngsters who aren't absolutely set on becoming professional musicians. In those cases, teaching is directed towards the nurturing of good, constructive listening and the cultivation of good taste. Many conservatoires, on the other hand, merely drill their students for a professional career.

There's a great deal of competition, and places are being cut back more and more.

That's a difficult situation, especially for budding orchestral players. For every post that's advertised, hundreds apply – not all of them, unfortunately, sufficiently qualified. Take string players: how many of them have read and studied Leopold Mozart's wonderful treatise? Or pianists: how many know and understand CPE Bach's *Essay on the True Art of Playing Keyboard Instruments*? That's why teaching is important to me.

What are, or should be, the basic principles?

My goodness, they already begin with how someone sits at the piano. Many people have an impossible posture – you can see that before you hear it. No decent sound can ever come out of that. Everything much too stiff. And you notice just as quickly if someone doesn't breathe properly. All that is relatively easy to learn. I get students to sing something. They make a fuss about it, but never mind: they feel how necessary it is to breathe and phrase, and that can then be transferred to the piano. Although technical and mechanical things shouldn't be neglected, they're never the most important point.

What happens if someone comes up with a concept or an interpretation which doesn't accord with your view? Are you tolerant, or do things get serious?

It's not too serious. Fundamentally, I'm very unprejudiced. If what the pianist has to say seems meaningful, if the score is treated with respect, we can happily talk details. As far as those are concerned, I'm broad-minded. I don't impose my own interpretation: it's not about me. What's important is the composer, the work, the text. Alfred Brendel coined a nice term for it – the 'awakening kiss'.

The piece has its own rules?

Always. For instance, if someone plays Beethoven's Op.111 and in the introduction already irons out all the contrasts, that's no good. Those *sforzandos* aren't mine, they're Beethoven's. With tempi one can often have more of a free hand – most free probably with Bach, least with Mozart.

Then structure, harmony, melody and rhythm all come into it. The only things you can't analyse are inflection and character. For those you have to have antennae, or you have to grow them. So that, to put it crudely, the 'Appassionata' doesn't emerge as a joke, but a drama. Or that Haydn's C major Sonata No.50 isn't a tragic piece, but one full of humour and wit. After that one can talk at length about the spiritual dimensions and specific moments of a work. And that, I freely admit, is something that gives me pleasure.

Is it possible or desirable for a teacher to influence a pupil's character as a performer?

In the majority of cases it's difficult or impossible. Let's consider my masterclasses: eighty people apply, out of whom I can take ten. I will already have heard many recordings made by those taking part, which despite my experience in these matters can still lead to disappointment, since some recordings are clearly better than the 'offenders' actually are. Or it can be the other way around. With auditions, there are fewer errors.

Do a lot of young people play for you?

Yes, while I'm on tour or also at my home. Some of them simply want a reference or a recommendation. As a rule, their intentions, whether good or not so good, can easily be seen through. If I think someone is gifted, I invite them to take part in my masterclasses. But I wouldn't like to claim that I have great aptitude for teaching like Sándor Végh or Ferenc Rados. I sometimes lack patience. And to come back to your previous question, I don't usually manage to make a moderately gifted pupil into a great artist.

That also has something to do with the fact that great performers are first and foremost preoccupied with themselves – that's to say, with their own art.

But sometimes the two can go together. Not with Chopin, who hardly had a single good pupil, but with Liszt, who left several significant pupils: Sauer, Rosenthal, d'Albert, Lamond.

Teaching is also a very personal matter.

There are times when it acquires an almost medicinal aspect: the teacher is like a doctor and the 'patients' come with their problems, both physical and psychological. Like a good doctor, a teacher very soon sees where the weakness lies. But unlike with medicine, that's not the end of the matter, because the composer and the music still await. We should never forget that we are all servants of the work itself.

How do you get around the fact that some pupils are in danger of becoming copies of their teacher?

That can be tricky, especially since you only become aware of it rather late in the day. What's important is to nurture the student's personality, so that you can develop something individual out of it. Of course, there are occasions when you decide to refer a pupil to another teacher.

Horowitz had pupils whom he would have done better to send to other pianists. Ivan Davis and Byron Janis tried to imitate the master in many ways.

Murray Perahia told me that as a teacher Horowitz was

immensely interesting, as well as wise and tolerant. Admittedly, by the time he met Perahia, he had been a wise old man for a long while.

The profession and critics

Let's talk a little more about the so-called music profession, about the power of the market, commercialisation, and critics and their value.

The 'profession' has undoubtedly acquired unpleasant aspects. Speaking personally, I'm not adversely affected by them. Sándor Végh told me that he no longer understood the mechanism of success after he'd taken up a second career as a conductor late in life. I have to say, in all honesty, that my kind and my character don't fit in with the current musical scene at all.

What has changed? Was it all better before, as people often assert when they're in their older years?

It was not all better before. But for one thing, I miss many artistic personalities who are unfortunately no longer with us. And for another, I think audiences no longer listen as well as they used to. The same goes for concert promoters: they used to have much better judgement as to who was a good Beethoven or Mozart player. One has to be careful not to idealise 'the good old days', but all the same Klemperer told a story of people coming to him and raving about young conductors who would do a fantastic 'Eroica', to which he answered, 'Spare me the raptures, if you don't mind. I often heard the symphony under Mahler.'

Pianists of old?

When I think of Annie Fischer, Serkin, Arrau, Richter, Michelangeli – my God, they really were amazingly good. Some of the piano celebrities of today aren't in the same league, yet are praised to the skies by the commercial lobby. Maybe we've lost self-confidence as far as culture goes.

In those days perhaps the public was much more likely to play an instrument, take part in chamber music and be able to read a score. That's no longer part of middle-class education.

Exactly. No one was ever born with good taste, but education and training, as well as the fact that music lovers also played, were important for the development of listening and for leading to higher standards. What is true emotion? What is true sensitivity? And what, on the other hand, is mere kitsch? Standards have already changed. Think of Chopin: for him, good taste – *le bon goût* – was the alpha and omega. Even as he lay on his deathbed, he opened up Voltaire's *Dictionnaire* on this key entry.

What is good taste?

That's very hard to define, and it differs according to the epoch. When I asked the great and wise Sir Isaiah Berlin about it, he couldn't give me an answer. Look at the women in Rubens' paintings. On the one hand, they don't correspond at all to our concept of what constitutes a beautiful woman, but on the other hand, we would never come to the view that they are ugly or mere kitsch. With Fernando Botero things are somewhat different . . .

Will we ever escape from the pitfalls of commercialisation?

I fear not. That's why I give more and more so-called lecture recitals. I play the music and talk about it in order to draw the audience's attention to certain things.

The abomination of arrangements is also part of the 'profession': the 'Goldberg' Variations for string orchestra and at the same time coming out of the loudspeakers in a store.

I really don't know where this epidemic comes from. There's probably even a transcription of the 'Goldberg' Variations for balalaika and brass! The keys are changed, as well as the voice-leading. A young flautist came to me and told me she played Bach's F minor Concerto in its version for flute. Rubbish! It doesn't exist. Some flautist or other transcribed it – and of course had to leave out the left hand. Entire chamber orchestras have taken to this abomination, because they think their repertoire is too small. It would be better if it stopped, and more new pieces were com-posed. In earlier times, the situation was different. Think of Liszt. He was a genius who realised that the demand for Schubert's Lieder was strictly limited. And so he made his piano transcriptions. These days, the position is completely different: anyone can listen to recordings of Lieder by Fischer-Dieskau or Peter Schreier.

Besides, it's fascinating to analyse well-known works and breathe new life into them.

I call that 'framing'. There is a frame, and, as I've already mentioned, with Chopin it's very strictly defined, with Bach it's very loose. But when it comes to a great work there are nevertheless a huge number of possibilities for its interpretation. Claudio Arrau once told a young musician that he shouldn't try so hard to be interesting. So, you shouldn't be afraid of so-called boredom – which, incidentally, doesn't have to be so at all. The only condition is that you have to know what you're doing. Otherwise you're just anarchic, or wilfully provocative.

You yourself are an extremely neat and tidy person.

I hope so – at least as far as my inner being is concerned. But when I'm on tour there's a lot going on in my surroundings that's more or less beyond my control. Take stage effects. These days, everything has to be rendered in visual terms through multimedia, and as a result there's a loss of aura. Earlier, when the door opened and Rubinstein or Richter stepped onto the stage, there was an aura in the hall – the atmosphere changed without any kind of funny business having been necessary. Just see how Oistrakh, Menuhin or Heifetz put their violin under their chin and simply stood there and played fantastically straight off. That was worlds away from the present-day rituals, which are like snake charming. Or conductors, for goodness' sake. My great role model, Otto Klemperer, 'did' absolutely nothing: his dignity and his aspect were like royalty, which didn't require any external apparatus. These days a lot of young conductors jump nearly up to the ceiling in the very first bars. Why?

Let's go back to your lectures. I remember an impressive evening at the Siemens Foundation in Munich, when you played and discussed both Bach's 'Golderg' Variations and Beethoven's 'Diabelli' Variations.

I felt the audience was very receptive and cultured. Perhaps one should give more courses to spread the art of listening. In the past, Leonard Bernstein gave lectures for children on the very highest level. To a certain extent, I follow that idea. Sometimes I give an introduction on the day before the concert – in London, for instance, for the complete Beethoven sonatas. People are very grateful for that. You can log in to the lectures for free at any time on YouTube.

That's the saving grace of the media, that they make it possible to revisit things like that.

On the one hand, yes; but on the other hand, the sound quality on YouTube leaves a lot to be desired. And usually, you only get extracts.

What's missing more and more are criteria and benchmarks. Which brings us back to music critics.

Criticism ought to be an important and nice job. But many newspapers give reviews less and less space. In London, for instance, almost every concert used to be written up in the leading daily papers. These days you need a magnifying glass to look for reviews. There are one or two exceptions: the *Neue Zürcher Zeitung* and the *New York Times*. But there's still a fundamental problem: most concertgoers wait until the review appears before venturing their own opinion.

That problem existed before, too, even if it was perhaps countered by a more cultured public which had its own view – despite the fact that Joachim Kaiser tried to set himself up as the leading arbiter as far as Germany was concerned.

You have to be philosophical about people like him, even if they've caused some harm from time to time. I could tell a story about that. When Iván Fischer was unhappy about a very bad review, his colleague Antal Doráti told him, 'Young man, take good note of this: in your career you will get 5000 good reviews, and 2000 bad ones. Their order is immaterial.' And another thing: I don't believe colleagues who proudly declare that they never read reviews . . .

Music criticism often used actually to be better: more competent, stylistically more assured, less impulsive.

One can, and should, be more demanding and, from time to time, more stern. But there should be such a thing as good manners, even for critics – written and unwritten laws of decency. We're all human, and humans should not be harmed.

A journey into the past

Tell us about your origins, your family, the cultural background you were born into and in which you grew up.

I was born in Budapest on 21 December 1953, into a Jewish middle-class family. My father, a gynaecologist, came from Gáborján, in northern Hungary. My mother was born in Debrecen, the second largest city in eastern Hungary.

She was the youngest of three daughters, and she already wanted to become a musician at an early age – that's to say, a pianist. That wish was never fulfilled, because her studies were abruptly terminated by the Second World War. In the wake of the Nazi persecutions, in 1944, the whole family was deported. In Hungary, the deportations came later than elsewhere: the Budapest Jews were the last to suffer this dreadful fate, and luckily the thugs weren't able to complete their work. It's important to know, too, that at that time both my parents had been married once before.

How did that come about? What were the conditions and the consequences?

My mother's first husband was sent to a camp and was employed as a forced labourer. He died there of typhoid fever. The Hungarian overseers burned him alive, together with the other typhus sufferers, locked into their barracks. My mother never got over that.

Did she have children from her first marriage?

No. My father was also sent to the camps, but thanks to his profession as a doctor he managed to survive. However, his first wife and their four-year-old son were murdered in Auschwitz. In this connection, I should report that arrangements had already been made to send my mother's family – her two sisters, my grandmother and other women and children – to Auschwitz, too. By a stroke of luck, the Allies had bombed and destroyed the railway line that led there. As a result, the transportation in the summer of 1944 reached Strasshof, near Vienna. There, the deportees had to carry out hard forced labour in the fields, but fortunately my parents survived and eventually returned to Hungary. They soon met, fell in love and married. I am the only child from their union.

So you had a half-brother. How does this knowledge affect you?

Of course, I think of László, and what would have happened if he had survived the camp. I also think about my relationship to my father, who died when I was six years old. But everything I know about the past and its terribly sad circumstances was told to me later by my mother.

When did your parents' return to Hungary take place? And how did they manage to build up a new life in the aftermath?

That was after the end of the war. My parents met in 1946–7. Incidentally, my father's side of the family produced many doctors: gynaecologists like my father, but also internists. In Thomas Mann's book about the origins of *Doktor Faustus* there's a Dr Schiff. His biographical background was that he was Thomas Mann's house doctor when Mann lived in California. This Dr Schiff was a cousin of my father's. It's also true that at that time the two hadn't been in contact with each other for a long while.

How did things go on from there? At first, my parents lived in Debrecen, which is where my mother came from. Then they moved to Budapest. The centralisation of the country began to come into effect, and so the capital city offered more possibilities. My father was appointed as consultant doctor in a large hospital. But my mother gave up any hope of a musical career. All the same, there was a piano at home – and that had consequences.

Did your mother tell you what her own musical aspirations were? What she would have liked to become and what were her feelings when she gave it all up?

I never found out exactly. But I knew something from her ambition to be a good piano teacher. She never saw herself as a concert pianist: she suffered too much from stage fright. All the same, she could play pieces by Beethoven and Chopin, for instance, very well. These were the influences under which I grew up. My father was an amateur violinist, but I never heard him play. He wasn't particularly fond of the piano. Many doctors at that time were very musical. Several of my father's friends got together every Sunday afternoon to play chamber music in private homes.

That was an essential element of the way middle-class cultural circles saw themselves, despite communism?

Yes, amateur house music was a significant part of the musical culture of a city, and it was those music lovers and amateurs that produced the best possible concert audiences.

Did you hear chamber music as a very small child?

No, that came only later, when I was about eight.

What part did Jewish tradition play in your childhood?

The Jewishness had already been secularised by then, but my grandparents were still orthodox Jews. They celebrated the festivals and followed the religious rules scrupulously.

On the other hand, I was conditioned by the social and political situation in Hungary at that time and was a complete ignoramus as far as religion was concerned. And there was something else, perhaps a sort of suppression: after the Holocaust, we gave up religion – which, after all, hadn't helped us in the midst of catastrophe.

That's an important point. After the Holocaust didn't the question come up, not only for Jews but also for Christians, of where was God in Auschwitz?

Oh yes. That was the big question and, of course, to this day it stands as a huge challenge to us all. It will never be resolved. But the hardest hit were women left on their own, and religious people. If there is a God, how could he permit all this? As a rule, the communists gave such questions short shrift. According to Marx's doctrine, religion was the opium of the people – and so in Hungary, too, all religions were suppressed and not suffered gladly.

In private circles, it was nevertheless possible to go on pursuing one's own creed.

Certainly. But when open society doesn't offer the room and the opportunity to do so, it becomes difficult. Many people nurtured their religion in private spheres. I imagine that even my parents didn't become atheists or materialists all of a sudden. In any case, outwardly you had to play along: that was an unspoken law and consensus among the populace. And, in the end, times were still hard: you had to survive, though in a different way.

Would it be right to say that your parents had a spiritual side which they continued to nurture in private?

You could put it that way. They were no longer religious Jews, but of course for all that they were quite deeply steeped in Jewish tradition. On the other hand, one led one's life in a rather pragmatic way. My parents and my grandmother, for example, fasted on Yom Kippur; I, on the other hand, didn't. They explained to me that the rites were intended to make us think of the dead and our forefathers.

To what extent is the life of those days preserved in memory? Are there still any documents of family history with photographs and other evidence?

Yes, there are. After my mother's death, I cleared out her house. I found a great deal concerning my father, as well as photos of Lacika, the deceased son from his first marriage. His first wife was known to me, to the extent that there was a large portrait of her hanging in our house. My mother was never jealous of her.

As a child, to what extent were you preoccupied with this past, which was at once fascinating and overburdening?

It was told to me by my grandmother on my mother's side, who was a strong personality. We called her Nanóka. The early death of my father at the age of only 65 was the result of lung cancer. He was an inveterate chain smoker who inhaled strong tobacco by the packet. I was a very late child for him. I was told that after his traumatic experiences of persecution he absolutely didn't want another child. But my mother insisted.

Luckily for us all. How great was the difference in their ages?

My father was born in 1896 and died in 1961. My mother was born in 1916, so she was 20 years younger than him.

A great love? Or rather an alliance that came out of friendship?

I presume they really loved each other. After the war, my mother couldn't go back to her old house in Debrecen, because it had been partly bombed and, on top of that, other people were already living in it. So she had to rent other lodgings, and found them in my father's house. He owned a large property which he also let out. Both of them were single, so out of that grew an attraction which later led to marriage. It's true that she never forgot her first husband, who had been her truly great, deeply romantic love.

Moving on to Budapest, how did your father's work go?

His work as a consultant doctor fell in the time of the worst years of communism, at the end of the forties, before I was born. The General Secretary of the party was Mátyás Rákosi, of whom one would have to say that he was a Hungarian Stalin, a madman, a dictator with an iron fist. That meant – not only for my father – that it was imperative to join the Party. He had never had anything to do with communism before, but he had to become a member because otherwise he would never have had a position of that kind.

Realising that nothing would come out of music, my mother enrolled at a commercial college and took studies in other fields. She already spoke German and French very well. At that time, export–import companies came into being, and she obtained a position with the Chemolimpex company, which sold chemical products. This meant that she had to travel a great deal. At first her business trips took her through the Eastern bloc, and, later, occasionally to the West. That was a huge privilege, because travelling was denied to 'normal' people, or was strictly limited. The West didn't even come into it.

Let's talk about this first phase of communism in the early fifties – that's to say at the time you were born. Were there a lot of convinced communists in Hungary, or at least people who, in the watershed of 1945–6, were enthusiastic about belonging both socially and politically to the big brotherhood?

There were the old communists who had been active in the resistance during the time of the Second World War. Their roots reached back to 1919, when Béla Kun established the Hungarian Soviet Republic, which was overturned in the same year, after only 133 days. And in addition there were famous intellectuals like the philosopher György Lukács, who acted as ideologists. But at that time all this represented a minority. Let's consider the Jews who survived after 1945. Many of them said, not unjustly, that they'd already been a hair's breadth from death and were only freed by the Soviet army. That wasn't propaganda – it was true. When people talk about the Second World War these days, the role of the Russians in the defeat of Hitler is often underestimated. No country did as much, despite the secret pact between Molotov and Ribbentrop. The decisive factor was the liberation. With the benefit of hindsight, we know that the luckier ones ended up in the West, and that those who were less fortunate had no possibility of escape – for them, all that remained was a cult of nostalgia for the homeland. It should also be mentioned that the Holocaust was not only driven by the Germans: parts of the Hungarian populace also propped up the mechanism of death.

And so, in the aftermath, many Jews turned to communism out of gratitude to the liberators. Yet in most cases the enthusiasm didn't last long, even if some people went along with it until the 1980s.

When did people first realise that this was a dangerous and misguided regime?

Many people already realised that under Rákosi. In any case, anyone who wasn't a complete idiot must have been aware of it. It was a dreadful time. Resistance was useless. There was no mercy. Instead, there were executions and show trials, just like under Stalin. Prominent people were put to death. Only the 1956 uprising marked a pause. Before that everything was bad, and at its worst at the beginning of the fifties. Which prompts me to remember that 21 December is not only my birthday, but also Stalin's and my father's.

It's lucky we're not astrologers.

Indeed. But 21 December, with its longest night of the year, was also the most hated day in Hungary because of Stalin. He died a couple of months before I was born and there was a sigh of relief.

Was that felt immediately?

Yes, it was noticeable at once. This one single person triggered off so much. The difference between Stalin and his successor, Khrushchev, was realised very quickly. You have to know that the Hungarians have a tendency to be slovenly – that's why to a certain extent communism was bearable in Hungary. Under János Kádár, people talked about 'goulash communism'. The regime couldn't rule the people as brutally as was the case in the GDR, and of course in the Soviet Union.

Was there also a repressed middle class that mourned for the old Austro-Hungarian monarchy?

I'm sure there was, but the old aristocracy had to keep quiet. Anything to do with the old world order and old society was stamped and labelled – and that even included children. If you had the wrong ancestry – bourgeois, or even aristocratic, like the Esterházy family, for instance – it was nearly enough to merit the death penalty. These people were stripped of their property and forced to live in impossible conditions in the remotest village, merely because of their ancestry.

'Class enmity' in one's own country.

Yes. That's why nostalgia was not without its dangers. Conversely, that slovenliness I mentioned enabled a culture of jokes. To exaggerate a little, you could say we survived this whole epoch thanks to our jokes. The Hungarians are very witty, and they always have great jokes at the ready. One had to be terribly careful, however, where and to whom one told political jokes.

From what age did you manage to follow them?

Very early, from the age of four or five, because I've always had a feeling for them. I've loved jokes for as long as I can remember.

What was the policy towards children at that time under the communist regime?

The policy towards children in the fifties was to encourage as many births as possible. And this was on the orders of a special ministry. At the same time, people knew they simply couldn't afford several children, despite the fact that they would receive a certain amount of child benefit. There were even abortions, which were strictly forbidden.

That brings up the question of why you remained an only child.

When I came into the world, my mother was 38 – a relatively late age to have a child. On top of that, it was a difficult caesarean birth and my mother nearly bled to death. My father left the operation to a colleague of his who was known as a specialist. In those days a caesarean was by no means a routine operation. After that my parents decided – and I must say understandably so – that there was no question of having any more children. For myself, I was naturally sorry not to have any siblings – whether a brother or sister was immaterial.

Did you have a happy childhood?

Yes, a loving, sheltered childhood, and later, too. Unfortunately, my father couldn't look after me for long because of his illness. I remember his continual coughing. As a doctor, he was well aware of what he was suffering from. We had a large house in Buda, where there is a lot of greenery and hills. Pest on the other hand is grey and flat. Obviously, Buda was much prettier. My father managed to acquire a house in the so-called suburb at a favourable price. If I wanted to play in the garden, I was often told: 'Be quiet, we mustn't disturb your father.' As a small child, I didn't understand what that was all about. I can hardly remember my father anymore. We had little contact, and yet my father was incredibly kind, and when he was in the mood, he sang folk songs.

Your mother was probably not a typical housewife. Under those political and social circumstances she could scarcely have been one, even if she had wanted to?

Perhaps there was no need for her to work, but she wanted to, for financial reasons, too. My father earned well for those days, though he no longer had a private practice. My grandmother on my mother's side lived with us. She was the one who really brought me up. She was called Ilona – a wonderful lady and a wonderful housewife. She cooked and baked splendidly, and she took care of the entire household, too. Without her, my parents wouldn't both have been able to pursue a profession.

Did your mother love her job?

She liked it, although her business trips sometimes meant she was away for weeks at a time – in Poland, often in Finland and Denmark, sometimes in Vienna.

Did she tell you about her trips?

Yes, in detail. In addition, she always used to bring me toys.

Of course, we had no conception of the West. Everything connected with foreign countries seemed magical to us. But suddenly foreign countries gained a surprising significance. In October 1956, there was the big uprising, during the course of which the border to the West was opened up so that many people could leave the country. Among them was my cousin, Ágnes, and her husband, János Kaposi. Two years later, my aunt, Magda, and her husband, Imre – Ágnes's parents – decided to emigrate and join their daughter. Astonishingly, the authorities didn't prevent this family reunion. The destination was England and I still vaguely remember how we went with our relatives to the railway station. Everyone was crying and I was the only one who didn't know why. The fact that England would later become a similarly important destination for me was naturally something that was still being written in the stars.

Was emigration a topic of conversation at home?

Yes. A large number of people left in 1956, especially many Jews. Because 1956 was in part a wonderful revolution, a rebellion against the Soviet Russians. At the same time, however, this uprising had its dark side because a total amnesty was proclaimed, which was particularly to the advantage of the old fascists and the former Arrow Cross Party which became socially acceptable again. Under law, they would have had to remain behind bars, but in this way they were granted their freedom.

Were there many of them?

Very many, and all absolutely dreadful people. Suddenly, a few neighbours began threatening my parents, making throat-cutting gestures. That, of course, was directed against the Jews and against those in office who were also Jews. The most prominent among them was Rákosi. Since other highly placed officials and members of the secret service were also Jews, communism was again linked with Judaism, just as Hitler had ranted about. That was another reason why the idea of emigration was spoken about at home. But at the same time, my father felt that he was ill and so no longer had any room for manoeuvre.

That would have demanded a different kind of strength?

He told us, 'Look, I'm not the healthiest of people, I'm already over 50, nearer 60. What will I do abroad with a diploma that's not valid there? I can't start a new life all over again.' And so, we stayed.

From her travelling experiences your mother would have been motivated to follow her sister, Magda, and support the idea of living abroad?

Let's put it this way: if my father had seized the initiative, she would have supported him. But things never got that far. Besides, my mother led a quite acquiescent life right up to the time when I left Hungary, in 1979. I had to take this step without my mother having the slightest idea about it. She actually never understood my decision. She always said: 'This is our country. It's true that there's a lot wrong with it, but nevertheless one must stay here out of conviction and duty.' It was only in the autumn of 1956 that the window had stood open for the family – but only in a hypothetical sense.

You didn't live poorly at that time, did you?

No, rather well, actually – much better than average. Of course, things weren't exactly luxurious; but to have your own house in those days was an enormously big privilege. As a rule, people lived in very cramped conditions. As in the Soviet Union, the elegant middle-class houses from the nineteenth century and the turn of the twentieth were divided up into small communal dwellings. Many families had to live very closely together and, on top of that, had to spy on each other. In comparison with those impossible conditions, we had an almost wonderful life.

Could one notice how the Party officials lived?

The Party officials were spoken of, but one didn't really know how the elite lived. Perhaps there were whisperings here and there, but nothing more. That was forbidden territory.

Was there any feeling of solidarity with the other countries under the thumb of the Soviet empire?

I really couldn't feel anything like that – quite the opposite. The Hungarians seemed positively to hate all their neighbours. They hated the Rumanians and the Slovakians because of the Treaties of Trianon and Versailles, since they lost their territories and lived from that time on as minorities. To this day, that's a big and controversial chapter in itself. The only people they didn't hate, and still don't hate to this day, were the Poles. But Poland isn't a neighbouring country. There's a saying which goes: 'The Poles and the Hungarians are brothers!' That dates back to the time of the struggle for freedom in 1848, when a Polish general by the name of József Bem served in the Hungarian army. He became a folk hero. There had already been a link between the royal families of Hungary and Poland in earlier times. But that never went for Czechoslovakia, Yugoslavia or Rumania. Yugoslavia was an interesting case, because for the people there things were better under Tito. But that, in turn, provoked envy.

What did your mother tell you about her trips to Yugoslavia?

Well, we Hungarians were allowed to travel to Czecho-slovakia or Rumania, as well as the GDR. But travel to Yugoslavia was a good deal more complicated. Anyone who actually obtained permission thought it was like a trip to the French Riviera. My mother occasionally went there on account of her job, and she told me fabulous things. When I was able to travel to Dubrovnik for the first time during the communist days I was completely fascinated. It was unbelievable – almost too beautiful, like paradise. By com-parison, Hungary was a desolate, grey country.

Would your mother have been allowed to take you with her on one of her business trips?

No. Completely out of the question. Goodness knows what these business trips were like. She never travelled alone, but always in a group, and one suspected – or perhaps didn't suspect – who the spy was. But there was always an ob-server there who wrote a report afterwards. The fact that the spouse or other family members stayed at home was a guarantee that people would return.

Tell us more about your childhood. What were your very first experiences?

Music came very soon. We had a primitive radio early on, which could broadcast just two stations. Music streamed out of it constantly. And my father, as an amateur violinist, had old records – 78 rpm shellacs. The first one I can remember was the Mendelssohn violin concerto with Yehudi Menuhin, conducted – though I didn't know it at the time – by George Enescu. Menuhin's name, on the other hand, was already known to me. My father loved him. The two of them even looked somewhat alike. People told me later that I sang more than I spoke – which is something I can remember myself. And then there was this piano: not a grand, but an upright made by the Viennese firm of Lauberger & Gloss. In retrospect, I would have to admit that it was a pretty terrible instrument, but at that time I found it magical. Already, at the age of four, I tried tinkling away on it with all my fingers, to imitate the tunes which came out of the radio or the gramophone.

How did your mother react?

She was astonished. But I'm grateful for the fact that she never said: 'He's a *Wunderkind.*' I was altogether a quite normal child. Then the idea, or rather the question, arose: the child is musically gifted, what should he take up? Piano lessons? They also said that I was very wild, and difficult to keep under control.

Is that the way you saw things?

No, I thought I was quite normal, though I had an

unbelievable amount of energy. When my mother had to work, I sometimes made my grandmother's life difficult. It's true that I loved her deeply, and it was mutual. But a child has to be able to let off steam sometimes. That was not unnatural. So they began to wonder in the family what I could do – for example, sport. I was passionately keen on playing football, though not in a club. But up to my tenth year I played much more football than piano. As an only child, I was tempted more and more to go onto the streets of the district, where there were a lot of children.

How were your relations with friends and companions, to other families?

To start with, they were very good. The first time I heard the word 'Jew' I was five years old. At home, that wasn't a topic at all. But we were the only Jewish family in our district: all the others were Christian, mostly Catholic and a few Protestants. Many of them came from Swabia, just as there's a large Swabian minority in Hungary as a whole. They emigrated in the nineteenth century, or even earlier. They hardly spoke any German, though they had German names. The latter is true of many Jews – my own surname is an example. But when it became dangerous to be Jewish, even before Hitler, many Hungarianised their names.

In order not to attract attention?

That's right. Take Sir Georg Solti. Solti's name was originally Stern. Or Eugene Ormandy, who was actually called Blau. Doráti was once Deutsch. Their parents thought a change of name might help their children. My family stuck to Schiff. I did some research in the Diaspora Museum in

Tel Aviv and I found that this name was already assigned around the fifteenth century in Frankfurt. Those are the first traces of Jews by the name of Schiff. Later, one had to pay a lot of money for names like that. Above all, Jews could buy better names during the Hapsburg monarchy at the time of Joseph II. Whoever could afford it, and wanted to, was called Rubinstein from then on.

Were there already strong signs of anti-Semitism in Hungary before Hitler came onto the scene?

I wouldn't say stronger than in other countries – not stronger than in Poland, the Ukraine or Lithuania, but equally strong. When I was five, the neighbour's child, Attila, told me: 'You're not allowed to play football with us anymore.' He was younger than me – a real little mouse. I said: 'Why?' 'Because you're a Jew.' 'Why is that a problem?' 'You killed Jesus.' I went home in tears. My grandmother explained to me what it was all about. That was my first experience of this problem. Later I could play football with my comrades again. But the episode hurt me so much that I haven't got over it or forgiven it to this day, although little Attila was probably completely innocent. He was just repeating parrot-fashion what he had heard – but from whom? From his dear parents; or in the Catholic church just around the corner, where the priest preached it.

How did your parents behave outwardly?

They were aware of the dangerous situation under which we had already suffered enough. They always said – and it's something I would later rebel against – one had to assimilate and adapt. In my opinion, one neither can nor should.

At the same time, people weren't unfavourably disposed towards us. My father was highly regarded in the neighbourhood and many of these people were his patients. He was an outstanding doctor and they were very grateful to him for that.

And so little Attila's attack was an existential experience for you?

Absolutely. My father was already very ill, so I couldn't talk to him about it, though I could to my mother and grandmother. They didn't try to hide anything. They said, more or less: 'Yes, we are Jews. That's absolutely no problem. But we live in this country, and we represent a minority. And so it's better not to talk about it.' But I, on the other hand, was haunted by it for a very long time. At kindergarten, things were still all right. I was certainly the only Jewish child there. But at elementary school – I was twelve or thirteen at the time – a boy came up to me once and said, 'I come from a Jewish family, too.' So, we were two Jewish children out of forty-two. Of course, there were also indirect hints. Christmas, for instance: at Christmas we were always kept away from the celebrations. The authorities, true to Karl Marx, taught that religion is the opium of the people. For the same reason, the Catholic church was attacked, too. All the same, these children went to Mass every Sunday. Then, for example, there was the Protestant Confirmation. People asked me, 'Why haven't you been confirmed?', and I was ashamed. In short, I always felt this sense of otherness, of rootlessness, without being able to find an alternative. There was a community and we were the exceptions, or the ones who were excluded from it.

How large was the percentage of Jews in the Hungarian population?

Larger than you would think, especially in Budapest. The Nazis invaded Hungary on 19 March 1944, but as allies. Hitler and Miklós Horthy had signed their notorious pact. That's when the deportations began – 600,000 Jews were deported from Hungary, at first from the provinces. After that Budapest's large Jewish community was terrorised by the fascist-leaning members of the Arrow Cross Party. Towards the end of the war, when the transportations were no longer happening, thousands of Jews were driven into the Danube and shot. However, the 'final solution' couldn't be carried through to its conclusion before the end of the war came, and liberation. Today, around 100,000 Jews live in Budapest. In many places in the provinces they were completely wiped out. There are perhaps 100–200 Jews still living in Szeged, for instance, where I once gave a concert in aid of the renovation of the synagogue.

Another flashback: what was daily routine in the kindergarten like?

I have to confess that in those days discipline wasn't my strong point. That only changed later. I rebelled, revolted, hated the kindergarten teachers, who really were dreadful because they treated the children unkindly.

So discipline and punishment were on the cards?

Exactly. On top of that, the food was terrible. For instance, they served up broiled pigs' liver. Disgusting! And, like most children, I also hated spinach. Anyone who didn't eat up was locked in the cellar. Sometimes to avoid being punished I hid my leftovers in my trouser pocket. We dreaded these rules because my mother and my grandmother tended to side with the staff. They probably thought it was the only way to keep such a wild child in check . . .

Was this regime sometimes carried out in your parents' house?

That occasionally happened. My mother was more forgiving than my father. He wanted to be firm, but no longer had the strength. He was very strict. I don't know what would have happened with my music if he had lived longer. When I started piano lessons, I was about five and hadn't begun school yet. I loved improvising. My father used to ask angrily: 'What are you strumming away at? Practise and play what your piano teacher gave you to learn!' And so I had to practise scales and Czerny etudes, but nothing more free. My mother was much more open. She was happy about my improvisations. I never merely strummed away, I tried to invent structures and to experiment with sounds. But my father demanded strict discipline. After his death, I had only women around me and became a spoiled 'little prince'.

In 1960, I went to elementary school. Not the nearest one to us, but an excellent school which bore the name of János Arany, the great nineteenth-century poet who wrote wonderful poems and ballads. He was one of the first to translate Shakespeare into Hungarian, although he hardly knew any English. I learned a lot at that school.

Was this school there in pre-communist days?

It had a different name then and was an all girls school,

run by nuns. That all changed when most of the religious schools were closed. In my time, the school was already co-educational. I went there until 1968. We learned physics, mathematics, history, geography, languages – all of that was very interesting. The only mandatory language was Russian.

Did you like learning Russian?

Not at all – precisely because it was obligatory. Everything you do out of duty, you generally don't like. Although this was the post-Stalin era, we were treated, as before, very harshly. Because there was a shortage of Russian teachers, opportunists entered the teaching profession.

The different alphabet, a different cultural and political background – how did you get on with all that?

The alphabet didn't pose any particular problems for me. What got on my nerves were the texts on, for instance, the history of the communist party or agricultural work on the collective farms. We read neither fairy stories nor great literature like Chekov, Pushkin or Gogol. So we all found Russian lessons rather trying. But I could get over that, because I began to love languages at a very early age. Today I'm very grateful that I learned Russian and can still manage it to a certain extent. Other languages weren't on the curriculum. It was only later that one had the choice of taking German, English or French.

Did your parents speak German?

My parents did speak German, yes; and when they realised

that we weren't learning any German at school, they made sure I learned it privately. I took lessons twice a week with a German neighbour, Aunt Ilma. I was seven or eight at the time. I thought it was marvellous, though the subject was hard and the aunt very strict. A curious observation: after this I didn't speak any German again for a long time. When I got to know my wife, Yuuko Shiokawa, we spoke English together at first. Yuuko was living in Salzburg and when I went there, we suddenly realised that I spoke fluent German!

When did you realise that the high-flown stories of communism were actually mere ideology?

Fairly early. At home we kept our distance in any case. I didn't have to take part in all that. Yet I was advised to be careful about what I said and to whom I said it. And so, of course, fear and mistrust were instilled in me. Some things were compulsory – for instance, belonging to the Pioneers. If I had refused, I would have been expelled from school. It began from the first to the fourth grades with the so-called Little Drummers. We had to wear a blue neckerchief and had to take part in the marches on 1 May, Workers' Day, and sing the obligatory songs. Then from the fifth to the eighth grades we became Pioneers: a red neckerchief, more marching, louder singing. Then there were the Pioneers' camps: living in tents, frying bacon on an open fire. From time to time, bread and dripping, very occasionally even goose liver. It all had its funny side, and I looked on it with humour.

When did you become aware that you are a witty person?

Very early on – perhaps when I was five or six. I really liked laughing, and laughed a lot more than I cried. So I was a cheerful person, and on top of that I loved jokes, both political and dirty. I had a favourite uncle, Ferenc, or Feri Bácsi. He was the husband of Theresia, my mother's middle sister, who had also remained in the country. On Sundays, either they came to us for lunch or we went to them. Feri was a successful lawyer, a wonderful person and a great music lover. He had a huge record collection of thousands of discs, and it was through him that I got to know a lot of music. I could tell him my rude jokes, which made him laugh his head off. That's how I became aware of the fact that I told them well, which I enjoyed. I soon began telling jokes like that in company, or at school, which caused me problems: the teacher would say something, I would say something funny in response – whereupon the whole class would burst out laughing. So I wasn't exactly a hit with the teaching staff.

Were there ever any punishments imposed?

Misdemeanours were noted in a so-called index book. But the consequences weren't exactly tragic. There were warnings, but no punishments. It never got to the stage of my mother being summoned to appear before the school authorities. With other children, that could sometimes happen.

Were you a good student?

Not a star pupil. But learning came easily to me, though I wasn't particularly brilliant at maths. In natural sciences I was unlucky with my teachers: the quality of teachers is terribly important. They were better in the humanities. I got through maths and physics rather dutifully, probably a bit grudgingly, and graduated in them later with difficulty. In the end I had to have private lessons at home in order to pass the final exams well.

History: was that an interesting subject for you?

The schoolbooks were pure propaganda. And today, I'm afraid it's even worse. When ideology rules the country, history is written and rewritten at will. It went without saying that we had to admire the Russians. What was drummed in as a result was that the Austro-Hungarian age was anathema, capitalism is pure exploitation and imperialism brought with it nothing but injustice. Lies, pure lies. Our history and geography books were teeming with statistics: which countries produced the most coal? The Soviet Union was always ranked first, of course. Always pure propaganda. Even the Holocaust wasn't mentioned – it was a taboo subject.

Why is that?

For one thing, because of the Hitler–Stalin Pact; for another, because they didn't want to admit that Hungary's history in this respect needed to be re-examined. That's still a problem to this day. At that time, they taught us that the Nazis and fascists had invaded Hungary. But the fact that there were also Hungarian fascists was never mentioned. In that case, who and what were Horthy and the Arrow Cross Party? Horthy was just as taboo: he wasn't hero-worshipped yet, as he is today, but a veil of silence was drawn over him. Then there was talk of the partisans: all the Hungarians were partisans, they all belonged to the Resistance, they all fought heroically against the Nazis. Nevertheless, there was a certain amount of scepticism going around. You could allow yourself to smirk about all that, and later even to laugh. The 'superior wisdom' of the schoolbooks or the radio was treated somewhat mistrustfully – a healthy mistrust.

At the time of the 1956 uprising you were three years old, so you probably have no memories of it.

I remember that huge Russian tanks suddenly appeared. That made an enormous impression on me and at the same time it instilled a good deal of fear in me. We lived on a main road where the bus passed by, but suddenly there were tanks instead. It was like an earthquake. I asked my parents what it was. 'Those are Soviet tanks,' they said. The rest is a blank. The fighting took place on the Pest side.

How was the big uprising treated afterwards in the country, in the city and at school?

It was underplayed. The whole occurrence had to be described as a counter-revolution, and in no way as a revolution. According to the communist leader János Kádár it was the work of reactionary forces who were trying to overturn the ruling world order. We defeated them, thank God . . . What really happened, I don't know. One wasn't allowed to talk about it. At school there was calm, silence, taboo. As everyone knows, a lot of people fled abroad following the events.

Did no one from your family take part in the revolution?

Not actively, but Uncle Feri worked as a civil judge before he became a lawyer. As a Jewish judge, he had sentenced many war criminals after the war who went on to be executed. In those days the death penalty was still in force. Feri was terrified during the uprising. If the rebels had won, things would have become extremely uncomfortable for my uncle.

Did he have to deal with the insurgents, too?

No, because he was already a lawyer; he no longer held the position of a judge.

Did people notice, or feel, that after this revolution something in the country had changed compared to how things had been before?

Times became much harder and darker. But, fortunately, not for very long. Kádár came to power. It's true that he was Moscow's man and was responsible for the execution of Imre Nagy and his colleagues, which made him deeply disliked at first. But in the course of time he realised how to make himself popular. He was even a success with my mother: she loved him.

How long was Kádár in power?

Almost an eternity – that's to say, until the spring of 1988. Then he had to stop, because he was simply too old. He became a father figure, and, as I've already mentioned, stood for 'goulash communism' in the country. Nevertheless, his regime was ruled with an iron fist and with Moscow's grace.

Were you politically engaged at any time in those days or did you think of yourself more as an observer?

I was a close observer, although at home the word was:

'Don't get involved in politics, child – leave that be.' The warning was clear.

Perhaps your parents were afraid you could still become a revolutionary.

Probably. Though in those days I wasn't that interested in politics. In any case, after the 1956 revolution there were no longer any alternatives. Where would there have been any? There was no underground movement, either.

Was Stalin a subject at school?

He was *persona non grata*. Khrushchev had toppled him from his pedestal. So with us, too, it was as though he had never existed. After Stalin's death all the schoolbooks had to be rewritten. That all happened in a trice. History came out without him.

Let's go back to the fine arts. When did you have your first piano lessons?

In 1959, when I was five years old, with a woman teacher. It was never a man: women determined my younger years almost exclusively. It was my mother who decided who should teach her son. She didn't want to take the task on herself, and that was a good thing. Of course, she could have given me piano lessons, but she quite rightly decided there should be a certain distance between us. Daniel Barenboim would probably see things differently, and would say he's grateful that his father taught him.

Who was your first teacher?

Uncle Feri's circle of acquaintances included an Aunt Elisabeth. Her pet name was Bözsi Néni (Aunt Bözsi), and she was a teacher with an excellent reputation. It was absolutely like paradise in Budapest in those days, because there were hundreds of aunts like her. Not a single man. Beyond that there was an ingenious system of music schools. There was one in every district of Budapest. They were elementary level – not conservatory or college – and free. But at that time, I was too young to go to a school, so I went to Aunt Bözsi at her home. It was a long way off, by bus and tram, with two changes. She lived in the centre of Pest, in a tiny one-bedroom flat. There was a real grand piano – not an upright, but a genuine brown grand. So, I know a time when not everything was black . . .

You were very talented, so it could have been expected that you would already have been sent for lessons when you were three or four.

That would have been too soon. Five is fine, and early enough. In any case, my parents never had such special ambitions. There was no talk of a *Wunderkind*: you studied piano, just as you learned German. That was part of it. My mother had piano lessons when she was a child and so did her two sisters. It was a part of overall culture, like languages, ballet and later dance school.

So to begin with you were, or seemed to be, normal?

Definitely.

Can you remember your first lesson?

Vaguely. I wouldn't say Aunt Bözsi was a particularly kind person. She was rather stiff, smoked continually and wore incredibly bright lipstick – vermilion red. And so the cigarettes always had a garish red colour. On top of all that, Aunt Bözsi was rather old – well over 60. To begin with I had to learn to read music. I managed that quite quickly. Then I had to learn to sing what I was reading; and after that came theory.

Was singing important?

Every child has to sing. As far as playing went, I began with very simple Bach preludes. Bartók's children's pieces came very soon after that. On the one hand the composer, who died in 1945 in America, was thought of as contemporary, and on the other hand he was already fully integrated into music teaching.

Were there people who found him too modern?

Bartók wasn't unreservedly loved, but he was respected. Some people found *Mikrokosmos*, above all, too radical. We found much of it too dry, too hard. But Aunt Bözsi decided I had to learn it. She was convinced by Bartók and thought he was marvellous. Basically, she was right. But I also had to learn Bach, Schumann's *Album for the Young* and things of that kind. A couple of years later, a Russian delegation came to Budapest, led by Dmitri Kabalevsky. He was very gaunt and tall. I had to play him Soviet pieces from the large repertoire for children, among them a piece of his. The Master was very satisfied.

When did people notice how talented you were?

That happened only gradually. In the beginning I was just a very musical child. I believe I've stayed the same to this day. And that was Aunt Bözsi's basic philosophy. Much later, when I came to London for the first time – I was around ten years old – I met a very well-known piano professor, Ilona Kabos, a legendary teacher who had taught a lot of great pianists. I played her a Bach two-part Invention and a Haydn sonata and she said, 'Why do you play such easy pieces?' And I told her that for me they weren't easy. Aunt Bözsi gave me these pieces because she thought the repertoire was suited to me. But Ilona Kabos mortified me: 'Just think about it, I have other pupils of your age who are already playing all the Beethoven sonatas. Now, go and learn Beethoven's Op.22, the third Chopin Ballade, etc.' I tried, but there was a real conflict between us. I went back to Aunt Bözsi and she was horrified. 'What? You haven't got nearly that far.'

With hindsight, who was right?

Fundamentally, probably both. But to this day my opinion is that young pianists play many things too early. On the other hand, you need the challenge. You need inspiration, vision. Maybe Aunt Bözsi held me by the reins for too long, slowed me down. I went to her for eight long years, during the whole time I was at elementary school, until 1967–8. And yet, I'm extremely grateful to her, because her teaching was very good preparation: basic and tasteful. Only the posture I learned with Aunt Bözsi was a problem. You can see on a film how I played, admittedly well, but with terrible posture: my nose almost touching the keys. Aunt Bözsi's colleagues noticed this straight away and took her to task for it. She answered: 'Yes, I know. But on the other hand, he's so musical. And I'm no policewoman. He should be left alone. He'll learn that later for himself.' That was admittedly true, but only under very difficult conditions. It was hard to get out of the habit without losing any of my musicality.

There comes a point where it's clear that a child is not only gifted, but more than that: a real force. When was that for you?

That happened in my time with Aunt Bözsi. Later, I entered the music school system I've already mentioned. I matriculated in the central music school. I was still going to her, though not at her home, but at a school where she also taught. I have to add that the system of schools of that kind formed a wonderful network. There was a central administration and also senior teachers who travelled around as inspectors. The word quickly spread as to who were the most gifted pupils. At the end of the school year, children's concerts were organised. We were chosen and assigned to the large hall of the Franz Liszt Academy. For those who were allowed to appear there, it was a huge honour.

You were eight or nine?

Yes. I was allowed to play there for the first time with an orchestra. I performed Mozart's D major concert rondo K.382. It caused quite a stir. Teachers had come from abroad to study the justly famous educational method founded by Kodály. Some of them had even travelled from Western Europe or the USA. The children had to play for the teachers – small pieces, rather than large ones.

Was that for pleasure or duty?

I did it gladly. I took to the stage from an early age, and that's something that has stayed with me. When I play for people it's completely different from my living room. I'm pleased to share what I have with others, and to give of myself. I noticed quite soon that people listened to me. It's a talent that was discovered quite early on.

Were people saying at that time, he's going to become a pianist?

No, not for a long time. I was twelve when I decided that was what I wanted to do. I no longer remember a specific event that led to that decision. The whole thing has to be understood as a gradual process. My mother took me with her to concerts when I was quite young. I sat on her lap, without a ticket. In 1962, Sviatoslav Richter came back to Budapest. He played Beethoven's Op.22 Sonata, and Schubert's Three Pieces D.946 and the 'Wanderer' Fantasy. I was hugely impressed, and I remember it down to the last detail. Richter was demonic, a madman. In addition, this experience took place at a time when we hated everything Soviet . . . So when I was twelve or thirteen, it was clear to me that I wanted to become a musician. I was still at elementary school when, in 1968, a competition for young talent was announced on Hungarian TV. *'Ki mit tud?'* – 'Who can do what?' There were various categories, and the event, which took place every three years, was hugely popular in Hungary. It was really designed for older children from secondary school, but I was allowed to participate and was chosen by my school. The surprising result was that I won that competition, the only one from which I've ever come out on top.

It made me famous overnight. Everyone watched it. You had to get through three rounds, plus preliminary rounds in each category. You had to recite poems, for instance, or sing hit songs. I was in the classical music section and my rival was a virtuoso on the accordion. There was a panel of experts which included the well-known music critic András Pernye and the composer Emil Petrovics.

A star was born?

I wouldn't put it like that. I became very well known, which gave rise to envy as well as enmity towards me. After that, things went like this: at the age of fifteen I went to a high school for music students. In the mornings, the timetable was taken up with 'normal' subjects; in the afternoons there was time for music and practising. The system of musical education in Hungary was divided into three levels: lower level until you were 14, conservatory or middle school until you were around 18 and, after that, an entrance exam for the college at the academy founded by Liszt. I left out the middle level, the Conservatory, and went straight to the Academy, where Professor Pál Kadosa was head of the piano department. Along with Aunt Bözsi and the director of the music school, I paid Kadosa an introductory visit at his home.

Were you prepared? Were you nervous?

I was probably prepared, yes. Nervous? No. Kadosa turned out to be a very charming old gentleman. I thought of him as an uncle. After I played to him, he said he would accept me. But all the same I had to pass the regular entrance exam, despite the fact that Kadosa had seen me on television. So I took an exam in one of the teaching rooms at the Academy. Around fifteen piano professors were there, not all of them favourably disposed to me. I played Bach, a Mozart sonata, something by Chopin and something by Bartók. Everything went satisfactorily, and so I came into a preliminary class that had been specially set up for me, because I was still too young for the regular class. The additional subjects I had to take were harmony, general music theory and music history. As the youngest there, I met the other students. Zoltán Kocsis was somewhat older and so he was already in the first class. He already played very well at that time. At the same time, I was still going to the music secondary school, which turned out to be a waste of time in the long run, however. When I spoke recently to Iván Fischer, who also went there, he said it was a miracle that with all that dreadful teaching we weren't completely illiterate.

Was that to do with the system? With communism?

What ruled above all was sloppiness. The people who taught there were neither well qualified nor did they have anything to do with music. I always had the feeling that I was treated with animosity, because I was good at music. And most of my classmates didn't become musicians, although that's what the purpose of a music secondary school should have been.

Beyond education, how was the politico-social situation?

It gradually became more relaxed, a bit more open and less relentless. It's true that you had to be a member of the so-called KISZ, the association of young communists. But I was discharged from this society – indeed, thrown out

– because I had forgotten to pay the membership subscription, which wasn't even high. That didn't do me any harm at all: it just shows that in those days everything happened rather sloppily. On the other hand, we were still living in and under a communist dictatorship.

Was your temperament a problem?

My surfeit of jokes was regarded as somewhat subversive.

How long did you live in your parents' house?

I lived at home until 1979, when I left Hungary. That was quite normal in those days, especially for children in Budapest.

Your relations with mother and grandmother were good up to the end?

Yes, excellent, wonderful. Both of them spoiled me in a very delightful way, though they were strict. My mother would regularly ask me: 'Have you practised enough today?' That held true up to her death. In those days, it drove me mad. I was a good student, too, and never had any real problems, and in the last two years I could even have private lessons at home. I only needed a special private tutor for maths. My shaky algebra probably had something to do with the fact that I was taught by an old woman who was as dry as dust.

After that, you took your final exam, which you passed with flying colours.

I took that when I was 18. It wasn't hard. I was helped by a

Russian teacher, Ferenc Sztupár – a curious individual. He came from the Ukraine, and was a great communist, and at the same time an unbelievably nice fellow. He was always wanting to help us. During Russian lessons, we wanted to play football in the corridor. Agreed – though with the rider: 'But don't make any noise!' Before the final exam, he told us what would come up in it. In addition, he particularly helped those who were musically talented – in complete contrast to some of the teachers in the music school, who reacted to music with almost panic-filled hatred.

How was your social life? Were you an introverted loner or more sociable?

School was sociable, and that went for me, too. I always had very good friends in class, liked being among people, was friendly, approachable and not inaccessible. I was only rather shy as far as girls were concerned in those days. Of course, I wanted them to like me. As a result, I was totally ignored. That only changed when it became clear that I played the piano well. At the time of the Beatles, pop music was very 'in'. I heard them on the radio, and realised that with girls, Mozart wasn't necessarily the right choice. So I played them Beatles songs – with the desired result. 'Yellow Submarine', 'Yesterday' – very good songs! It's true that my first approaches to the fair sex remained wholly platonic . . .

The Rolling Stones were stronger fare.

I liked them a good deal less. The Beatles, however, were melodious and invented very nice harmonies. On the other hand, I immediately knew that wouldn't be my world, even though when I was young I kept up with pop music to a certain extent. That happened inevitably through parties and dances. We all went to dance school. First, we learned classical dances, and then modern ones – tango, rumba, samba, cha-cha-cha, twist. We heard the music via Radio Free Europe, where great things were broadcast. I had a tape recorder, so I could record the music and learn the songs. In theory, we weren't allowed to listen to this radio station, which was financed by the CIA.

So there were dances in the cellars of Budapest?

Parties, house parties. The grown-ups weren't exactly keen. It was always a bit chaotic. But we liked going there to dance, listen to music and tell jokes. I never smoked, but the others did. I tried it but didn't like it. Same thing with alcohol. In short, my youth was very proper. I think on it with pleasure: it was a nice time, very secretive and romantic. What I see today is much less mysterious. Everything is available, everything is in the open – total transparency. Where are the surprises, the romanticism?

At that age one is extremely receptive and constantly expanding one's horizons in musical and general cultural interests. About composers: in those days, you weren't at all well disposed towards Wagner. What about other composers?

My favourite composer was Brahms. That's quite unusual. He enthralled me enormously, above all the D minor Piano Concerto, which I still think of as a work of genius. Then the First Symphony, which I listened to with my uncle on a recording conducted by Toscanini. That literally sent me into ecstasy. I was around fourteen. Bach was also already a strong presence and the same is true of Mozart. On the other hand, I didn't feel particularly close to Beethoven yet. Of course, I liked the symphonies, as I did Schubert's. My first visit to England contributed significantly to a broadening of my horizons. That was not only a great privilege: I was also stimulated by many new things.

How did a child from a socialist country in the Eastern bloc come to travel so far, and to England?

I had relatives there – a small clan that had left Hungary. The trip was made possible by the fact that I received an invitation: my relatives invited me for the summer holidays. The authorities looked into it and graciously decided that I was allowed to go.

Did you have your mother's support?

Of course. But just as self-evident was the condition that we weren't to travel together. My grandmother had often visited the 'English' relatives, but always alone. Someone had to remain at home for the reasons I've already mentioned. I travelled by plane from Budapest to London Heathrow. My first flight – very exciting, but not a pleasure. To this day, I still don't like flying, but you can't get around it. In any case, I flew with the Hungarian company Malév, which no longer exists. I was met and taken to Surrey, where my relatives had a nice house, and I spent a couple of months there during the long summer holidays.

How did you get on with the language?

I couldn't speak a word of English then, but I learned extremely quickly, which was what my relatives wanted. They wanted to take my father's place and give me a good up-bringing. Learning English well was very important. I had to go to an ordinary school in Esher, Surrey, every day. It was like being thrown in at the deep end. The children were always joking about me because I came from 'Hungary – hungry'. But they accepted me, and I managed to assimilate well, for example, by playing cricket with them. It was really funny and very different – all a bit eccentric. The food was terrible – a real disaster. All those cooked vegetables! The only thing I liked was custard.

Did you go to London, too?

Yes. I often went to concerts in the Royal Festival Hall and the Royal Albert Hall. At that time, there was the difference between the greyness of Hungary and the theatre life of London. At first, I didn't understand anything, but it was wonderful. I got to know the Schubert songs. I heard re-cordings by Peter Pears and Benjamin Britten, which I liked very much. Britten's piano playing was unique. In a nutshell, I was able to breathe a very cultural atmosphere.

For a twelve-year-old, Schubert's Lieder were quite demanding.

That's true. But they were good groundwork, because when I went to the Academy at the age of 14, and had my first lessons with György Kurtág, I was well prepared for the part of his classes that was devoted to Schubert's Lieder.

Which musicians did you hear in England?

Clifford Curzon, who later impressed me at a concert

in Budapest – a fine musician, but a complex character. Solomon was already no longer playing. I missed Klemperer, which I still regret to this day. I rate him extremely highly. It shouldn't be forgotten that Klemperer was at his best during his time in Budapest. After the war, and after he'd suffered a stroke, Aladár Toth, Annie Fischer's husband, who was a music critic, and then director of the Budapest Opera, engaged him as music director. At the end of the forties and the beginning of the fifties, Klemperer conducted the most wonderful operas and concerts there. Those performances set benchmarks.

Did you have more journeys like that?

Every year until I was about 16. Then the authorities suddenly turned down my applications. Why? Because I was approaching the age of military service. For a male graduate, two years of military service were obligatory. There was no escaping it. Dreadful. But somehow, thank God, I did get out of it. The director of the Academy, Dénes Kovács (a first-rate violinist, by the way) had good relations with the ministry and the government and he managed to get the best instrumentalists exempted from military service.

Which English experiences and insights were decisive and formative for you?

Many of them. Especially my meetings with the musician George Malcolm. In fact, I had got to know Malcolm in Hungary, through acquaintances in England. I'll have more to say about that in a moment. The same acquaintances opened a door for me to several émigrés from Hungarian Jewish circles who were living in London: the pianist Peter

Frankl, for example, the violinist György Pauk and the teacher Ilona Kabos whom I've already mentioned. Peter Frankl's wife, Annie, belonged to the same group. She was a pianist and her father, who was a doctor, had been my father's best friend. Small world . . . This father was a cultured man who played in string quartets. I had already played to him when I was twelve and the general impression was that I was very talented – still a child, of course, but a remarkable one. The upshot was that I was scheduled to appear at Lady Margaret Lamington's salon, where house concerts took place. The influential critic Andrew Porter, who in those days was writing for the *Financial Times*, was there. Among the regular guests was the well-known art historian John Pope-Hennessy. And so, I presented myself to this circle of about 30 music lovers. When Lady Lamington died four years later, she left me 500 pounds – a lot of money in those days. I went to the piano showrooms of Jacques Samuel on the Edgware Road and bought myself my first decent piano stool. It cost 25 pounds and was shipped from London to Budapest, where products of that quality weren't available.

A stool with red velvet, like you use these days?

No: black leather. With the money I had left over, I was able to travel to a masterclass which George Malcolm held at Dartington Hall in Devon a couple of years later and pay the fees. I mention this because Lady Lamington wrote to me and told me that her good friend George Malcolm was about to come to Budapest to give a concert. He would need a page-turner, because he never played from memory. I was about twelve and was extremely keen. I wasn't exactly a virtuoso yet, but I could read music very well, and Malcolm was delighted with my services. He gave a harpsichord evening in the large hall of the Liszt Academy: the English virginalists, Couperin, Rameau, Bach, and Scarlatti to end with. It was wonderful: I was in absolute raptures. Malcolm was highly imaginative and compelling. As a person, he was nervous, and before I went to him he'd been an alcoholic. A doctor had a serious talk with him and he came off the bottle with great self-discipline. When I met him, he always drank only fruit juice, coffee, tea and water. On the other hand, he was a chain smoker and puffed away at strong Gitanes and Gauloises incessantly. With those, he drank black coffee – not exactly good for your health, either.

Did Malcolm become your teacher?

You can't really put it that way. On the occasion of his harpsichord evening, I was allowed to play for him, and that was something I always did either when I was staying in England or he came to Budapest. He wasn't really my piano teacher, but he stimulated me in important ways and, above all, he had a lasting influence on my baroque style. He also encouraged me to play the baroque repertoire not on the harpsichord, but on the piano. He himself much preferred playing the piano to 'his' instrument.

Why didn't Malcolm appear in public as a pianist?

He could never have made an international career. The time simply hadn't come when the baroque repertoire could be played on the piano. Harpsichord evenings, on the other hand, were perfectly acceptable. On the EMI recording of Bach's 'Brandenburg' Concertos under Klemperer, Malcolm played No.5, with its big cadenza, sensationally well.

Didn't he want to persuade you to take up the harpsichord?

No. It was much more important to him that I should play 'his' repertoire properly on the piano. He was vehemently against too much pedal. What was of decisive importance to him was a perfect legato and the various possibilities of articulation. His harpsichords satisfied him in those respects: the instruments had various pedals with which you could create different colours, and even make a crescendo. In that way, you could obtain orchestral effects. Wanda Landowska played in a not entirely different style. But, of course, in those days there were already purists who were angered by him and attacked him vehemently. But Malcolm was someone who had a sense of humour and didn't allow himself to be influenced by that. He was simply a brilliant articulator – when he spoke, too, incidentally. I've seldom heard anyone speak such beautiful English, and he used to correct me constructively, too.

When did he die?

He died in 1997. He was 80 and died happy. He was a very religious Roman Catholic, and towards the end he realised that his time had come. He was very important to my life. He was really a renaissance type – extremely versatile, and rejecting any kind of specialism: conductor, organist, soloist on the harpsichord, clavichord and piano. On top of that he was a continuo player and a conductor of the Royal Air Force band! In addition, he composed witty pieces – for instance, an outrageously amusing fugue in mock-Bach style, 'Bach Before the Mast'. Malcolm gave me many and varied things. I'm very grateful to him.

Then you went back to Hungary: the hard grind of reality in the East.

I couldn't travel at all any more – just to neighbouring countries. From 1969 to 1973–4 I lived and played almost exclusively in the Eastern bloc.

Let's consider the Academy for a moment. Now it was getting serious and there was more competition.

That's true. But to start with I went to Professor Kadosa's preliminary class which had been set up especially for me. He was not only the best, but also the most important teacher, who trained all the pianists who were any good or became good. But because he was a busy man he had an assistant who was no less than the wonderful composer and musician György Kurtág. Kadosa was a good composer, too, and as a pupil of Kodály he cultivated a clear-cut, folk-like style. He had the reputation of being a fine pianist, too. Unfortunately, I never heard him in that capacity.

But he must have given you a lot of pointers and guidance?

Of course. I think Kadosa himself no longer played owing to a hand injury. But he spoke of his heroic years as a virtuoso, when he played Beethoven's Fourth Concerto and people said it was better than Dohnányi.

Dohnányi was the great hero in those days?

Exactly. That's why Kadosa's remark was the height of modesty . . . Because Dohnányi was amazing – a legend in the Academy. Kadosa always taught the overall view, without going into details. His pupils had to bring a lot of pieces to their lessons, which lasted exactly an hour – not a minute more or less. This highly concentrated lesson covered everything. Kadosa said little, but what he said was in very good taste and to the point. For instance, when it was Chopin: 'Don't play so sentimentally here.' Or, 'Be clearer, more articulated'; or, 'more legato'. In the Beethoven sonatas, the transitions were important, and the unity of the pieces. 'Don't play mechanically, please; don't be so aggressive: make music expressively, with tenderness.' And alongside this were the lessons with Kurtág. When Kurtág stopped being an assistant, in 1969, Ferenc Rados took over. After that we studied chamber music with Kurtág, and piano with Rados. He was just as demanding as Kurtág and, on top of that, he was very focused on the technical aspects of the piano. He criticised my posture at the piano vehemently, and he was right. Posture is critical for the sound, the tone and other aspects. It's important to sit correctly. Many young pianists sit badly and move too much. And good piano playing or violin playing needs to be convincing from an aesthetic point of view, too. Just look at Horowitz or Rubinstein or David Oistrakh. Richter was something of an exception. Glenn Gould is a poor example. And while I'm talking about Gould, I also had, and still sometimes have, the bad habit of singing out loud. Meanwhile, you don't really hear what's going on: you lose control.

One could object that you played so well that you no longer needed to hear at all.

That might have been true with Gould. You can say a lot about him, but you really can't claim that he was uncontrolled. All the same, the cantabile has to come from the piano, not from singing along. You may think you play in a cantabile style, while you're actually performing very percussively, and the singing covers it.

Who did you profit more from? Kurtág or Rados?

Both. The teaching assistants were of course rather merciless. Rados was sarcastic or cynical; Kurtág by comparison was never unpleasant – on the contrary, he was very kind. He could praise us highly for an individual note or a phrase. Occasionally he even liked a whole piece. Rados, on the other hand, almost never liked anything. Never. To him, it was always dreadful – and for us, very frustrating. Nevertheless, for me he was of central importance. A lot of his pupils ran away; many of the girls cried and never came back. But he wasn't truly mean; at heart he wasn't malicious. Basically, he meant well. And he was just as dissatisfied with himself as he was with others. I was terribly fond of him, also because he wanted to prepare us for the world, the cruel world – by which I mean the world of music. Prepared in that way, nothing should surprise us anymore. In this, he was right: I can't remember a single instance in which he was wrong.

The catchword of development: was there an agenda for that, or did it happen, so to speak, of itself and overnight?

There was an agenda in that every half year we had to take an exam. What we had to play was more or less laid down: something by Bach, plus a classical sonata, then of course Chopin and perhaps a piece by Schumann, or something twentieth-century, by Bartók, for instance.

Who chose the repertoire?

The teacher provided the ideas. Several of the students were already very advanced. Zoltán Kocsis, for example, brought pieces with him which he had learned unbelievably quickly – difficult pieces like the Etudes of Bartók and Debussy. His repertoire wasn't prescribed to him. For me, it was different: my teachers stipulated what was to be learned and performed. So I had to learn Bach's three-part Inventions systematically, but not the 'Goldberg' Variations. Everything was graduated. Besides the Bach, there were a couple of Mozart sonatas, Schumann's *Papillons*, shorter pieces by Chopin and the Third Ballade. All the same, that was quite a step forward from Aunt Bözsi's province.

How did you feel about the exams?

They were dreadful. I hated them. They were held in the small concert hall of the Academy. Relatives were allowed to be there, but it wasn't open to the public. The professors sat there, with Kadosa always right at the front. It had clearly always been the same. There's a story that when Bartók came in the thirties, he didn't greet anyone. He was truly a hermit. Then Dohnányi came in. He was the director of the school. The two men were close friends, and they embraced. Bartók didn't deign to look at the others – not out of arrogance, but because he was so reserved. His son, Péter, later wrote that his father described the Academy as the 'evil house'. He disliked teaching and never taught composition, only piano, simply to earn money.

Bartók was not only a great composer, but also – and you can see that from his pieces – a brilliant pianist.

He could play the piano amazingly well, though he wasn't really interested in that. What interested him was his composing, and his ethnographic work. He thought of himself primarily as a researcher.

Going back to the exams, how exactly did they proceed?

I was always very nervous, which I otherwise almost never was. On top of that, I felt that some of the professors disliked me on account of my having taken part in the TV competition at that time: I had got too far for them. And, in fact, my popularity in those days bore no relation to my ability. I was regarded as a conceited child, and I was anything but. Under this presumption I played a classical sonata. Repeating the exposition was forbidden; and at the start of the recapitulation Kadosa cried: 'Thank you – enough!' It was terrible: always this 'Thank you – enough!' I was never able to give of my best at exams, because I felt such antipathy towards them. I played decently, but with more mistakes than there really needed to have been because I was trying to overcompensate for the difficult circumstances. The result was unsatisfactory. If you try too hard, things don't work out.

Was there any rivalry with other students?

Yes, but much less at that time than later. I was so much younger than the others. My fellow students were very nice to me. They liked me, which was a big advantage. Kocsis liked me in those days, too, but not later. I thought very highly of him – he was an unbelievably talented person.

Did you hear the other pianists? Was that useful to you?

That was very important to me then. To say something else about Zoltán Kocsis: his lesson came after mine, and I stayed on so that I could hear him. At that time, we used to listen to each other. After that we stayed together for a long time, and sometimes played four hands – usually orchestral pieces on two pianos: symphonies by Brahms or Bruckner. In short, we listened, learned, and studied a lot which didn't directly have anything to do with the piano. We heard records at home. Kocsis was very advanced, and unlike me he also studied composition.

Was that the rule: piano and composition?

It was exceptional for someone to do both. Later, he gave up the dual lessons because he needed more time for the piano. In those days he inspired me a great deal, and his difficult character hadn't come to light. Years later, we made a recording together for Hungaroton of Bach's concertos for two pianos. It was a disaster: one of the few recordings I still can't accept to this day. It would have been better if it had never happened. We drifted apart. Kocsis had begun to imitate Glenn Gould. Sometimes Gould himself teetered on the edge of parody; and when somebody copies him, it becomes caricature: sharp, hard, unbearable.

So no elective affinity?

The opposite. We didn't fit in with each other at all. I couldn't play in that manner and didn't want to. But at the time of that Bach project he was the stronger of us. The conductor, Albert Simon – a wonderful musician, incidentally – said to me: 'You're a little fellow, and you're playing with a genius. So fit in with him'. I was still young and so I did what was wanted. I had too much respect; I should simply have run away.

Were there any competitions where you could prove yourself ready for a possible career?

Student competitions. I hated them. I would much rather have gone back to England. That's why I applied for the famous Leeds International Piano Competition, in 1972, and was eliminated after the second round. (The first prize was won by Murray Perahia, who played quite wonderfully.) It was a matter of indifference to me – I wasn't a bit sad. I found myself on a long path, in search of myself, too. After my early success in the TV competition, where I was celebrated as the public's favourite, my self-confidence had suffered a bit. On top of that, I suppose, came the onset of puberty. My teachers didn't spoil me in any way, and that was a good thing. And at least Kadosa believed in me and was never mean to me.

He acknowledged your musicality?

Immediately. Perhaps others did, too. But then something happened which pointed in another direction. Once Rados told me to send my mother to him. When she arrived, he read her the riot act: 'What are you thinking of? Your son is a great big nobody. What we need in our school is talents like Dezsö Ránki, Zoltán Kocsis and others; and what do you think your son is in such company? A nonentity. Don't ever forget that.' My mother ran home crying and was utterly dismayed. For me the incident had a positive effect, inasmuch as I said to myself, 'Damn it all, I won't allow my mother to be so sad. I'll work much harder and will show Mr Rados that it wasn't all a waste of effort.'

When was that?

Around 1970. In the following years, I developed a great deal. I practised very intensively and with great perseverance – six hours a day. And in any case, Rados was the best teacher I could have had for piano technique. On top of that, he always bracketed technique together with musicality and tone quality. For example, you had to phrase two notes together – one deep in the bass, the other quite high in the treble – with one finger, without using the pedal, and create the illusion of playing that widely spaced interval *legatissimo*. Rados himself could play these notes in such a way that he really breathed life into them, and they didn't die away. Then there was balancing chords, the transparency of polyphony. I learned these things slowly but surely; and then, for instance, by way of Brahms's D minor Concerto, which was already a big step forward. For Leeds, there were so-called preparatory concertos. Rados had agreed to play the concerto in public with me on two pianos. I was in seventh heaven. It was an indirect way of showing his praise – even if he still thought I was a nonentity. And yet, for this nonentity there was still a ray of hope . . .

What was the situation as regards instruments in those days? Their quality, was, after all critical for the experiments in tone and sound which you've just been describing.

Shortly after my success in the TV competition, my mother bought a medium-sized Blüthner. That was a substantial investment at the time. It's true we weren't poor, but we weren't exactly well-off, either. On the one hand, the piano was a luxury on which my mother used up her entire savings; but on the other hand, a good instrument was of course enormously important to me. I kept the Blüthner, which was a fine item, right up to the end of my days in Hungary. When my mother died a few years ago, I had it brought to Italy, where it was restored by Angelo Fabbrini. Now it's better than ever. The problem in Hungary was that there were hardly any decent piano tuners: one had the impression that they had died out after the war, and there was no progeny. Good technicians would have had to learn their trade at Steinway's or Bösendorfer in any case, and in those days that was an impossibility.

One of the most famous conservatories in Europe had—

—inadequate instruments, yes. That's how things stood. The old ones were often in poor condition. Once in a while a new Steinway was purchased, but there was always the problem of having it serviced. The pianos were seldom tuned, and never voiced. That obviously had something to do with the communist economics in the country. In the basement of the Academy there was a piano workshop, which was supposed to have been responsible for the upkeep of the instruments. But what did they do there? They took the new Steinways, robbed them of their mechanism, and cobbled together an inferior substitute at great expense. That went on for a long while, well beyond my time as a student. Upstairs there were instruments which weren't exactly unplayable, but which were not of real quality. In Hungary, I was never able to learn what a good instrument is, or can be. And it was no better in the Soviet

Union, although there was a worthy old man who took on tuning for Sviatoslav Richter and Emil Gilels. My craziest experience in these things was one of my first concerts in the Hungarian provinces. I found the piano was missing one leg and they propped the keyboard up with bricks. That seems like an absurd story, but it can teach you something. These days, young people think top quality should be taken for granted everywhere.

Apropos Richter. Which outstanding pianists did you hear at that time besides Richter and Annie Fischer?

I was blown away by Rubinstein who came to Budapest in 1967 and gave fantastic, unforgettable concerts. He played Chopin's E minor Concerto and Brahms's B flat on the same evening, with the Hungarian State Orchestra conducted by János Ferencsik. And then he also gave a wonderful solo recital. He played – not at the end, but to start with – Schubert's last sonata, which I was hearing for the very first time.

He obviously wanted to end with something virtuosic.

To him, the B flat Sonata was a curtain raiser. By cutting out the first-movement repeat, he got through it in 25 minutes. He followed it with a very impressive *Carnaval* and after the Schumann he played Chopin and Liszt, and finally the obligatory *Ritual Fire Dance* by Falla. The encores included Liszt's *Valse oubliée*, in which he suddenly had a stage-managed memory lapse. He turned to the audience and said, '*Pardon, j'ai oublié.*' Unbelievably charming. Many people said Rubinstein was at his best in those late years: his tone, his sound, his aristocratic appearance, although he was of small stature. His posture was perfect: that impressed me a great deal.

Emil Gilels must have come to Budapest often, too.

Strangely enough, in those days I never liked him. I don't really know why. He made a few wonderful recordings, but when I think of my experiences of live concerts – Budapest, London, New York – I have to say that one concert was weaker than the next. It's true that he was an extremely nervous person who had an attack of stage fright before every concert.

All the same, Gilels had a wonderful touch.

A beautiful touch, yes. His sound was beautifully full and round. When he played Tchaikovsky, the sound carried with full strength, without his having to force it. One of his finest recordings is of Grieg's *Lyric Pieces*.

What did you think of your fellow countryman Géza Anda?

I heard him three times in Budapest in the early seventies, shortly before he died. His Chopin Etudes impressed me at that time: they were commanding. Whether or not they were all really good, I can no longer say. Then, in 1972, Maurizio Pollini came to Budapest for the first time. He was already a sensation and I immediately understood why. At the same time, I knew that could never be my style – but at the same time I was aware that my own style lay far ahead of me. Everything seemed somehow unreachable to me.

Now you're exaggerating.

Not at all. It was fundamentally a matter of a specific atmosphere. Let me explain that in more detail. People like Kurtág or Albert Simon or Rados formed a sort of guru system. They were great personalities and fantastic musicians, as everyone knew. At the same time, they were know-alls who knew everything better. Only when these gurus had given their blessing did you count for something. Without that blessing, you didn't exist. That needs to be said, for once.

It sounds rather unpleasant.

That's how it was. There's a story that illustrates it quite well. It's about the great musician and pedagogue Leó Weiner. Weiner was also a fine composer, and from the twenties to the fifties he taught chamber music to nearly everyone. Later, if I spoke to Sir Georg Solti or Sándor Végh the conversation would soon turn to Weiner, with reverential tones: he was the person from whom you could really learn music! So he was the link between us, although I could no longer study with him. Kurtág and Rados were also among his pupils. In his teaching of composition, Weiner was an absolute master in analysing, for instance, works by Mozart, Beethoven or Brahms, which he revealed down to the smallest detail. And so to the story: at the beginning of the thirties, Toscanini comes to Budapest with the New York Philharmonic. The whole city is excited. An hour before the concert, someone passes by the window of a café. There sits Weiner eating a risotto or a paprika chicken. The passer-by says: 'Leo, Toscanini is paying us a visit, and you're sitting in a café eating chicken!' Weiner replies, 'Look, my friend, Toscanini is conducting Beethoven's

Seventh. If he conducts it as I imagine he will, there's no need for me to go. I know exactly what it's going to be like. If he doesn't perform it the way I think he will, it'll just be poor, and it won't be worth being there.'

Is that the moral of your story?

That's my basic story. It's absolutely typical of the way strong personalities ruled the musical world in those days. You had to play every single piece to them. Then you were told if it was good or bad. That made you feel very small. That's why it became more and more important for me to get away with my rucksack, which was already filled with various things, on my shoulders, and escape into inner and outer freedom. The first person to help me on my way was Sándor Végh.

When was that?

I had already heard Végh in 1972, at the Summer School of Music in Dartington, Devon. Végh, who was teaching violin there, had left Hungary shortly after the war, and was regarded as a dissident. I took part in his class and had to play to him. He encouraged me and said that what I was doing was wonderful. He told me I shouldn't be so downcast and should believe in myself. Just a small example: to this day, I still play with my mouth half open. Why? So that I can breathe. Many people play with their mouth firmly shut. They don't breathe. It sounds constipated. Végh told me, 'I play with my mouth half open, too. The diaphragm has to be open. That provides space and air.' A first hope of gaining experience by being close to Végh was fulfilled. Things were working out.

It also shows that you were quietly working at that time, steadfastly increasing your assets and creating something which would bear fruit later.

Exactly.

But at the same time a situation like that is rather frustrating. One can't always live only on what one has in reserve. And on top of that, there was your rebellious side.

Certainly. It's not true, either, that I was always made to feel small. I was also lovingly looked after. And in communist Hungary there was also a concert system which nurtured talent. Kadosa and Rados spoke for example with Éva Lakatos, the director of the Filharmònia (National Concert Agency), about organising a series of concerts for young soloists. As a result, there was a performance of Mozart's Concerto for three pianos K.242 with the Hungarian Chamber Orchestra which took place in the Music Academy, and I was to play the third piano part together with Dezsö Ránki and Zoltán Kocsis. The audience was enthusiastic. After that we recorded the work for Hungaroton, this time with the Hungarian State Orchestra under János Ferencsik. That was my very first recording.

Was that your first real concert?

And in borrowed coat-tails! That was in 1970 or 1971.

What came out of it?

Everything was absolutely fine, and a great success. After that I had to give a solo recital in the small hall of the Music

Academy. I think I played well: the complete two-part Inventions of Bach, Beethoven's Op.126 Bagatelles and then the four-movement A minor Sonata by Schubert, which is a rather difficult piece. The audience was very taken with me and remembered the little TV star from the past. People were even sitting on the steps.

That was quite something.

Yes – not a real explosion, it's true, but it brought me a grant from the Filharmònia. I was still a college student, but at the same time you could be a scholarship holder or a soloist of this same organisation. In concrete terms that meant a monthly amount on which you could live comparatively well. In return, you had to give a certain number of concerts throughout the country – around 20 a year. A few in Budapest, but mostly in the provinces. The orchestras were often bad and the conditions miserable. Of course, there were also cultured towns with for the most part a cultured audience. Western Hungary was more developed than the east, both economically and culturally. Within that framework I was able to build up a repertoire, before I appeared abroad. So even these small concerts brought valuable experience with them.

Did you enjoy them? Were they strenuous?

Both. The travel was fine, and for the most part I had a company car. On these tours a sort of compère came along to introduce the events, so we travelled as a team.

*You've already spoken about your first recording for
Hungaroton. What came out of that?*

I've mentioned Mozart's Triple Concerto. After that things
went rather slowly. A solo disc of Bach – the D major
Toccata, the fourth English Suite, the Partita No.5 and the
Chromatic Fantasy & Fugue. I would have liked to have recorded some chamber music, too, but that only came later.
Chamber music had been important to me since my childhood. Later, older musicians asked me to play something
or other with them. That needed a good deal of versatil-
ity. I performed the two Brahms Op.120 sonatas with the
viola player Pál Lukács, who was outstanding and should
have been world famous. But with the exception of Annie
Fischer most of the musicians who had stayed behind in
the country in 1956 were only known locally. I gave a lot of
concerts with Lukács.

In those days, you were able to travel in the Eastern bloc?

That's right. Because I should have done my military service, I wasn't allowed to travel to England. So I asked myself
where else one could study. The answer lay in masterclasses
that were advertised in Weimar, which was in the GDR. In
addition, there was the Franz Liszt University of Music there.
So I took part in masterclasses, or summer courses, with Tatiana Nikolaeva and Bella Davidovich. With Tatiana Petrovna,
I studied Bach; and with Bella Michaelovna, Prokofiev (the
Third Sonata) and Tchaikovsky (the First Concerto). Both
were excellent pianists and musicians. With the German
pianist and organist Amadeus Webersinke, who was also outstanding and excelled as an interpreter of Bach, I was able to
work on the 'Goldberg' Variations for the first time.

Not at the Budapest Academy?

No. At first it was important for me to be able to work with a pianist who knew the piece well and played it often, in order to get to know the inside view of an expert, so to speak.

Did your teachers never suggest that you should go for a while to the Moscow Conservatory?

Not directly. But it would have been logical. It wasn't possible to go to Vienna. I had got to know Russian teachers in Weimar, and that was something I had liked. So I acquired a little of the 'Russian School', which usually instils itself in your whole body. In Vienna they taught you how to play from the wrist. Professor Rados had been in Moscow for years and had also studied there. That led him to have a high opinion of the Russian school. All the same, for me to study in Moscow was something that never came about. The only exception, but from an entirely different aspect, was that in 1974, I was called into the Ministry of Culture and was informed: 'Comrade Schiff, you are representing the country of Hungary in the International Tchaikovsky Competition.'

The form of address was still 'Comrade Schiff'?

Comrade, yes. I replied that I didn't want to, and that I didn't like competitions at all. Moscow, Russian music – that wasn't my home territory. But there was no excuse: an order is an order. Comrade Schiff is off to Moscow!

That was instead of military service.

You could put it like that.

And then, were expectations fulfilled or was it bitter frustration?

I had to tell myself to make the best of things, without expectations. I knew how the Soviet Union functioned. The Tchaikovsky Competitions had always been very political as it was. Just take the case of Miklós Perényi, who later became a great friend of mine. In the sixties, he had to go to Moscow, too, and was eliminated after the first round. But I can assure you he's the greatest cellist in the world. There's none better. In brief, I learned a lot: Tchaikovsky's *Seasons*, some of Rachmaninov's Etudes. I had never played a single note of Rachmaninov before, but I was already fond of Tchaikovsky. Then there was Shostakovich's Prelude and Fugue in D flat – an outstanding piece. And of course, there was also an obligatory piece by a Russian composer – Pirumov's Scherzo, a rather ghastly thing. Preludes and Fugues by Bach were part of it, and so were a study by Liszt and one by Chopin, plus a Mozart sonata. Two big concertos, one by Tchaikovsky and the other a free choice. I plumped for Brahms's D minor Concerto again, and to my great surprise I got through the first round.

How long did your preparations take?

A long time – a year. I was well prepared, though, above all through Professor Rados again, who was great. The first round was nothing, really, but at least I had got through it. From the second round onwards, I earned the audience's favour. In short, I was awarded the shared fourth prize. Remarkable, when you think that the winner was called Andrei Gavrilov. It was obvious that a lot of politics was going on behind the scenes. To the whole paraphernalia you can add the fact that we were put up at the Hotel Rossija in Moscow. We laughed ourselves silly at the Spartan fittings. On every floor sat the notorious babushkas, whose job was to make sure that no trespassers got in. Once when I took a walk to the church right nearby, with its onion-shaped design, I went inside. I just wanted to take a look and explore a little. There I saw a whole load of people equipped with headphones: the army of watchdogs who were spying on our hotel. I've never fled so quickly in my life. It was just dreadful. On the other hand, the Moscow audiences were fantastic – without doubt the best, and not only in Russia: quick to show their enthusiasm and palpably warm.

Was that your first visit to Moscow?

No. I had been to Moscow once as a child, part of a delegation of music schools. That was in 1966, even before the TV competition.

You were 13 – just a child.

Yes, a 13-year-old in Moscow, with the obligatory red neckerchief of the Pioneers. It was an exchange programme. We had to play something, and I was amazed at how well the young Russians played: much better than us. There was Vladimir Feltsman, for instance. He played Chopin's G minor Ballade. And I came with a tiny piece by Kabalevsky. All the same, I liked everything a lot. We were in the Palace of Congresses and we went to see *Swan Lake* performed by the Bolshoi Ballet, and the famous GUM store on Red Square, with its toy department. By 1974, some of the veneer had already peeled off, and I saw it with different eyes.

Were your contributions to the Tchaikovsky Competition recorded?

In the late eighties or early nineties I was in Canada, and I did a radio interview in Toronto – a sort of talk show. The interviewer said, 'We know that you're no great admirer of Liszt and don't play anything of his. Well, here's a bit of evidence to the contrary: we're going to play you the Liszt Etude *La leggierezza* which you performed at the time of the Moscow Competition.' I was somewhat puzzled and surprised: I played very nicely. Apart from that, nothing is documented, apart from a Rachmaninov *Etude-Tableau*, which I played rather less well.*

Were you a great young hero with your countrymen when you got home?

I wouldn't say that. But they were satisfied. At the same time, my success died down into a typical Hungarian attitude: what does it matter? So what? But I had a lot to do and went on working hard. It had been an important step.

What effect did the prize have on your further career?

I earned greater prestige and respect. The Moscow Competition is very hard and also politically significant. The audience sided firmly with me. That gets noticed very soon in Moscow – even more then than now. As far as Hungary was concerned, the recognition was palpable, because Hungarian pianists had never won prizes in Moscow before. I

---

* I have now discovered that almost my entire contribution to the Competition was in fact recorded and was recently released.

got my prize money in roubles, with which I was able to buy a whole heap of books and records, and I also received a medal which I still have somewhere or other.

How do East European audiences react to concerts and artists, in comparison, let's say, to Western audiences?

At that time, I couldn't really make any comparisons, other than with England. As a rule, people react more spontaneously and warmly, and with greater feeling in East Europe. But I already noticed that in England the applause was much more subdued. That hasn't changed to this day. You play a Brahms concerto in the Royal Festival Hall: people clap, you come back onto the stage, and that's it. That doesn't mean that people didn't enjoy the concert, but it's just not customary to applaud too much.

Proverbial British understatement?

Perhaps. The mood is already much livelier in Berlin or Vienna; and as far as East Europe is concerned, under dictatorship life was a daily grind, and art, concerts and music were an oasis of paradise. People didn't go to cultural events out of a sense of duty – they were happy to do so. They were not spoiled. So when Sviatoslav Richter came to Hungary it was a real event. Richter was a living legend.

Already at that time?

Already at that time, yes, despite the sense of mistrust towards most Soviet Russians. They personified the occupation with all its conditions, including the language. It's true that Richter, Oistrakh or Rostropovich didn't fall into that category. They were celebrated cult figures. Richter's concerts merely had to be announced: there were no advertisements, no posters – nothing. Everything happened at very short notice. At 7 in the morning there was an announcement on the radio that Richter was going to play such and such a programme in the evening – sometimes without any details of the pieces – and the hall was full to the rafters. A police cordon controlled things as necessary. The mood was unbelievable. Then the following thing happened: at the end of the seventies, I happened to be in Glasgow, where I was rehearsing Beethoven's Piano Concerto No.2 one morning. Suddenly, word spread that Richter was playing in Glasgow that evening. Off we go! The hall was only a third full. Richter played fabulously. The reaction was lukewarm – that was a shock to me.

Are there still such strong differences between audience reactions in the West and East?

I have to say, unfortunately not. The world has changed, and after the Wall came down other priorities took hold. Since then, people travel all over the place, they buy everything, everything is readily there on sale, at least for the majority. And yet in Russia, concert audiences are still excellent.

At that time audiences' musical education was probably on firmer ground. Old school, so to speak?

Without doubt. As far as the status of music in the home is concerned you can see just how much has changed. People make far less effort these days.

On the question of your subsequent development: you were 21 at that time and had your first successes abroad. How did your career go after that?

As I said, I became a soloist of the Filharmònia. Experts, who knew a lot about music, saw to the programming and travel arrangements, which were agreed among themselves.

So they were a kind of concert management?

Yes, a national concert management. Some concerts took place under better conditions than others. Sometimes it was appalling: ignorant audience, bad piano, deepest provinces; sometimes better. The instruments were never particularly good. For a long time, I had no idea of what a good piano could sound like. But beginning on poor pianos also has its advantages: you have to learn to make the best of it.

Richter described provincial experiences like that in some detail.

He even said that a less good instrument inspired him more. I wouldn't go that far. But what he meant is obvious: the overcoming of obstacles.

Were there other pianists who were active within the same system?

There were many of us, both older and younger. But what was interesting was that although we lived under the same egalitarian communism, some of us earned more than others. At the beginning of the month you could collect your fees. There was a list which you had to sign, so you could immediately see who earned what. That almost always led to heated arguments. The system was ridiculous, and yet at the same time those were happy days. I held this position right until I left Hungary. But my conditions became better all the time. My fees were raised, I got a grant from the Music Academy and another from the foundation which Ditta Pásztory, Bartók's widow, had established. Things were actually going very well, because the cost of living was generally low.

Of all the countries in the Eastern bloc Hungary was the most liberal in those days.

With hindsight, yes. That's true in any case as far as music is concerned, because music is an abstract art. When I talk to my literary friends, I can see that things were difficult for many of them, because language is easier to control. A censorship official passed or rejected books or banned authors. That gave rise to an atmosphere of fear.

As far as any message was concerned, music was much more innocuous.

None of the musicians was oppressed. Perhaps not everybody sees it that way, but that was my experience. Talented and less talented people made progress, almost every composer was issued by the state music publisher, and their works were disseminated through Hungaroton records. After the Wall came down, people said that only the privileged few had got on, but that wasn't true.

Was there a musical avant-garde who experienced more difficulty with their compositions?

There was. Up until the sixties and seventies there was an official line, and even the best composers like my teacher Kurtág had to toe it. For example, he composed a Korean cantata in the early fifties. Then, in the wake of John Cage, came experimentalism. Musical happenings took place. Officially that was frowned upon but tolerated. I found most of what came from that niche musically worthless.

Which intellectual circles did you frequent in those days?

My friends came mostly from the world of music. They came from liberal circles which were interested in music and art. We often got together in private lodgings and listened to music: many of them had large record collections. But we also read literature or talked about philosophy. There were a lot of discussions. Whether or not we were spied on, I don't know. There was no danger – at least, not any longer.

Who were your closest friends?

Above all, they were musicians. Imre Rohmann, for instance, with whom I played a lot of piano duets. Zoltán Kocsis was a close friend. Then the violinist Miklós Szenthelyi and the clarinettist Kálmán Berkes. On top of those, there were scholars of the arts. We felt at ease and grumbled a lot about politics. But things were going well for us, and we even felt some gratitude for that.

You went to England several times and then also to Moscow. But you didn't have any other foreign experience yet.

No, absolutely none. There was an organisation called Interconcert which was responsible for concerts abroad. There was one department for West Europe, and one for East – all very politically biased. Various heads of department managed various countries, and you had to discuss and plan everything down to the last detail with these gentlemen – all very laborious and time-consuming.

That's where the decisions were made?

That's certainly the impression I had. But fundamentally these people were powerless. They didn't have the slightest influence over whether one was engaged in Switzerland or France. Most things happened by chance or through acquaintances. One time, I received an invitation to go to Denmark – I still don't know why. My first official invitation came from the town of Aalborg. If you had a head of department who didn't like you, the invitation would disappear into the waste paper basket. Or they would write, 'Schiff is not available.' There were thousands of incidents of that kind. All rather Kafkaesque. Well, never mind: I was able to play the Schumann concerto in Aalborg and no one cast a critical eye on me, as they did in Hungary. I felt free. And gradually I came to realise that I would have to leave my homeland if I wanted to get anywhere. The environment was too constricted. The fact that Annie Fischer was the only Hungarian pianist who lived in the country and was internationally known at the same time gave me further food for thought.

But for the moment there were further engagements abroad.

There was an Interconcert protocol. For example, there was a list of exchanges that were possible between, say, Hungary and the GDR. Annie Fischer in Hungary and Peter Schreier in the GDR had the top place every time. I was approximately in 35th place. My equivalent in the GDR was perhaps Peter Rösel. And so artists of the same ranking were exchanged for concerts. That's how I got to play in the GDR and in East Berlin. The audience was fantastic, and the concerts were very good. You could still feel the traditions of the old German provincial towns with their country theatres and orchestras which played operas, operettas, ballets and symphony concerts. Whole series of evenings were sold out. You got paid 500 East German marks per concert, which you absolutely had to spend. I bought myself scores and editions of facsimiles from the East Berlin State Library in Unter den Linden, some of which I still have and use.

And how did your travels in other countries of the Eastern bloc go?

In other countries my experiences were less pleasant, whether in Rumania or Bulgaria. I could tell a story which in retrospect is funny. One day we were called in to the Budapest Ministry of Culture, where we were received by a highly placed female official who had the reputation of being an absolute martinet. 'Dear Comrades,' she said to us soloists, 'it's time to do something for Hungarian contemporary music.' You have to know that in those days there were Hungarian Cultural Institutes rather like the West German Goethe Institute all over the place, both in the East and West. She went on: 'We're forming squads of three or four musicians, and we're deciding who is to play what and where.' That's how I was assigned to Zoltán Kocsis and the clarinettist Kálmán Berkes. We went to Sofia, and hardly had we arrived when we were summoned to a talk with the director and the head of the cultural department. It was ten o'clock in the morning, and both of them were already quite drunk. Through a cloud of vodka, they told us we had to make the programme a bit more popular. Could any of us play the accordion? 'Yes, Comrade Schiff is a first-class virtuoso on the accordion,' my friends said. I was dumbfounded and didn't venture to contradict them.

You were on dangerous ground.

When we got to the concert hall it was full to the rafters with soldiers who were there purely out of duty. Short haircuts, vacant looks. Before our eyes a Bulgarian folk ensemble was performing, with three brilliant virtuosos on the accordion. I got into a panic: I didn't even know how to open out the instrument. I could already see my next destination: The Gulag Archipelago. Our escape route was this: Berkes announced that we were going to play *Cage Music* by János Duma. Duma was the name of a janitor in Budapest. Then they hung the accordion around my neck. The letters C-A-G-E were marked in red crayon on the rows of buttons – and we were off: 15 minutes of complete cacophony. But it was a huge success! The audience went wild; the officials sent a glowing report to Budapest. All's well that ends well.

Did you travel into rural Rumania and Bulgaria?

I have pleasant memories of Rumania, which was very beautiful. In Bucharest, there was a first-rate hall, the

Athenaeum. I also travelled through Transylvania, which used to belong to Hungary, but was assigned to Rumania after the Treaty of Trianon, which led to frustration and an explosive situation which persists to this day. I would have liked to play in Prague, too, but that didn't happen – with one exception which was of decisive importance to the further course of my life.

What was the story there?

At Interconcert there was a mean-spirited person. The man had previously been a priest but had left the church and become a fanatical communist. In 1978 he told me they were going to form a piano trio with the Czech violinist Václav Hudeček and a Russian cellist called Igor Gavrish. I said, 'Excuse me, I don't know these people. How do you know we're suited to each other?' The official ignored me and wouldn't countenance any objection. We were to go to Prague, where there was a meeting of all the socialist concert agencies, and we had to appear. On our programme was the first Beethoven trio in E flat, which I knew very well because I had studied it with Kurtág. I soon noticed that Hudeček was actually a very good violinist, but he had had almost no chamber music experience. The same was true of the Russian cellist: he had almost no idea about the Viennese classics. We were not unsuccessful, but I didn't feel comfortable. After I came home, the official decided that our trio was now established, and would be sent on tour. I was not in agreement: we weren't suited to each other at all. But the bureaucratic gentleman just said, 'If you don't agree, I'll put paid to you for the rest of your life.' That was pure bluff, but it scared me. In retrospect I can say, Kafka all over again! At that time, I saw it differently, and was haunted by the thought that I had to leave the country.

Let's talk a little more about your tours in the Eastern bloc. They must have been physically strenuous: cold, inhospitable, dubious food, precarious instruments. How did you cope with that?

Luckily, I have a good constitution. On the whole, the food was no problem; but the cold was more difficult. But I'm not hypersensitive.

Discipline, a sense of order – 'living by the clock', as Alfred Brendel once described his existence.

Yes, you have to be very disciplined. One of my main tasks was to give tours of a high standard, and at the same time to practise regularly. Organisation is key. Today, all of that runs with impeccable smoothness. Previously? I can't really remember, but clearly it went well.

Did you have a specific repertoire for these concert trips?

It was mostly mixed, and planned ahead by the Hungarian National Agency. I had to play the programme in Hungary first, and that also went for works with orchestra. That's why I hate Liszt's E flat Concerto to this day, because I had to play it then. A Hungarian pianist? Then it had to be Liszt! Once, I think around 1975, I played that warhorse at the Komische Oper in Berlin with Maxim Shostakovich conducting. It was a huge success, and I had to play three or four encores. I preferred to play Tchaikovsky's B flat minor Concerto, which I also recorded later with Solti in Chicago.

To those I added, for instance, Prokofiev's First Concerto and Third Sonata, as well as some of Shostakovich's Preludes and Fugues. At the same time, I turned increasingly to Bach, Mozart, Haydn and Schubert, but deliberately less to Beethoven. On the other hand, there were in any case Schumann, Brahms and Bartók. And so I gradually put together a wide repertoire.

And how was it with tours in the West in the early days?

There was nothing much for a long while. When I was very young, I was chosen by a Dutch producer to appear on television in Hilversum. I was to play the finale of Brahms's D minor Concerto and of Mozart's E flat K.271 with the Netherlands Radio Orchestra. And that was it. The organisation on the Hungarian side was poor: they had no wish, or weren't able, to build on artists' successes abroad.

When did you first go to West Germany?

In the late seventies. Somehow, I ended up in Bochum, where I played Tchaikovsky's B flat minor Concerto. And that was my only concert in West Germany before I left Hungary. I should add that I took part in another competition following the one in Moscow – Leeds again. I shared third prize with the French pianist Pascal Devoyon. The first prize went to Dmitri Alexeev and the second to Mitsuko Uchida. The level was high.

And what followed on from that?

The result was that the doors to the West opened further, because the Leeds competition was a big affair. The final round was broadcast 'live' by the BBC. In that round I played the D minor Concerto of Bach. After the concert, people told me: 'It's a pity you played the Bach. With a bigger work you would have won.' Yet the Bach was on the list of choices, and there are worse pieces . . . My teacher at that time, Professor Kadosa, was on the jury. He said the same thing, but, conformist as he was, he didn't put in a single word for me. The Bach specialist Rosalyn Tureck was on the jury, too, and she couldn't stand my playing. As the High Priestess of Bach interpretation, she acted as the Chosen One, and saw everything quite differently from me. Fortunately, things went better for me with Charles Rosen. As a jury-member the brilliant American pianist was on my side and praised me highly afterwards. He went further and told his manager at Columbia Artists, Thomas Thompson, about me. The latter came to Budapest specially to hear me and booked me on the spot. I'm still grateful to Rosen. He was also a first-class writer on music, and the author of quite exceptional books – *The Classical Style*, for example.

But you still hadn't managed to break through?

No, but I was making more and more contacts, some of them through Leeds. And on top of that, Interconcert organised a so-called Interforum at the Esterházy Palace in Fertöd, on the border between Austria and Hungary. Young soloists were presented in the glorious concert hall where Haydn worked. There were people there from record companies, as well as critics – around 50 people in all. I presented a mixed programme, and out of that came a good many invitations – Denmark, Limerick in Ireland – and gradually one thing led to another. But in all honesty, I have to say small fry. I didn't play in France, hardly at all in Italy, seldom in Spain – though in the Teatro de la Zarzuela in Madrid, in the presence of the Queen, I played the complete concertos of Bach, alternating with Kocsis, which was very nice.

And America – when did that begin?

That happened – at last, I have to say – in 1978. And I must also add that it was very difficult for a completely unknown pianist. I played in Carnegie Hall – not a solo recital, but with the Franz Liszt Chamber Orchestra of Budapest. I performed Bach's D minor Concerto and Mozart's E flat K.449, and even got good reviews in the *New York Times*. Alongside that I made my debut with a Sunday afternoon recital in Orchestra Hall at Symphony Center in Chicago: Haydn's F minor Variations, Schubert's A minor Sonata D.845, the *Dance Suite* of Bartók and Schumann's *Humoreske*. It all went very well. In the same year I made my debut with the Chicago Symphony Orchestra in Bartók's Third Concerto under Ferencsik. I have a recording of it, and I can say that I still stand by that performance.

Progress in small steps. Wasn't that sometimes rather depressing?

I didn't see it that way. Shortly afterwards I appeared for the first time in Vienna with the Hungarian National Philharmonic Orchestra, again with Bartók No.3, which went very successfully. As an encore I played a movement from a Haydn sonata. Afterwards a critic from the *Kurier* daily paper came up to me and asked what the encore was . . . The next day, her damning review came out. One way or another I made slow progress. My great wish was to be able to appear at the Marlboro Festival. I was a great admirer of Rudolf Serkin, the festival's leading light, and of course of the great cellist Pablo Casals. How could one get from Hungary to Marlboro? I asked Thomas Thompson, who made the appropriate contacts – and, miraculously, I was invited for the summer of 1978 without having to audition.

No doubt there was plenty of chamber music there?

Chamber music is the very meaning of Marlboro. My meetings with Serkin and above all with Mieczysław Horszowski were wonderful. Horszowski was already very old at that time – around 90. Contact with Serkin was more difficult. He was always friendly, but rather uncommunicative if you asked him anything. Everything needed a lot of time, there was no fixed formula for the music. That much became apparent to me. Serkin was extremely demanding, both of himself and of other pianists.

And how was it all organised?

We were divided into groups. One of the older musicians instructed the younger ones like a coach. We had to rehearse, for which a huge amount of time was allocated. Concerts were given, some of them informally in the dining room. The concert hall had been built out of a barn, and the paying public came there. But there was never any announcement of what was going to be played. After the rehearsals a committee decided what each group was to play. Everything was difficult, there was a lot of pressure, and also a lot of competition. I wasn't to play anything in public for several weeks, and that made me extremely nervous. Serkin wanted to put me to the test that way.

Then he asked me to play to him but cried off at the last minute. One time, we were studying Brahms's Piano Quintet. Serkin came to the rehearsal and offered to turn pages. No sooner had he sat down next to me than he began to turn at the wrong moment. He wanted to find out if I knew the piece from memory – which I did. But in the end we weren't allowed to play the Brahms. Serkin found it not good enough, and he was probably right. But to tell the truth, Serkin was hard to please, even if I learned a lot from him. All the more pleasant was Horszowski, whose playing reminded me of Schnabel's. I visited him often, turned pages for him and went for long walks with him. On one occasion I asked him, 'Mr Horszowski, how should I play? I like playing somewhat freely, with rubato.' He answered: 'We all love our own rubato, and don't like our neighbour's at all.'

How long did this festival last?

A long time – seven or eight weeks. I went back there twice more. The second time, in 1979, I met Yuuko Shiokawa, who was to become my wife. It was the only summer in which Serkin wasn't present: he wanted to take a holiday for once. As a result, it all went like a dream for me, and everything ran like clockwork. I no longer had to overcome any obstacles or hindrances. My groups were very good, and I wasn't bad, either. I had known Yuuko by name. She was already a celebrated violinist and played a great deal with Rafael Kubelík, whose protégé she was. She also played with Karajan and the Berlin Philharmonic, both in Berlin and at the Salzburg Easter Festival. She was rather like a star without any of the airs and graces that go with that status. We understood each other completely right off. At our first meeting at lunch I offered her a peach, which she accepted. We became closer, played many sonatas together, especially Mozart. Mozart was more or less the ambassador of our love. But the inconsiderate committee never put us in the same group, which made us both suffer a lot.

Then came the time when you decided to move to the West.

It was just at this time that I decided not to go back to Hungary. I had had enough, and I had prepared myself to take this step for a whole year.

Did your soon-to-be wife help you in that?

Indirectly, yes. But many friends in London helped, too, in telling me not to go back. But still I hesitated: could I really do that to my mother? My grandmother had died in 1975, and my mother was left alone. She always said to me, 'I know you're dissatisfied with many things in Hungary. But after all, Hungary is your home, your country. You have to live here, and in any case I need you! I can't manage alone.' And so I found myself in a deep quandary. But in the end I told myself that I had to live my own life and follow my own path alone. I could take care of my mother from abroad. And that's what happened, actually a little too late.

Why?

It would have been easier if I had left when I was 22. It's no small matter to give everything up and start again from scratch. But having to subject myself to the system had become dreadful and undignified, despite the fact that I had grown somewhat used to it.

How did it happen from a practical point of view?

I couldn't arrange my emigration legally – I had to leave the country illegally. In August 1979, I was on tour in England, shortly after Marlboro. I sent a registered letter to Interconcert, and informed them that I was not coming back, adding as a postscript, 'Many thanks for everything.' My English agent helped me in this. A close friend from Budapest happened to be in London and he took my letter back and handed it over to my mother personally.

What was the political significance of breaking away like this?

Politically it was terrible, because illegal emigration counted as a criminal and punishable act. However, my escape took place at a time when such 'cases' were not unknown. One or two years earlier, the soprano Sylvia Sass failed to return, and at first that caused quite a stir. She stayed in London, and had an exclusive contract with Decca. In the beginning, they simply refused to accept my case. When I played a couple of concerts with the Hungarian Radio Orchestra under György Lehel in Graz in the autumn of the same year, the authorities sent my mother there, with orders to bring me back. She had convinced herself that I had done something stupid. After such a long time under communism, the best person in the world had become a bit influenced by the ideology. She knew the West well on account of her occupation, but all the same she thought Hungary was a good country, and gratitude to one's homeland was a duty.

Can you give any more precise details?

The journey to Graz was perilous – by which I mean one had to be watchful. My London agent, Terry Harrison, who had a weakness for thrillers and knew many stories about the Cold War, organised everything as well as could be. I was staying in a different hotel from my mother. The authorities from Interconcert were also present at our meeting. They wanted me back and assured me that absolutely nothing would happen. Absolute rubbish! Later, the situation was cemented. I came to an agreement with the authorities, not signing anything but demanding that nothing would happen to my mother and that she could visit me. In return, I would not seek political asylum in the West. So the whole matter became considerably more relaxed: I wasn't a political refugee and had no reason to say bad things about the regime. I wanted more space to myself, for my artistic development. It's possible that as far as the state was concerned, I was just small fry, and not worth taking much notice of. Permission was granted, and was legally valid, but as a precautionary measure for the next eight years I didn't go to Hungary. By the way, an Austrian passport would have been no help to me in the country of my birth. In 1986, the chains of the Cold War gradually began to be loosened in Hungary and elsewhere.

A move to England would have been an obvious step.

It would certainly have been logical to stay in England, because my relatives lived there: my mother's sister, my cousin and her husband as well as their children. They lived to the south of London. But I thought to myself, be courageous and do something completely different – go to New York!

That was a new world. And I also thought that that was the headquarters of the very demanding and very powerful Columbia Artists agency. I realised that it would be difficult, and that there were no guarantees of security as there were in Hungary. Nevertheless, I left for New York, completely alone.

A real story in the spirit of the American pioneers.

Fortunately, it wasn't quite as wild as that. I already had several friends there, and I found a small apartment on the Upper West Side in Manhattan. A former good female friend of mine also lived there. The building housed many musicians, including Peter Serkin, who lived two floors above me. There was practising going on in practically every apartment. It wasn't exactly quiet, but no one got worked up about it.

Did you have your own piano?

I had to rent one and I had no money at all. It was difficult. At first I lived in a single-room studio, though it was quite spacious. To begin with I slept in a sleeping bag and ate at McDonald's – not exactly my favourite restaurant. To begin with I couldn't give any concerts. I quickly came to realise that America can be a ruthless country. If you read the book *My Father* by Bartók's son, Péter, you feel how the great composer suffered there and how he eked out a meagre existence in his illness. Unlike him, I could at least work. A recording came my way with the flautist Carol Wincenc, whom I knew from Marlboro. That brought in a couple of hundred dollars.

Was that already for Decca?

No, Decca wasn't even beckoning on the horizon. It was a small label. The managers at Columbia Artists said, 'Yes, András, we'll work for you, but nobody in this great country knows you, and it will take a long time. It's true that you've already played in Chicago and Carnegie Hall, and had reviews for that; but that doesn't amount to much. We'll take care of publicity for you, and do a flyer and brochures.' Columbia also organised so-called Community Concerts: as an artist, you travelled across the States, sometimes played in large towns, but more often in small ones, sometimes in concert halls, sometimes in basketball stadiums or ice-skating rinks. Often symphony orchestras from the Eastern bloc would appear, and perhaps a Cossack choir, or a circus troupe, a singer, a pianist. People could take out a subscription and were happy to do so. I played from Washington to North Carolina, in Milwaukee, Pennsylvania and San Diego. I spent a lot of time travelling by air. The fee was usually $400 an evening. Only later did I realise that even so I was heavily in debt to the agency. The publicity was expensive, and I had to absorb the costs by instalments. It was all quite tough. To put it plainly, I was destitute.

But America wasn't your only field of activity: you already had good contacts in Western Europe, too.

I did have concerts in Europe, and they were somehow more civilised and didn't entail publicity costs. In my first years of 'freedom' I financed my American life through European concerts. Of course, that involved much flying to and fro, which was expensive, and very complicated because I only had a Hungarian passport. I needed a visa wherever I went, and for the USA I had to have a so-called Re-entry Permit. One needed a lawyer for those documents, and, later, to get a Green Card. A bottomless pit. Lawyers worked by the hour, and so of course the longer they worked the more they earned. Sometimes I really didn't know where I would get the money from. For that reason, I stayed for a long time in my small apartment, until I found a two-bedroom apartment in the same house, which I held onto until 1994. So I know New York rather well – both its good and less good sides.

Why did you stay so long?

The concerts gradually became more attractive, and the fees, too. In the end, I could give up the Community Concerts – which had also included pianists like Charles Rosen and Claude Frank. When Mr Thompson died, I was looked after by his assistant Gregg Gleasner for a further few years. Then I changed from Columbia Artists to Shirley Kirshbaum, who had her own agency. She is still my agent for the United States.

A second mainstay had been recordings with Hungaroton.

After the Hungaraton recordings, there was a surprise move to Decca. That Hungarian singer Sylvia Sass, who emigrated to London before me and was under contract to Decca, wanted me as her partner in songs by Liszt and Bartók, and Decca agreed. In the meantime, I also had a house in London. And so we met up in Vienna in 1980, and recorded the disc in the Sophiensäle, which subsequently burned down. The acoustics were excellent and the producer, Christopher Raeburn, soon became an important figure in my artistic life. He was a real gentleman who could have stepped straight out of a novel by Dickens. In a break, during the recording, he asked me if I played any Mozart. I told him Mozart was one of my favourite composers, and played him the A minor Rondo. It was recorded, without comment, and suddenly I received an invitation from London to record Mozart sonatas. Decca was planning a complete recording for the Book of the Month Club in America. They already had some recordings by Wilhelm Backhaus, Alicia de Larrocha and Vladimir Ashkenazy, but around half the sonatas were missing.

Were you really prepared for an album like that?

There were several sonatas I had never played and the time-frame was short, but I didn't have too much work on my hands and I knew the music and its style very well. In those days there was a team of five or six people working on recordings – from the producer to the sound engineer to the truck driver. We recorded in Decca's London studios, and I was given a week to record ten sonatas. Already at that time my philosophy was that recordings were not meant to last for ever. What I played, and how I played it, represented my current thinking and insight into the music. But, as I always have been, I was one hundred per cent prepared. Everything has to be just so: preparation is half of the recording process. I am against editing and cutting different takes together. Small corrections are all right, but my approach has always been the same: I play the work through three times. One of those performances must be good, or I won't have been sufficiently prepared. And so we managed to complete the recordings within the space of three days, and the question came up of playing the complete sonatas. That worked out well, because the sonatas that were missing happened to be the ones I knew particularly well, like the C minor K.457, for instance.

Could one call that a breakthrough as far as recordings were concerned?

Yes and no. I still didn't have a contract with Decca: they were cautious and wanted to see how I would develop. At the same time, I had several contacts in Japan, which I had visited regularly since 1976. For Denon and for King Records, which was a subdivision of Decca, I recorded three Haydn sonatas, and a Schumann disc with the *Humoreske*, the *Arabeske* and *Papillons*, as well as an all-Bartók programme which has remained my only solo Bartók recording. On top of those there were three Bach concertos in London with the English Chamber Orchestra under George Malcolm, and a Bach recital for King Records. Then at last in 1982–3 I got an exclusive contract with Decca.

Was that the long-desired goal?

I was hoping for more. Decca's artistic director, Ray Minshull, was very competent, but at the same time an extremely difficult person. We had a complicated relationship. He wanted to be my father-figure. There was something military about him, he was like a colonel out of the colonial army, with his pipe, his resolute manner and strongly preconceived ideas which clashed with mine. Already in the first year we worked together I said to him, 'Let's do two Mozart concertos, and we absolutely must have Sándor Végh.' He said, 'Nonsense. Végh is a great chamber player and has a good string quartet, but he's not a conductor at all, and certainly not a star conductor. We have really fine people under contract: why don't you do it with Peter Maag?' He was really convinced that Maag was one of the greatest conductors, especially for Mozart. In the end, he gave way, and Végh and I recorded Mozart's concertos over a period of 15 years. I managed to get my way, but Minshull never forgave me. Things came to a head around 1994, and I switched to Teldec for five years. For them I did the five Beethoven concertos with Bernard Haitink and the Dresden Staatskapelle, as well as the three Bartók concertos with Iván Fischer and the Budapest Festival Orchestra. After five years, I was the one who didn't want to renew the contract. A fortunate meeting with Manfred Eicher and ECM resulted in a new change, and in extremely important recordings from Bach to Schumann and Beethoven. I'll have more to say about those later.

Were there other conductors with whom you worked at that time?

I did the Mendelssohn concertos with Charles Dutoit, but more important to me was Antal Doráti. I learned a lot from him, we recorded the Schumann Concerto and Chopin's F minor Concerto together, with the wonderful Amsterdam Concertgebouw Orchestra. Decca's star was, or course, Sir Georg Solti. I had wanted to play with him for a long time, but he always declined. That mainly had something to do with his aversion to Hungary. He had suffered a great deal there, and had been driven out twice – first, as a Jew, and then, under communism, as a musician. In the end we did get together for recordings, for instance Dohnányi's Variations on a Nursery Song. Solti had been a pupil of Dohnányi. At first, we spoke only English, but later we switched to our mother tongue. It's curious that following his death Solti was buried in Hungary, because his antipathy had been genuine.

Getting back to biographical details, what drew you to London at that time?

For all my long love of England, I couldn't go on living with my relatives in Surrey. Through an acquaintance I found lodgings to rent, and in 1983 I bought my own small house – at first the upper floor, and later the whole property. I'd been aware for a long time that London was one of the world's major centres for all forms of culture and cultural events. Nothing has changed as far as that's concerned, but in the meantime I find it better to divide my life between the Old and New Worlds. I commute less and live for longer periods in one or the other.

Did you feel gradually at home with English culture?

I was cosmopolitan, and still am, but I always liked the English manner and speech. I admire the art of speech and theatre, from which I benefit above all in the realm of articulation.

Were all doors open to you quite quickly in England?

Not at all. It took much longer than in America for me to be able to play with the great London orchestras. Thanks to Yuuko, in New York I gained the sympathy of Rafael Kubelík, and after I had played him some Schubert and other things, I made my debut with him in Mozart's G major Concerto K.453. We had further plans to work together, but his health prevented them from happening. Things were much harder in England, and all over Europe. All the same, thanks to the mediation of my Munich agency, Hörtnagel, from 1981 onwards I was able to take part in Gidon Kremer's festival in Lockenhaus. Then I received an invitation to go on tour with the Bamberg Philharmonic under Eugen Jochum, with concerts in Munich, Augsburg, Düsseldorf, Nuremberg and Duisburg. Jochum was delighted with my Mozart playing. At that time, as I still do, I played the basso continuo in the *tuttis*, as Mozart himself wrote it. I didn't reckon with Joachim Kaiser, who tore me to shreds with the curious argument that it was absurd to play the continuo. The 'Kaiser' or imperial authority on the piano had laid down the law. The next day a change had come over Jochum, who barely wanted to talk to me any longer and said I was not to play continuo any more. He had read the review. German faith in authority . . .

Kaiser caused a lot of damage. To Alfred Brendel he was always a red rag.

I couldn't agree more.

And then Austria came into sight as a possible place to live.

That was above all for practical reasons. In America, I had a Green Card, paid taxes there and intended to acquire citizenship. But that turned out to be complicated. The authorities felt that I travelled too much: for naturalisation I would have had to live in the country for at least three years without interruption. None of my lawyers had informed me about this. When I told the whole story to my friend Hans Landesmann, who was then the director of the Vienna Konzerthaus, he advised me to try Austria. In special cases, above all for scientists and artists, the procedure there was relatively uncomplicated; and as things turned out I obtained a passport after a couple of months. That made my everyday life easier at a stroke. On top of that, my wife Yuuko was already living in Salzburg, where I registered officially and applied for citizenship. We married in 1987.

Why had Yuuko settled in Salzburg?

She was born in Kamakura, in Japan, and she grew up in Peru, where her father worked for Mitsubishi. It was there that she was discovered as a child prodigy. Friends wanted to send her to the Juilliard School in New York, but she preferred Europe and came to study in Germany. Her teacher in Munich was Wilhelm Stross. When he died, she moved to Salzburg, where she came under the protection of Sándor Végh, who taught in Düsseldorf before Salzburg. Yuuko moved into a small apartment by the Salzach river, and after that we bought a house together there.

Then Jörg Haider came to power, which was unpleasant.

When Jörg Haider began to strut the political stage, it was the end of our peace in the country. We left Austria for Italy.

What were your first experiences of concert life in Austria?

My very first experiences were when I was still living in Hungary, and was a visitor to Vienna. We've already spoken about those. Later, I played cycles of Bach's works, at first in the Mozartsaal in Vienna, and then also in the Musikverein. In 1982 I made my debut at the Salzburg Festival together with Gidon Kremer. That all went smoothly and pleasantly.

Kremer had already engaged you for Lockenhaus. What was the atmosphere like there in the early days?

Extremely relaxed and creative. Wonderful musicians met up there, and that's how I got to know Heinz Holliger, Aloys Kontarsky and Krystian Zimerman. The public was distinctly favourable and faithful. Most of the concerts took place in the old castle, and they were always sold out. The programmes were only announced on the previous day, which added to the impromptu character. The concept was new, and it proved its worth for 30 years.

And then Italy. Why this change of location?

As I mentioned, we were nauseated by Haider and his right-wing populism, and so we had to leave. But where to? Yuuko and I had rented rooms in Florence a couple of times, and spent holidays there. It was beautiful. And so we decided to keep a lookout for a place to stay. Our violinist friend Éva Szabó helped us search for a suitable house, and since then we've been living in the hills above the city, and we have enough room to be able to practise undisturbed. All the same, I didn't cut my ties with Austria completely, because in 1989, I founded the festival in Mondsee, in the Salzkammergut, which I ran until 1998: once again, Hans Landesmann had given me good advice. As far as festivals are concerned, I also came to Ittingen, in the Swiss canton of Thurgau. Heinz Holliger and I directed the festival there for 19 years, until 2014.

But your festival in Vicenza will carry on?

Nothing should change there. It is also the home of my orchestra, the Cappella Andrea Barca. I founded it in 2000, after I had given a couple of concerts in the Teatro Olimpico, and had been overwhelmed by the beauty of Palladio's architecture. At the end of April and beginning of May we always play three or four programmes, rehearsing, making music, living together – wonderful!

Cappella Andrea Barca – András Schiff.

Something occurred to me as far back as 1997, on the occasion of the Salzburg Mozart Week which takes place each January. Earlier, I played recitals and concertos there – for a long time with Sándor Végh. After he died I just wanted to stop, but Josef Tichy, who was director of the Mozarteum at the time, talked me out of it and suggested I should form my own ensemble. And so I hit on the Italian translation of András Schiff. Some people still think the musician Andrea Barca actually existed. My wife plays in the group, as well as musicians who had been with Végh. Several of the members belong to the older generation, which is no disadvantage. Retirement is absurd – in music, too – as long as one is still hale and hearty. We perform during each Mozart Week, and organise a small tour around that. Then comes Vicenza, and after that there's always perhaps Lucerne or the Schubertiade at Schwarzenberg. So, appearances in manageable and measured doses. Chamber music is very important, even if we're playing orchestral works. Up to now, I haven't issued a single CD with the Cappella Andrea Barca.

How did you come to start conducting?

Initially, from the piano. With the marvellous Chamber Orchestra of Europe we performed Bach's keyboard concertos, and because those went very well I continued with Mozart. The Philadelphia Orchestra invited me, and so one evening we performed together, including Schubert's 'Unfinished'. The Chief Conductor at that time, Wolfgang Sawallisch, gave the green light, although he wasn't always an easy customer. One time he insisted on teaching me how Beethoven's C major Concerto was to be interpreted. And so my conducting developed further, though as far as this activity is concerned I am self-taught. The important thing is to be able to listen. In any case, I don't want to neglect my piano playing.

So there's no sudden pressing need to conduct Mahler symphonies.

Absolutely not! But Bach's *St. Matthew Passion*, yes. That also benefits my piano playing – as does Mozart, when I conducted *Cosi fan tutte* and in dealing with the voices was able to gather experiences for my piano playing. Of course, there are many components – above all the collaborative music-making – that differ from orchestra to orchestra. Mutual respect is vital. Bernard Haitink presented me with some batons, but I wouldn't begin to know what to do with them. I conduct just with my hands, which have to be free.

Up to now, which has been the most extreme among piano concertos that you have conducted yourself?

The Dvořák Concerto, for instance, and recently even both

Brahms concertos. The slow movement of Brahms's B flat Concerto, with its wonderful cello solo, accrues quite new colours. With the Chamber Orchestra of Europe, I directed Bartók's Third Concerto from the piano. On the whole, I now concentrate more and more on the piano and chamber music. Mozart's concertos are the exception.

Let's get back to your recording career. We've already spoken briefly about how you came to ECM and its artistic director Manfred Eicher. Is this your final destination?

I think so. Our first meeting took place in Zürich in 2000. We weren't unknown to one another, and we took a liking to each other right away; and so began a close and friendly collaboration. Manfred's company is a one-man show: he decides everything from A to Z – completely different, for instance, from my earlier experiences with Decca. In addition, ECM is a very creative label, in the realm of jazz, too. It appeals to open-minded and varied purchasers, and that's also important. We never signed a contract: there's just a genuine gentlemen's agreement.

Certainly, revenue from physical discs has declined drastically thanks to the digital revolution.

Absolutely. Previously, half of my income consisted of profits from recordings. These days, it's barely around five per cent. ECM and their artists have of necessity a great deal of idealism. What's important is that ECM make every CD into a real artistic endeavour, including the booklet cover and notes. At all events, those can't be 'downloaded'. In addition, Eicher keeps all the recordings in his active catalogue, even the ones that don't sell so well.

Which of your ECM recordings brought you your first great success?

Without doubt, Bach's 'Goldberg' Variations.

Did ECM influence the attitude of the public towards you?

That's something you'll have to answer yourself! ECM doesn't stand for the mainstream. As an example, when I was once playing in Munich in the Haus der Kunst at an ECM event, I suddenly felt it was possible even in Munich to reach a younger audience. I didn't feel constricted, as I do for instance in the Herkulessaal.

Are you completely free as far as repertoire is concerned?

Of course Manfred Eicher and I talk it over. One advantage is that in the realm of the piano concerto I've already recorded practically all the important pieces for Decca and Teldec. To be honest, I've made more than enough recordings, but always only after having lived with a work and performed it often. Perhaps I'd still liked to record Brahms's B flat Concerto again. There are a few things missing in the solo repertoire, too – for instance, some of Haydn's splendid sonatas. On the other hand, I'm not wild about documenting my entire musical activity. Sometimes people come up to me and say, '25 years ago you played that differently.' Sure. So what?

It's striking that you've included many live recordings, especially for ECM. What was the reason for that?

Not to disparage the studio, but the concert hall produces

something more intensive. One feels the element of risk-taking in the live recordings of the Beethoven sonatas, and the works by Schumann and Bach.

And how did the transition from LPs to CDs work out for you?

Digitalisation evens out some of the dynamic subtleties. Everything becomes more constricted, outbursts are cushioned, the quietest moments are in danger of disappearing. With LPs, the sound spectrum is livelier and more natural. I find the old mono recordings with their special aura very beautiful. All the same, as a storage medium the CD is more practical.

Disregarding questions of repertoire, how did your artistic career develop in terms of concert activity? We've heard about the early stages, the path that led to England, to the United States, to Austria. How did it go from there?

In the meantime I play almost everywhere, though I have areas on which I concentrate. In Europe, for instance, Switzerland, with its beautiful old concert halls in Zürich, Basel, Bern and Geneva. I've always had a love-hate relationship with Vienna, but musical life without Austria would be absolutely unthinkable for me. I like Germany, because it's a country that has no centre. It's a home of music, and I love the provinces, where there are so many beautiful places. I really like playing in Neumarkt, for instance, in the Upper Palatinate. I'm altogether attracted by the charm of the small towns, often more than by the large cities.

France is somewhere you haven't so far won over.

I feel the French simply don't like my piano playing or the other things I do. Perhaps they'll accept me when I'm 70. Alfred Brendel also had to wait for a long time as far as the French were concerned. I myself love France and its culture. Who knows, perhaps I'll still be able to learn the great cycles of Debussy. However, Parisian musical life strikes me as rather bizarre.

What are your other experiences of this kind?

I've played a lot in Spain and Portugal, and even more in my adopted country, Italy. I love Scandinavia, in particular Denmark, where I was welcomed at an early stage and was awarded prizes. Eastern Europe has acquired a quite different meaning since the fall of the Wall. There's a phenomenally good new hall in Katowice – perhaps the best in Europe. For all my political reservations, I'm happy to go to Russia, especially St. Petersburg, with its wonderful hall. I give a good many concerts every year in the United States, on both coasts as well as in mid-USA (Chicago, Berkeley and Michigan universities). Canada is also within my orbit. Israel is very important to me, though I'm not in agreement with the politics of the government. On the Asian continent it's above all Japan, but increasingly also China and South Korea, where there's a hall that seats 2,500 – the Seoul Arts Center. Believe it or not, the average age of the concert-goers is 20. The tremendous urge to learn is palpable – as are some strange customs. In China, they spit and take photos on their mobile phones. And finally, there's South America: Buenos Aires, with its unique Teatro Colón; and Rio de Janeiro and Mexico City.

Do you choose your programmes according to the place?

No. For instance, I've played Beethoven's last sonatas in Vienna, Zürich, London, New York, Moscow and Buenos Aires, but never with the thought that the audience here or there could be insufficiently mature for them. You have confidence, and it's mutual.

Where do you see yourself at home? You have a house in Florence, one in London, and an apartment in Basel. How does that feel?

The older I get, the more comfortable I feel in Switzerland. That has something to do with questions of security. England is always a place that means a great deal to me: I really feel at home there. That goes for Florence, too, of course. The way my life played out, I never felt at home in Hungary – even as a child. I was always the outsider, and at the same time one had to keep the Jewish side secret. Today, I'm terribly concerned about political developments in Hungary. When I think of earlier times in the old Budapest, it almost makes me nostalgic. The hall in the Academy of Music sometimes felt like a living room: there was still an aura of the old bourgeoisie. All that disappeared a long time ago.

But that's true of all countries.

Less so. I can still feel that aura in Vienna, as well as Berlin and London. The audiences are older, but sensitive and cultured. There's no problem about organising concert series of string quartets or Lieder recitals in those places. The same holds true for Switzerland.

Have you developed friendships with other pianists? Pianists are rather like lone wolves: that goes with their instrument.

We are indeed lone wolves. All the same, I've developed one or two good friendships, for instance with Radu Lupu, Peter Serkin, Richard Goode and Daniel Barenboim. We all belong more or less to the same generation.

In the meantime, you also teach. What led you to refuse to do that for so long?

When I was 19, I tried to teach chamber music at college. Admittedly, that didn't last long. Today, I know I want to pass on what I've learned myself. On top of that, there's my dissatisfaction with the way music is performed. That's why I try to share, and to discover and nurture new talents. By the way, that begins right from the start with manners – etiquette! Knowing how to behave is not an unimportant matter. Many young people not only think they are tremendously gifted, they make sure everyone knows it. Unfortunately, the piano competition industry promotes a sport-like approach which often doesn't have much to do with music.

Winners of competitions could often expect a great career. These days, that's all changed for the worse.

Alas. Again, that's part of the inflated importance of competitions. Globalisation also favours a unified style which is fostered by the juries. That's why I began by offering masterclasses and alternative series of concerts – for instance at the Gstaad or Schleswig-Holstein festivals. I no longer advertise the courses: after I've heard young people somewhere or other, I invite them myself.

Has the profession become very much objectified as a vocation?

Yes. And on top of that young people these days are very spoiled. Everything can be called up on the internet. No one is prompted to read the complete versions of Proust or Thomas Mann – the synopsis will do. I can see the complete contents of the Louvre in the form of a catalogue on the web. The effort, and often the ambition, of really wanting something goes by the wayside.

Can this evolution still be counteracted?

Probably not. But one can cultivate oases, for example in places like the Teatro Olimpico in Vicenza. Those concerts take place regardless of listening figures, and all the better for that. More and more people play the piano, above all in China, whereas in Europe the numbers are gradually diminishing. Why? As I've said: people are spoiled and lazy.

Are you a religious person?

That's hard to say. In any case, I'm not an atheist – more of an agnostic. I can't say that I believe in God. I experience my religion, my religiosity, through art. That to me is evidence of some higher force, of a spirit and a soul. Life after death? Who knows? You can't rule it out, and you also can't prove the contrary. I find it hard to believe that every thought that ever came into the world simply dissolves into nothing. There's a further life inherent in every note, every thought, perhaps in the cosmos. But I must stress one thing: I have a strong aversion to any kind of fundamentalism and dogmatism. The teaching of original sin is absurd. Of course, one makes mistakes in one's life, and feels guilt. But to live in fear of punishment – that's appalling. One can forgive, but certain things are unforgiveable and should never be forgotten.

You have achieved things that will have a permanent life.

Perhaps. I hope so! Some things will last, others not. In any case, a lot of it has been documented. I sometimes think of those creative figures who produced masterpieces. Those stand up for ever and are timeless.

Looking back on your life, are there some things that you would fundamentally have wanted to do differently, or should have done differently?

As far as details are concerned, without doubt. But on the whole everything has gone more or less just as I could have wished. Certainly, there was some luck involved. It would be presumptuous of me not to have been satisfied with things. Whether or not I would have been a good father, I don't know. My lack of children was not intentional, it just happened. On the other hand, not having a large family is certainly no handicap to the life of a musician. My self-discipline requires a firm rhythm. I can't imagine how Bach could have created his huge body of work while so many children were running around in that small living area

You seem to be reconciled and content with everything. All the same it shouldn't be forgotten that you experienced hard times and privations, and had to build things up over a long period.

It wasn't easy by any means. In the end, things worked out as they did. There's probably not much more to say about it.

Part 2

POLITICS, MUSIC &
MUSICIANS

No hunger for Hungary

The following letter from me appeared in the *Washington Post* of 1 January 2011:

Hungary's role in the EU is questionable

Congratulations on your leader in the issue of 26 December, entitled 'The Putinisation of Hungary'. Unlike Viktor Orbán's Hungary, Vladimir Putin's Russia is not a member of the European Union. This formidable and influential institution is not only a business and trade organization, it also claims to represent common European values. In view of the latter, is Hungary ready and worthy to take on the presidency of the community, as it was scheduled to do last Saturday?

The latest news is indeed alarming. People's tolerance levels are extremely low. Racism, discrimination against the Roma, anti-Semitism, xenophobia, chauvinism and reactionary nationalism – these symptoms are deeply worrying. They evoke memories that we hoped were long forgotten. Many people live in fear.

The latest media laws are just the last link in a sequence of shocking events. Many of these concern the arts. The EU presidency is an honor and a responsibility. The EU and the United States must keep a careful watch on Hungary. The EU must set the standard for member countries. We must guard and respect our common values.

January 2011

This innocuous letter elicited a storm of protest in Hungary. The publicist Zsolt Bayer (a close friend of President Viktor Orbán) published an inflammatory article in the daily newspaper *Magyar Hírlap* attacking me, the EU delegate Daniel Cohn-Bendit and the *Guardian* columnist Nick Cohen, describing us as 'putrid excrement'. He wrote about 'that Cohn', and deplored the fact that 'unfortunately, we have not managed to bury a person like that in the Orgovány woods. (In Orgovány in 1920, following the collapse of the new communist Soviet republic, hundreds of people, above all Jews and those suspected of being communists, were horrifically tortured and murdered.) In anonymous posts on the internet, I was tarnished as a 'Jew-pig' and a 'traitor and denigrator of his country'.

On 15 August 2012, a friendly match took place in Budapest between the national football teams of Israel and Hungary. As the band tried to play the Israeli national anthem, the local crowd (better described as the mob) began whistling and shouting, screaming and howling like a chorus from hell: '*Rohadt mocskos zsidók*' ('Filthy rotten Jews'). The Hungarian national anthem which came after it (a very nice piece of music, incidentally, composed in 1844 by Ferenc Erkel) was played and listened to without disturbance, and in solemn silence. The whole spectacle was recorded: you can enjoy it on YouTube. The crowd behaves like this because it is allowed to – it doesn't have to fear any consequences. Some circles not only harbour Holocaust deniers, they even breed Holocaust proponents to whose profound regret not enough Jews were murdered at the time. It's true that there is no official anti-Semitism in Hungary, but remarks and opinions of this kind are the order of the day, and have achieved drawing-room acceptance. President Orbán and his ruling FIDESZ Party (Union

An eight-year-old András plays a concert at his primary school, Budapest 1961

Young András with his father, Budapest 1960

Young András participates in a Hungarian talent competition, 'Ki mit tud?' or, 'Who can do what?', 1968

András's mother, Ilona Schiff, at the piano

Pianist Rudolf Serkin

András Schiff with Polish pianist Mieczysław Horszowski; Yuuko Shiokawa stands in the background, Lucerne 1981

András Schiff with violinist Sándor Végh during the recording of the Beethoven sonatas, Salzburg 1983

András Schiff with the great Hungarian pianist Annie Fischer, Budapest 1986

Wedding of András Schiff and Yuuko Shiokawa. Conductor Rafael Kubelík stands beside them as witness, Salzburg 1987

András Schiff performs Mozart, Salzburg

András Schiff and Swiss oboist and composer Heinz Holliger play
Schumann, Debussy and Kurtág, Milan 1990

Dietrich Fischer-Dieskau, German baritone and conductor, with András
Schiff, Berlin 1993

András Schiff
works on the
recording for
Brahms's first
concerto with
conductor Sir
Georg Solti,
Vienna 1989

Mezzo-soprano
opera singer
Cecilia Bartoli
rehearses with
András Schiff for
a joint recording,
Salzburg 1993

George Malcolm,
harpsichordist
and composer
with András
Schiff, recording
Mozart's Works
for Piano
Four-Hands on
Mozart's own
Walter fortepiano,
Salzburg 1993

Yuuko Shiokawa rehearsing,
Mondsee festival 1995

András Schiff performs Bach: *Senza*
pedale ma con tanti colori

György Kurtág at piano, András Schiff stands beside him, Mondsee festival
1998

András Schiff conducts and performs with his chamber orchestra, the
Cappella Andrea Barca, at the Teatro Olimpico, Vicenza 2002

of Young Democrats) refuse to condemn these evil tendencies because they don't want to antagonise potential groups of voters.

In a further reader's letter (published in *Die Presse* on 19 November 2013, and *The Guardian* on 11 December 2013) I wrote:

Shame and Disgrace

On 3 November 2013, when streets and squares had already been named after him in the provinces, a monument to the former 'regent' of Hungary, Miklós Horthy, was unveiled in Budapest – not in an obscure place, but right in the centre of the city on the prominent Szabadság Tér (Liberty Square). Horthy, who ruled Hungary from 1920–1944, was one of Hitler's closest allies.

Some people in their wisdom can of course argue that the statue is actually not on the square, but at the top of the steps leading to the 'Church of Homecoming', and that since the sacred place is public property one is free to do whatever one likes there.

While the monument was being blessed by the Calvinist minister – and neo-Nazi – Lóránt Hegedüs Jr, Márton Gyöngyösi (a member of the extreme-right Jobbik Party) gave a speech. According to him, Horthy was 'the greatest statesman of the twentieth century', and one who could be mentioned in the same breath as St. Stephen, St. Ladislas, Ferenc Rákóczi, Lajos Kossuth and István Széchenyi.

The mind boggles. It is common knowledge that the period under Horthy was one of the darkest chapters in Hungarian history, and to glorify it is outrageous and shameful. To judge him otherwise is in no way a matter of opinion: the anti-Jewish laws, the deportations, the tragedy of the River Don (where, in 1943, the Hungarian troops were massacred by the Red Army) are all bound up with Horthy's name. Neither God nor the politics of the extreme right can absolve him of this shame.

It is shocking to find a large proportion of the Hungarian population ignoring and denying these historical facts. Admittedly, they have the right to do so, because at last freedom of thought and opinions is permitted in Hungary. So if someone puts up a statue of Horthy or Ferenc Szálasi (the latter was Head of State and Prime Minister during the fascist dictatorship of the Arrow Cross Party from 1944–5) in their church, vegetable garden or stable, it's purely their private concern.

Antal Rogán, the party whip of the ruling FIDESZ party, is worried about Hungary's negative reputation abroad. He has every reason to be worried, but the country has only itself to blame. There are no statues to Hitler in Germany or Austria, because they are banned by the constitution. In the same way, no Mussolini monuments can be erected in Italy, none for Pétain in France, Antonescu in Romania or Tiso in Slovakia. (All these countries are EU members.)

The hundreds of people who took part in a courageous counter-demonstration on Liberty Square, many of them wearing a yellow star, deserve our respect and admiration. There could, and should, have been many more of them. Their opponents – they were in the majority – were keen to see them sent to Israel or Brussels, or even thrown into the Danube, on whose banks thousands of Jews were murdered in Budapest between 1944 and 1945 by the Arrow Cross Party under Szálasi.

What I described in my 2011 *Washington Post* letter has unfortunately come to pass. Viktor Orbán and FIDESZ won the elections in 2014 with an overwhelming majority, which seems to have decisively strengthened their power and influence. They have more or less rewritten the Hungarian constitution. Important positions in business, law and even the arts are filled by FIDESZ apparatchiks and the party faithful. The forcing into line is reminiscent of the times and methods of Goebbels and Stalin. On paper at least, and theoretically, Hungary is a democracy, and yet there is no real opposition party. After the fall of the Wall, the socialists (the remnants of the years 1948–9 and their followers) had their chance, which they mishandled miserably: they lost their credibility through incompetence and corruption. And so it is not surprising that the FIDESZ party garners so many protest votes, or votes from people who are either too indolent to do otherwise, or – even worse – expect improvements from the extreme right wing.

Hungary's economic and financial situation is disastrous: the country is hopelessly in debt and can only keep its head above water through generous financial aid from the EU. Poverty and destitution are both shocking and deeply depressing, and many people languish in indescribable living conditions. The capital's streets are teeming with beggars, and hordes of the homeless occupy railway stations and underground passages.

Compared with this misery, the wealth of Orbán, his FIDESZ and its vassals, thrives. Anyone who wants to work, or simply exist, in Hungary has no choice other than to follow the paths of conformity, opportunism and careerism. In the last few years several hundred thousand young people, among them the most talented and intelligent, have left their homeland to try their luck elsewhere. (These days,

London counts as the second largest Hungarian city.) Their loss will cause Hungary irreparable economic, scientific and cultural damage.

Orbán and his government of course think otherwise. According to their creed there is absolutely no reason for dismay or complaint: the present leadership will allow the country to flourish; it is driving it towards an auspicious future, in a glorious and unstoppable triumphal procession. The government only complains when it sees itself as the victim of an evil international conspiracy of communists, internationalists and liberals. Our little Hungary (an area of 93,030 square kilometres, and with around 10 million inhabitants . . .) will show them, as we have shown others in the past: we suffered enough under the Mongolian Tartars in 1241 and 1242, the Turks from 1526 to 1686, the Hapsburgs from 1686 to 1918, and the Soviets from 1949 to 1989. So let us not be forced into a dictatorship from Brussels now. (Naturally, the Horthy years of 1919–45 have been left off the list: many Hungarians look back on them with nostalgia.)

Perhaps these ludicrous tirades shouldn't be taken at all seriously – they belong to the satirical realm of the 1959 Peter Sellers film *The Mouse that Roared*. Hungarian folklore is itself rich in fictional heroes, such as the Betyár (bandit) Sándor Rózsa or Mattie the Goose-boy (Ludas Matyi). Rózsa, the Hungarian Robin Hood, began his 'career' as a violent robber, and later took an active part in the 1848 revolution. Mihály Fazekas's *Ludas Matyi*, written in 1804, is a free retelling of a folk tale. It tells the story of a simple boy who was unjustly punished by the local squire, Dániel Döbröghy, with 50 lashes. The boy pays the lord back threefold. In both cases – Rózsa and Ludas – simple, poor people prevail over powerful rulers who have exploited and mistreated them. From this point of view, it becomes easier to understand why Orbán's words meet with an enthusiastic response from large swathes of the population. The president is by no means a compassionate person: nothing is more alien to him than to lend support to the poor and the elderly, the weak and the ill. Instead, he regales his supporters with torrents of demagogic words, with questionable patriotism and sanctimonious Christian slogans. One of his favourite weapons is the Trianon conspiracy. On 4 June 1920, a peace treaty was signed at the Grand Trianon palace in Versailles, according to which Hungary had to withdraw from two-thirds of its territory as a consequence of having lost the war. This was an emotional shock that penetrated deep into the hearts of the Magyars. To this day they have not got over the stipulation, which they regard as an unacceptable form of humiliation. And so during the time of his EU presidency, Orbán appeared on one occasion in Brussels bearing a gift in the form of a tapestry showing a 1918 map of Greater Hungary.

Self-glorification, self-pity. 'This nation has already suffered for all sins of the past and the future', it says in the *Himnusz*, the Hungarian national anthem, written in 1823 by the poet Ferenc Kölcsey. Others are always to blame for our misery – we would rather not look into the mirror. Instead, it's better to find scapegoats, whether the communists, the Roma, or – as ever – the Jews.

When the great writer Imre Kertész was awarded the Nobel Prize for literature, the Stockholm Academy received a pile of hate mail from Hungary, protesting against the conferment of the prize to a Jew who didn't deserve such an honour. Is the old joke, one wonders, only a joke? Question: 'What is an anti-Semite?' Answer: 'Someone who hates the Jews more than strictly necessary.'

It's not by chance that Viktor Orbán and the FIDESZ

party are in power: they were elected by the people – now for the third time, with a two-thirds majority. (The Italians, too, have voted three times in favour of their beloved Silvio Berlusconi.) The second largest party is Jobbik (the word means 'better'), an extreme right-wing, fascist alliance supported by around 20 per cent of voters. The liberal opposition is weak and more or less insignificant.

Democracy is a wonderful principle. It has its advantages and disadvantages, but so far no better system has been devised. Democracy can only function within the framework of a responsible society in which humanitarian values are universally observed. From this point of view, Hungary is still a very young and immature country. In its 'glorious' history it has never had the opportunity of learning and applying the basic principles of freedom. It lacks a tradition of democratic thought, of tolerance for those who think differently, of political maturity. With the fall of the Wall in the wake of the Soviet Union's collapse in 1989, Hungary, like all the other former satellite countries, suddenly found itself faced with new circumstances and systems of values. It met them fully unprepared for a situation which demands much time, over generations, in order to be understood and appraised. Hungarians have to look forwards, but without forgetting or falsifying their history. Dreadful mistakes of the past cannot be redressed, but they can be acknowledged, analysed and regretted. And one can learn from them. That is the most important precondition for dealing with future cases.

'No hunger for Hungary'. Unfortunately, the title fits the present situation. Let us hope that in the not too distant future it can be 'Hungary – with great appetite', even if that lacks alliteration and seems clumsy.

New York, December 2014

Postscript

Unfortunately, the present situation is not encouraging. On 3 October 2016, there was a referendum on the number of refugees Hungary should take in. The turnout was low – around 40 per cent – but almost all of those who took part voted against the admittance of refugees. A few days later the most important newspaper of the opposition, *Népszabadság*, folded. Officially, it was for financial reasons, but it is more likely that it was on political grounds. The paper had been very vocal and courageous in its criticism of the government. In April 2018, Orbán and FIDESZ won the national election for a fourth time, with an increased majority.

On the southern border of the country Orbán has had a high fence with barbed wire built, to keep refugees out. Some people build bridges; Orbán builds walls.

Who's afraid of Jörg Haider?

On 9 February 2000, I was to have given a piano recital at the invitation of the Austrian Embassy in Washington DC. A few days earlier, Jörg Haider and the Freedom Party of Austria were voted into power by an astonishingly large proportion of the electorate. Because of that, I felt obliged to cancel the concert. For the same reason I am withdrawing from my next engagements in Austria, at the Vienna Festival and the June Schubertiade in Feldkirch. I absolutely refuse to appear in this country as long as Mr Haider and his party form part of the government.

It cannot be denied that this election result is based on

a democratic decision on the part of the Austrian people. But is that the end of the matter? This wonderful country has its own peculiarities, and a different mentality from others. ('All cities are alike, only Venice is a tad different', as the Viennese satirist Friedrich Torberg said.) Frustration over the disintegration and loss of the Austro-Hungarian realm and the shock of two world wars lie heavily like dark shadows on the idyllic country of *Gemütlichkeit*. Austria's responsibility for its activities in the Second World War and the Holocaust has been suppressed, hushed up and hidden to this day, on all levels.

The legendary falsehood that 'Beethoven was Austrian and Hitler German' has almost become reality. Austrian Nazis, both bigwigs and small fellow travellers, were pardoned with extraordinary haste and soon regained their reputable place in society. On 21 March 2000 in Vienna, Dr Heinrich Gross – a Nazi doctor responsible for the murder and torture of 772 disabled children – was acquitted on the grounds that the 'poor 84-year-old man' was physically too weak to withstand his trial. In the post-war years this 'gentleman' pursued a brilliant medical career in Austria. Why was this trial delayed for so long that it degenerated into farce?

In central Vienna stands an attractive square. It bears the name of the former, much-loved mayor Dr Karl Lueger (1844–1910), who was nevertheless notoriously known for his openly propagated anti-Semitism. The young Adolf Hitler found in him an excellent teacher. In Salzburg there is a Josef Thorak Street. The name celebrates a sculptor who was the Führer's favourite. The list could go on. These examples are unmistakable signs that many Austrians are in sympathy with this past, while others – and this is no less despicable – think it wasn't so bad in those days, life can just go on in its usual way.

Enter Jörg Haider. His words and statements are like pouring oil on the flames. Politicians are responsible for their words: it won't do to invent excuses afterwards. Words can be dangerous: they influence the masses and are the root cause of evil deeds and their consequences. Hitler didn't kill anyone by his own hand, but it would be madness to play down the results of his rhetoric. It's true that Haider is no Hitler, and yet the situation is serious and can escalate. Twenty-seven per cent is a considerable figure, and there is always the danger that it will increase. Haider's withdrawal as head of his party is a deception. In the background, he still holds the strings of his marionettes in his hands. At the first opportunity, he will step forward as the saviour of his people.

A large percentage of Austrians are both outraged and astonished by the European Union's reaction. Permanently stuck in the past, they scent injustice and conspiracy. For the first time, the EU has acted unanimously against a member state. Legally, their action can be called into question, but ethically and morally hardly so. The community was founded in part with the intention of preventing the crimes and atrocities of the past happening again. It is true that the majority of its member states have to contend with radical right-wing factions, but those groups function on the margins of society, and evoke little sympathy. Numerous countries of the former Soviet bloc are waiting to join the EU, yet it's within these very states that alarming tendencies of nationalism and right-wing populism can be seen. These groups are now celebrating the success of Haider and the Freedom Party of Austria. The European protests are not merely necessary reactions against Austria, but a warning signal for future members.

How long will the protests and sanctions last? France, Belgium and Portugal are still pursuing a hard line, but increasingly softer voices can be heard from Finland, Denmark and other countries which would like to revert to business as usual as quickly as possible. The trivialisation of Haider's aims and intentions amounts to acquiescence, and inevitably makes them more or less socially acceptable.

Every free person has the choice of being a servant, a fellow traveller or an opponent of a political movement. Among artists, there are three kinds. The first refuse to become involved where dangers lurk: they avoid entering into murky territory. The second group behaves rebelliously and is convinced that in difficult times it is necessary to be present on the spot, fighting and protesting. Representatives of the third kind – and unfortunately there are many of them – believe that art and politics have nothing to do with each other. That is the position of the perpetual spectator who turns a blind eye. Looking at the band of fighters and revolutionaries, we can see that this movement comes mostly from the worlds of the theatre and literature. Depressingly enough, in the realm of classical music a deathly silence reigns – above all in the country of music which Austria is. Do writers and actors have more courage and a greater sense of justice than their musical colleagues?

My personal choice has been made: I am keeping away. It is a difficult decision, because without wanting to, I am punishing concertgoers. I hope, however, that my action will be understood, as well as the message it sends, and that the time will soon come when things can return to normal.

Austria is a wonderful country, blessed with many

outstanding people whose task is to eliminate the shame of right-wing populism. I should like to do everything to help them in this with the admittedly limited means at my disposal. It is true that a single voice is no more than a drop in the ocean, but silence would easily become a step towards complicity.

Florence, April 2000

Postscript

Jörg Haider died in an automobile accident in 2008, but his legacy lives on. In the latest elections of 15 October 2017, his Freedom Party received 26 per cent of the vote and was able to form a coalition with the People's Party. Fortunately, in the previous year the liberal Alexander van der Bellen won the Austrian presidential election, if only by a small margin. That was one of the good pieces of news in 2016. There were not many of those: 2016 was also the year of Brexit and Donald Trump. What has happened to the world? What is right or wrong? What good or bad? Who decides?

Bach on the piano

The year 2000 marks – among other, perhaps more earth-shattering, events – the 250th anniversary of the death of JS Bach. As in 1950 and 1985, there will be endless tributes and celebrations to honour the 'father figure' of Western music. Today his star shines brighter than ever, and his unique position at the summit of Mount Olympus has been universally acknowledged. With the exception of a few naysayers, who to their shame surreptitiously conceal their reservations about him like members of some secret society, most musicians and music lovers revere Bach as an ideal. They are right to do so: in all the various genres except opera – whether sacred or secular, vocal or instrumental – he created monuments of such unparalleled beauty, mastery and perfection that they are seen as the standard by which later compositions are judged, and usually found wanting.

Schumann once wrote that the *Well-Tempered Clavier* should be the daily bread of every musician. Paradoxically (or is it a bad joke?) of all instrumentalists, it is pianists who have the least experience of, and living contact with, Bach. Almost all violinists study the solo Sonatas and Partitas, all cellists learn the six solo Suites, and they go on playing them long after they have finished their studies. Not so pianists: after having played the Inventions as children, and probably some of the Preludes and Fugues as conservatoire students (because they are obliged to do so), once they have passed their final examinations they put the score back on the shelf, where it remains unopened, gathering dust. That is a terrible pity. A musician's life without Bach is like an actor's without Shakespeare. Why do so many pianists deprive themselves of the very best, and why are they content to waste their precious time on music of lesser value? True, we hear the odd Bach piece here and there – usually at the beginning of a recital as a warm-up exercise – but the number of pianists who play Bach regularly and with passionate involvement is small. They form the proverbial exception to the rule.

Let us try to examine this curious phenomenon more closely. There can be only three reasons for such abstinence: (a) one simply dislikes Bach; (b) one fails to understand him; or (c) one simply lacks the courage to play his works. Given its heretical nature, the first of these is highly unlikely; the second is at least conceivable; and the third the most likely. Do string players have a better understanding of

Bach? Certainly not, since they are less used to polyphonic textures. If pianists are not lacking in intelligence and understanding, and they like Bach's music, then what on earth are they afraid of?

Part of the answer lies in the false application of the word 'authenticity'. Many people consider it a mortal sin to perform Bach on a modern piano and are as scared of doing so as the devil is of holy water. They claim to be able to re-create the conditions and circumstances of the composer's time. Since the piano in its present form didn't exist then, in their opinion it should be banned, excluded, eliminated. This brotherhood of the Wise and the Good argues that Bach should only be played on the clavichord and the harpsichord. Similarly, Haydn, Mozart, Beethoven and Schubert are supposedly far more enjoyable on the fortepianos of their times. What, for goodness' sake, are we allowed to play on a 1990 Steinway? Elliott Carter, perhaps? Luckily, this view of authenticity hasn't got completely out of hand, authenticity doesn't threaten us with dictatorship, and there has so far been no ban on playing Bach on a 'normal' piano. (In this connection, Richard Taruskin's fine essay in the symposium *Authenticity and Early Music*, edited by Nicholas Kenyon, is warmly recommended.)

Of Bach's vast number of keyboard works, only three – the 'Italian Concerto', the 'French Overture' and the 'Goldberg' Variations – were specifically written for a harpsichord with two manuals. Most of the keyboard pieces were intended for the clavichord, a sensitive and lovely instrument of such delicate sound that most of its nuances are lost in a space larger than a drawing room. In his own preface to the Inventions, Bach writes of the *arte cantabile*, the singing way of playing. This explains his preference for the clavichord over the more brilliantly percussive harpsichord. No one knows the 'correct' instrument for the *Well-Tempered Clavier*. Some pieces suggest the clavichord, others the harpsichord, organ or pedal-harpsichord. None of these historical instruments can do equal justice to all of the Preludes and Fugues. The modern piano probably can. In the two 'abstract' masterpieces of Bach's late years, *The Art of the Fugue*, and *The Musical Offering* with its three- and six-part Ricercars, Bach declined to prescribe the precise instrumentation. We may assume that these works were conceived for a keyboard instrument, because they are eminently playable by two hands.

In his aforementioned essay, Richard Taruskin quotes Theodor Adorno's well-known view that there is such a huge chasm between the music of Bach and that of his lesser contemporaries that to convey its universal message we should not get stuck in endless arguments about the 'right' instrument. It is much more important, says Adorno, to ask ourselves how we play this music. And if it is to be heard not just in small rooms or on recordings, but in the concert hall, then the acceptance of the piano is a must.

But hold on a minute, says a protesting voice. How can you accuse pianists of neglect? Haven't they had their fair share of Bach-Liszt, Bach-Tausig, Bach-Busoni? They certainly have, and that makes things all the more complicated. Transcriptions represent Bach in the *Zeitgeist* of the second half of the nineteenth century. Just as in architecture, where many beautiful Romanesque churches were drastically altered by the Gothic and, worse still, the Baroque style, so those transcription specialists felt it necessary to add to the original musical text. Just as in the former field the external church walls were left in place while inside endless decorative elements of glittering gold and silver were added to glorify the Lord, so in musical transcriptions massive chords, thundering octaves and decorative passages were added, distorting the purity of Bach's counterpoint. Unfortunately, the original splendour of the vandalised churches is lost forever; but with Bach we can still go back to the original text and ignore the transcriptions.

In the famous Chaconne from the D minor Partita for solo violin – one of the peaks of all music – Bach erects a magnificent polyphonic structure rather like a cathedral, using only four strings. Busoni's version for piano blurs the wonderful hard-won structure, because unlike with the violin we no longer experience what is literally a struggle to achieve the seemingly impossible. On the violin, four-part counterpoint is extraordinary; on the piano it is quite normal. If the Chaconne is to be played on the piano at all, it would be better to do so by adhering to the original score in a practical way, as Brahms did in his transcription for left hand alone. That, however, would not accord with the spirit of Busoni's day, when the plain framework of Bach's text, without added octaves and other pianist devices, would have been regarded as dull and boring. Even today this dubious recreation is in the repertoire of many famous and less famous pianists – not least those who don't play a note of genuine Bach, or go to the trouble of learning real Busoni, such as the wonderful *Fantasia Contrappuntistica*. Nineteenth-century transcriptions were relevant in their own day, when original Bach was neither appreciated nor widely performed. Today, they feel anachronistic and contribute nothing to our understanding of the composer.

Bach was himself a great master of transcriptions, and he arranged around 20 concertos by various composers, from Vivaldi and Marcello to Telemann and others. Through these he studied and mastered the Italian concerto form, and went on to transcribe his own works: thus, for example, the E major Violin Concerto became the D major Keyboard Concerto. Several movements of the keyboard concertos are borrowed from various of his cantatas. It is both fascinating and rewarding to investigate how Bach alters the tonality and texture to fit the requirements of the keyboard instrument. He transformed the opening motive of the E major Violin Concerto in the new version, for instance, and completely changed its character. He restricted his arrangements to his own works and those of his contemporaries. Wisely, he steered clear of the works of Schütz, Palestrina and Ockeghem.

If we speak of a correct text, we must examine the choice of editions. Czerny, Busoni, d'Albert, von Bülow and many other prominent musicians – even Bartók – all edited Bach's keyboard music. Important publications were also produced by Bischoff and Tovey. Today, there are so-called Urtext editions published by Henle, Bärenreiter and Wiener Urtext, all of them based on the sources. There are two complete critical editions: the Bach Gesellschaft and the Neue Bach-Ausgabe. What criteria should we use in making our choice? Does the right edition exist at all?

Nowadays, Czerny and his followers are clearly out of contention; to follow their example would be tantamount to digging up the transcriptions again. Bischoff and Tovey both produced excellent editions, the latter providing illuminating analyses of the Preludes and Fugues. The editions under the banner of 'Urtext' are by no means identical in small details, and are all worth considering. Apart from the Bärenreiter, a major shortcoming of all of them is that they contain fingerings, by the editor or some other 'expert'. While some students and amateurs value this, most music lovers and connoisseurs regard it as an unwelcome annoyance. What they would like to have is beautifully produced critical editions which print all the sources, and in which nothing but the truth is reproduced, without the interference of editors.

For a more complete understanding of Bach's mind we have to consult his autograph manuscripts. Not even the best printed version can manage to reproduce the beauty, elegance, strength and energy of his handwriting. Those wonderful wavy lines are so suggestive that they show us how the music flows. This is an ocean that produces large waves, and we cannot impede their course! The manuscripts also give us an opportunity to read the notation in different clefs, whereas even a good modern edition uses only treble and bass. And those who worry about deciphering the manuscript should at least try to find pleasure in autographs, as one does in a handwritten letter from a person one loves.

Performing Bach's music on the piano – although completely 'unauthentic' – is not necessarily an obstacle to historical and intellectual awareness. The informative textbooks and treatises of Bach's time – those by Carl Philipp Emmanuel Bach, Johann Joachim Quantz, Johann Philipp Kirnberger and others – are all available in reprints, even for pianists! These sources will not teach us the latest secrets of performance practice, but they are a treasure-trove of information on style, aesthetics, ornamentation, free improvisation, figured bass and other aspects. In his *Essay on the True Art of Playing Keyboard Instruments*, CPE Bach wrote that in the end it was all a matter of *buon gusto* – good taste. It seems that in those days, too, there were plenty of people with the opposite – that is to say *cattivo gusto*.

The manuscripts give us very little information on certain aspects of interpretation such as tempo, dynamics, phrasing, articulation and ornamentation. Obviously, it was not considered necessary to put everything down in writing, since musicians of good taste would understand the music's style and character as a matter of course. The performer was expected to fill in the gaps following his musical knowledge and instinct. Bach himself apparently never played a piece twice the same way. Hence the numerous versions of the 'Chromatic Fantasy' and the French Suites.

Today, we are far removed from that glorious era, and we cannot, and should not, even try to reconstruct its habits and circumstances. We mere mortals must trust our instincts and use our imaginations instead of obeying the laws of a musical police state where the invisible finger admonishes: 'You mustn't do that.' The pianist should not become a slave of received opinion, but should function as a medium and recreator – a sort of second composer. Bach's text is sacrosanct, but it allows us the freedom to make certain choices and decisions of our own. The editions by Czerny & co. are not suitable because they rob us of this freedom. They represent the editor's personal interpretation, which offers only one among many possibilities. An interpretation in print forces other players to become thoughtless robots instead of using their own imaginations.

Bach rarely provided his own tempo indications. The first book of the *Well-Tempered Clavier* contains only five, the second book no more than three. The Inventions and many other pieces also have no markings. A few of the 'Goldberg' Variations are marked: No. 7 is a 'Tempo di Giga'; No. 15 an Andante; No. 25 – the work's emotional climax – an Adagio. The Suites and Partitas are mostly sequences of dance movements: Allemande, Courante, Sarabande, Gigue and other 'galanteries', as Bach himself called them. A familiarity with these types will enable the player to identify them elsewhere, associating, for instance, the C sharp minor Prelude from Book One with a courante, the F major Fugue from Book Two with a gigue, the B flat major Fugue from the same book with a minuet. Defining the exact tempo of a dance is both impossible and senseless. The secret lies not in the speed of execution, but more in the rhythmic characterisation.

Likewise, how slow is Adagio or Andante, how fast is Allegro or Presto? Andante means 'walking', and it is certainly more flowing than Adagio, but even an Adagio by Bach cannot afford Brucknerian spaciousness. Allegro means merry and cheerful, and even a Presto in the eighteenth century was not associated with supersonic speed. Bach is the most generous of all the great composers because his works can be played convincingly in many different tempi. In this he is the exact opposite of Mozart. A good tempo is suggested by the harmonic movement of the piece, and it allows the player to articulate even the smallest note values without haste.

The purity of polyphony and counterpoint requires the utmost clarity of execution. Pianists who want to achieve this must be aware of the deadly enemy – the sustaining pedal. This splendid device is an essential element of nineteenth- and twentieth-century piano music, but it is an invention that is ill-suited to the music of Bach, where it must be used extremely sparingly and with caution. Bach's entire output can, in fact, be played to its advantage without touching the pedal. (A similar attempt with any work by Chopin or Schumann would produce absurd results.) Just as modern string players unfortunately use vibrato continually and indiscriminately, so many pianists cannot take their foot off the 'gas pedal'. Absurdly enough, *senza vibrato* and *senza pedale* seem not to exist in the vocabulary of present-day music teaching. With the exception of the organ, none of Bach's keyboard instruments allowed a note to be sustained by mechanical means. Clearly, he wrote his 'clavier' music for the hands alone. If he wanted to involve the feet, he changed over to the organ. Of course, it would be foolish and dogmatic to ban the pedal in playing Bach: its use can be condoned for effects of colour, or to achieve spacious sonorities. But the pedal should never be allowed to blur polyphonic textures or to cover up an inability to achieve a perfect legato with the fingers alone.

The player must, furthermore, make his own choice in matters of articulation and phrasing. The old-fashioned way of performing Bach – the *sempre legato* still being taught in some conservatories – is gradually dropping out of sight, and period instruments have opened our eyes to the beauty and necessity of varied nuances of articulation. The ideal performance offers not only a perfect rendition of individual notes, the individual musical 'syllables' or 'words', but also of complete 'sentences' and sections.

Ornaments are an essential feature of Bach's style. Some of them are written out in full, others are indicated by abbreviations and signs. In his *Clavierbüchlein* for his eldest son, Wilhelm Friedemann, Bach included a table of ornaments to facilitate their correct execution. The writings of CPE Bach and others devote long chapters to the art of embellishment, and modern players should be familiar with these sources. That familiarity will give them the confidence to apply ornaments freely when they are not explicitly printed in the score.

Repeats should be observed because they give the listener a welcome second chance to hear a section. That doesn't mean that the second time should be a mechanical reproduction of the first. On the contrary: in binary-form dance movements decoration, articulation and nuances of dynamics acquire their meaning only with the repeat. Here again, it is *buon gusto* that dictates when and to what degree ornaments are appropriate: less is more.

In his harpsichord pieces, such as the 'Italian Concerto', Bach uses the directions *piano* and *forte* to indicate changes between the two manuals. Otherwise, there are no dynamic markings. But the idea that his music forgoes colours like a black-and-white photograph is mistaken. It is true that the modern piano allows for infinitely more colours and shades than its predecessors, but to use its full volume and resources when playing Bach would be to distort the music's meaning. Between the delicacy of the French Suites and the hugely dramatic Sixth Partita there are millions of colours to be discovered. Dynamics are also influenced by the size and acoustics of the venue in which the performance takes place.

Pablo Casals, one of the greatest of musicians and Bach lovers, once said that accents were the salt and pepper of music. By this he didn't mean the absurdly mechanical emphasis on the first beat of the bar, but rather a vital pulsation and the courage to underline the irregularities of the musical prosody.

Today, we are in danger of wasting valuable time in arguments over this and that instrument, or whether trills should begin on the main note or the upper auxiliary note. Let us acknowledge Bach once and for all as an essential part of our musical heritage. As an introduction to Bach's world, young children can almost begin their first piano lessons with the Little Preludes and the *Notenbüchlein für Anna Magdalena Bach*. Continuing with the Inventions, the road leads to the *Well-Tempered Clavier*, and, if the heavens are favourably disposed, eventually to the 'Goldberg'

Variations and *The Art of the Fugue*. Alongside this road they will find the wonders of the French and English Suites, the Partitas and many others. (To young students who try to take a shortcut and play the 'Goldberg' Variations before having studied simpler pieces, I would advise patience. You cannot scale Mount Everest if you haven't climbed any hills.)

Bach's influence on later great composers – from Mozart and Beethoven to Chopin and Bartók – is well documented. His art continues to fascinate and inspire most composers to this day. Bach, who was himself a deeply religious person, does not demand us to share his faith, yet the unique spirituality of his music unites players and listeners in a sense of community.

Florence, August 1999

Senza pedale ma con tanti colori: on playing Bach and the *Well-Tempered Clavier**

Pianists who play Bach are faced with some fundamental questions to which there are no easy answers. For example, what is the 'correct' instrument for the *Well-Tempered Clavier*? The clavichord, the harpsichord, the organ, the pedal-harpsichord? Is it permissible to play Bach on an instrument he never knew? If not, whom should we ask for permission? What are the right tempo and suitable character for a particular prelude or fugue, and how do we find them? How wide is the dynamic range in this music, and does it vary from instrument to instrument, or from venue to venue? How do we phrase or articulate a certain passage

---

* Booklet notes to CD recording, 2012 (ECM 2270–73).

or fugal subject? Do we need more ornamentation or less – or even none? Which is the best edition?

Each of these questions, and many more, has to be asked and taken into consideration. To answer them convincingly requires experience, intelligence and – to quote CPE Bach – *buon gusto*, good taste. Decisions have to be made, and it takes courage to play a piece in a certain way, knowing that it will not be to everyone's liking.

One of the biggest problems seems to be the use of the sustaining pedal, and not only in Bach. This ingenious device enables the player to raise the dampers, so that the strings can vibrate freely. Beethoven was the first great composer to use this effect consciously and creatively. In his famous C sharp minor Sonata Op.27 no.2 the entire first movement is to be played *senza sordini* – without dampers, or in other words with the pedal. The effect is magical: the different harmonies sound together, creating entirely novel sonorities. It would be reasonable to assume that pianists would follow the composer's directions – after all, Beethoven was quite a respectable musician, and he knew what he wanted. Wishful thinking, since ninety-nine per cent of performers ignore his wishes and diligently change the pedal at every change in harmony. Why? Because, they argue, the effect would have been different on Beethoven's fortepiano. Have these people ever played on Beethoven's Broadwood piano? No, they have neither heard nor seen it, and yet they know better. I am privileged enough to be able to say that I have played it and made recordings on it. The sound, the volume and the mechanics may be different, but that doesn't alter the actual musical idea in any way. A dissonance remains a dissonance, regardless of the instrument.

What does all this have to do with Bach? Rather a lot, in fact. On the keyboard instruments of his time the 'right-foot' pedal simply wasn't there. That means that he was able to play his keyboard pieces with no problem without the use of the non-existent pedal. It follows quite logically that the same works are also playable on a modern concert grand, with eight fingers, two thumbs – and no feet. (The one exception is the A minor fugue from Book 1 of the *Well-Tempered Clavier*, whose final bars can't be played with two hands alone, since this is presumably an organ piece. Here, one can judiciously use the sostenuto pedal – the middle of the three.)

Does all this mean that we have to deny ourselves the use of this invaluable aspect of the piano completely? Not necessarily. The pedal can be used intelligently and discreetly to lend help to the sound when playing in a very dry acoustic. But the damage that can be done through the indiscriminate use of the pedal should not be underestimated. The piano is not an automobile, where you have to keep your right foot permanently on the accelerator. String players and singers who use vibrato continuously, on every single note, are unbearable. The pedal is to the piano as the vibrato is to string players: both must be applied with careful control, and in moderation.

Intelligibility is essential with Bach. The clarity of the counterpoint and voice-leading must be self-evident: there is no room for confusion. Thus, a discreet use of the pedal can be tolerated as long as the player respects these rules. Nevertheless, in seeking easier solutions, are we doing the music any favours? There's no such thing as a perfect legato on the piano – it is an illusion. Although it is much harder to realise that illusion with the hands alone, it is well worth the effort. Bach's music is extremely demanding for performers and listeners, for professionals and music lovers alike. The composer certainly didn't want to make things easy for us.

An eminent pianist colleague of mine recently reprimanded me for my 'abstinence'. He argued that all the great pianists of the past played Bach with a great deal of pedal, and we should follow their example. I don't find his logic convincing. My teacher and mentor George Malcolm, a truly great musician and harpsichordist, taught me the art of playing without pedal, and the joy of clarity. There's a story attached to that: a successful young virtuoso pianist once came to him, asking if he could play him Bach's D major toccata. Malcolm agreed, the young man took his place at the keyboard with his right foot on the pedal, raised his arms – whereupon Malcolm shouted, 'Stop!' 'But I haven't played a note yet!' complained the young lion. 'No, but you were just about to.'

To me, Bach's music is not just black and white; it's full of colours. In my imagination each key corresponds to a colour. The *Well-Tempered Clavier*, with its twofold 24 preludes and fugues in all the major and minor keys, is an obvious repository for such fanciful ideas. Let us picture it. At the beginning there is the snow-white innocence of C major (only the 'white' keys); at the end there is B minor, the key of death. Compare the B minor fugue from Book 1 to the 'Kyrie' from the B minor Mass: they are both pitch-black music. Between these two poles we have all the other colours – first the yellows, oranges and ochre (C minor to D minor), then blue (E flat major to E minor), green (F major to G minor), pink and red (A flat major to A minor), the two browns (B flat major and minor) and grey (B major).

Of course, this is a very personal and arbitrary interpretation, and some may find it ridiculous or childish. But if you believe me that music is more than just a series of notes and sounds, then you will forgive me the sins of this little fantasy.

Florence, May 2012

Bach's 'Goldberg' Variations: a guided tour*

Se non è vero, è ben trovato – If it isn't true, it's well thought up.

In his Bach biography of 1802, Johann Nikolaus Forkel describes the origins of the 'Goldberg' Variations with the following anecdote: 'Count Keyserlingk, formerly the Russian ambassador to Saxony, often visited Leipzig. Among his servants there was a talented young harpsichordist called Johann Gottlieb Goldberg, a pupil of Wilhelm Friedemann Bach, and later of JS Bach himself. The count suffered from insomnia and ill-health, and Goldberg, who lived with him, had to stay in the room next door to soothe his master's suffering through music. Once the count asked Bach to compose a few keyboard pieces for Goldberg – light and happy pieces that would enliven his sleepless nights. Bach decided to write a series of variations, a form that had not previously interested him. Nevertheless, in his masterly hands, an exemplary work of art was born. The count was so delighted with it that he called it "my variations". He would often say: "My dear Goldberg, play me one of my variations." Bach had probably never been so generously rewarded for his music. The count gave him a golden goblet filled with a hundred Louis d'or!'

Se non è vero, è ben trovato. Like all legends, this one is of dubious authenticity. It is hard to understand why this work, published in Nuremberg in 1741 by Balthasar Schmid, does not bear a dedication either to Count Keyserlingk or to Goldberg. This, however, clearly shows that the work was

---

* Booklet notes to CD recording, 2003 (ECM 1825).

not a commission. No less unlikely is it that Goldberg, who was born in 1727, would have been sufficiently developed as a musician (at the ripe old age of 14!) to master the extraordinary musical, technical and intellectual difficulties of this work.

However, as with all legends this one also contains a grain of truth. Bach's works in variation form are few and far between. The rare examples are the *Aria variata alla maniera italiana* BWV 989 (1709), the Passacaglia in C minor for organ BWV 582 (1716–17), and the Chaconne from the D minor Partita for solo violin BWV 1004 (1720). The dates show that two decades separate the Chaconne from the 'Goldberg' Variations. Not until 1746 to 1747, with his canonic variations for organ on the Christmas song 'Vom Himmel hoch, da komm' ich her' (BWV 769), did Bach come back to this neglected genre.

Bach was a composer with encyclopaedic ambitions. In all the genres of sacred and secular music that he worked with, he reached heights that it would be unimaginable even to equal, let alone surpass. Had the circumstances of his life been different and had he become the court composer in Dresden, then no doubt he would have been the greatest opera composer, too. In 1731, our encyclopaedist embarked on a huge undertaking: the *Clavier-Übung* (Keyboard Practice), a collection of pieces of various styles written for different keyboard instruments. The first part (1731) contains the six Partitas. It represents the art of the baroque dance suite at its highest level. In the second part (1735), the *Italian Concerto* is juxtaposed with the *French Overture* (not bad for a composer who never set foot outside Germany). The third part is a collection of organ pieces: the Prelude and Fugue in E flat major, the four *Duetti* and several chorale preludes. In the fourth and last part, Bach wanted to finish with a crowning achievement, and thus the variations provided him with a real challenge. He probably felt a certain prejudice against this form. Many of his famous contemporaries had produced brilliant examples that had received widespread acclaim. Bach was never interested in cheap success, and so he set himself the aim of elevating the usually extroverted variation form to a hitherto unknown artistic and spiritual level.

The title page announces: 'Keyboard practice, containing an aria with different variations for a harpsichord with two manuals.' This is one of the three instances where Bach specifically calls for such an instrument (the others being the *Italian Concerto* and the *French Overture*). The theme is a beautiful aria which Bach wrote for his wife in the famous *Clavierbüchlein vor Anna Magdalena Bach*, in 1725. It is symmetrically divided into two halves of sixteen bars each. Present-day listeners must be careful not to be led astray by the beguiling quality of the melody and should concentrate above all on the bass line. If we stand in front of a cathedral, we are overwhelmed by its size and grandeur. Our eyes constantly drift towards the splendour of the towers and the cupola high above, while we tend to neglect the foundations on which the whole building rests.

This ground bass is like that of a passacaglia or a chaconne – it is the alpha and omega of the entire composition. There are 30 variations, after which the Aria returns in its initial form, thus uniting the beginning with the end. Bach clearly asks the performer to repeat each section. Were it not so, both the perfect symmetry and the proportions of the piece would be destroyed. Great music is never too long: it is certain listeners' patience that is too short.

Aller guten Dinge sind drei – all good things come in threes. Thus, the 30 variations are divided into 10 groups of 3 each.

Each group contains a brilliant virtuoso toccata-like piece, a gentle and elegant character piece and a strictly contrapuntal canon. The canons are presented in a sequence of increasing intervals, starting with the canon at the unison, until we reach the canon at the ninth. In place of the canon at the tenth, we have a quodlibet ('as you will') which combines fragments of two folk songs with the ground bass. The key remains G major for the most part, but with the shadow of the tonic minor in three variations (nos. 15, 21 and 25).

Let us go on a journey together, and allow me to be your guide. A guide should not talk too much, but it's essential that he has already taken this tour many times and can thus draw the travellers' attention to the essential details.

Aria
Our port of embarkation is in triple time ($\frac{3}{4}$), rhythmically similar to a sarabande, which has a gorgeous melody richly embellished with trills, mordents and appoggiaturas. Don't allow them to lead you astray. Always follow the bass line.

Variation 1
For a single manual, in $\frac{3}{4}$ time. Our journey begins with a brilliant and sunny two-part invention. The dance rhythm of complementary dactyls and anapaests recalls the spirit of the Italian *concerto grosso*.

Variation 2
For one manual, in $\frac{2}{4}$ time. A gentle piece with three voices, reminiscent of the trio sonatas for organ.

Variation 3
For one manual in $\frac{12}{8}$ time. Our first canon, at the unison.

Of the three voices, the two upper parts present the canon. The second voice imitates the first at the same pitch, a bar later. Meanwhile, the lowest voice follows the ground bass.

Variation 4

For one manual, in ⅜ time. Four imitative voices are joined together in this lively section reminiscent of a *passepied* – a French dance that is like a quick minuet. (Note the frequency of dance types throughout the work).

Variation 5

For one or two manuals, in ¾ time. A rapid toccata requiring the special virtuosity of crossed hands, and perhaps a homage to Domenico Scarlatti.

Variation 6

For one manual, in ⅜ time. Another canon, this time at the second. There are three voices. The subject in the alto voice is answered by the soprano a major second higher and a bar later. Against this the bass moves independently in continual semiquavers. Mozart used a similar device in the 'Ricordare' of his Requiem.

Variation 7

For one or two manuals, in ⅝ time. In his autograph score Bach wrote 'al tempo di giga'. The dotted dance rhythm of a gigue gives this piece its inherent character.

Variation 8

For two manuals, in ¾ time. Another brilliant two-part invention or toccata with frequent crossing of the hands. Although there are only two voices, the ingenuity of the figuration makes us imagine four or more.

Variation 9

For one manual, in $\frac{3}{4}$ time. Canon at the third, with three voices. This time the soprano leads and the alto follows a bar later and a third lower. A lyrical movement of the utmost simplicity and serenity in the *cantabile* style Bach favoured.

Variation 10

For one manual, in *alla breve* time. This 'fughetta' is in four voices, beginning with the bass, and followed by the tenor, the soprano and the alto at four-bar intervals. It marks the end of the first section (one third of the composition) with clear-cut finality. We may take a rest.

Variation 11

Having regained our strength, we continue with Variation 11 for two manuals, in $\frac{12}{16}$ time. This is an unobtrusive, mellow piece, of considerable virtuosity. The two voices (and hands) constantly cross over each other. As a result, the player often finds his left hand at the top, and his right hand at the bottom of the keyboard, which is not exactly a customary arrangement.

Variation 12

For one manual, in $\frac{3}{4}$ time. Canon at the fourth, in which the repeated crotchets of the lowest voice mark the ground bass, while the two upper voices give out the canon. The soprano begins and the alto answers a bar later, a fourth below. However, for the first time in the work, the answering voice is in contrary motion, or inversion. In the second half (from bar 17 onwards), the two parts change places. Now it is the alto that leads, and the soprano that follows. The extreme complexity of this texture is counterbalanced by the rhythmic vitality and rustic character of the whole piece.

Variation 13

For two manuals, in ¾ time. The two lower voices, bass and tenor, are joined in polyphonic harmony, above which an endless melody of singular beauty unfolds. Bach had already used this technique in the middle movement of his *Italian Concerto*. With it he paid tribute to the Italian art of written-out embellishments. This variation is closely related to no. 25: they are like sister and brother, feminine and masculine, lyrical and tragic.

Variation 14

How strong is the contrast to Variation 14 for two manuals, in ¾ time! It awakens us from our reverie with exhilarating explosions of trills, mordents, arpeggios and rapid sequences. Bach must have been very fond of crossing his hands and must have mastered the technique very well. His great contemporary Scarlatti, who used the same technique frequently, gave the habit up later, when – thanks to the wonders of Spanish cuisine – his stomach became an insurmountable obstacle for his arms.

Variation 15

We now come to Variation 15, for one manual, in ²⁄₄ time and marked *Andante*. This is the canon at the fifth, and the first variation written in the tonic minor. The diatonic ground bass is chromatically coloured. The alto initiates the canon, with the soprano answering a bar later at the fifth above. Like the canon at the fourth (no. 12), this one is in contrary motion. The slurred pairs of semiquavers sound like *sospiri* (sighs). This is music of the deepest sorrow, of lamentation. Note the extremeness of the final interval, where the lowest G in the bass joins forces with the highest D in the soprano – that's to say, a fifth spread over a compass of four-and-a-half octaves. This represents the desolate emptiness between heaven and earth. As this marks the middle of our journey, let us rest again and enjoy the silence.

Variation 16

The Overture which so appropriately opens the second half – Variation 16 for one manual, its first part *alla breve*, its second in ⅜ time – celebrates the French style. At the court of Louis XIV and his successors, this was the preferred type of music for festive occasions, produced by the great composers Lully, Couperin and Rameau. The first part, with its dotted rhythms, is stately and grandiose. The second, by way of contrast, is lively in character. Bach applies the French model with the astonishing mastery he had already demonstrated in his orchestral suites, and in keyboard works such as the D major Partita and the *French Overture* in B minor. Here, the jubilant first part gives way to a quick, light-footed fugato. The composition is so naturally artless that we hardly recognise our beloved ground bass, so cleverly is it concealed.

Variation 17

For two manuals, in ¾ time. After such a tour de force, it is sensible to relax, and this piece is a two-part invention based on sequences of broken thirds and sixths, ascending and descending stepwise.

Variation 18

For a single manual, in *alla breve* time. A canon at the sixth, in which the two upper voices (alto and soprano) present the canon in *stretta*. In other words, the second voice follows the first at a distance of only half a bar, overlapping with its second note. The bass line leads an independent life and is, indeed, far removed from the aria's ground bass. The merry dance rhythms (could it be an *Anglaise*?) show us that joyfulness and intellectual mastery can very well go hand in hand.

Variation 19

For a single manual, in ⅜ time. This charming little minuet creates the illusion of new sonorities, as though we were listening to a music box or musical clock.

Variation 20

This leads us straight into Variation 20 – for two manuals, in ¾ time. Another *pièce croisée*, a splendid display of artless virtuosity. The initial syncopations suggest a certain awkwardness, making the following rolling triplets sound even more effective.

Variation 21

From glowing daylight, we fall into the pitch-dark abyss of Variation 21, for one manual, in ¼ time. This canon is at the seventh and is in G minor, just as the canon at the fifth (no. 15) had been. In place of sorrow and grief, we hear music of intense despair, delivered with enormous passion. The bass line's wild chromaticism suggests a gigantic storm. If this is war, then what follows next must represent peace.

Variation 22

For a single manual, in *alla breve* time. This is strict four-part polyphony in the old style (*stile antico*). Let us imagine that after all this horror (of no. 21) we've come to a clearing, and from a distant chapel the sound of an *a cappella* choir casts its purifying effect over us. At long last, we can hear our lost ground bass again in its original clarity. In a work of 30 variations, it would have been logical to make a pause after no. 20. That would have been mathematically correct, but dramatically wrong. It would have been impossible to launch the canon at the seventh after a break: it had to grow out of the relentless energy and tension built up by the previous variation. Similarly, the dramatic contrast between nos. 21 and 22 could only be achieved by continuity, and at this point your guide begs you to enjoy the tranquillity and take another rest.

Variation 23

Let us resume our journey with Variation 23, which is for two manuals, in ¾ time. This is a witty show-piece which requires brilliant delivery. Try singing 'Ha-Ha-Ha' on the opening semiquavers, as if the gods were laughing on Mount Olympus.

Variation 24

For one manual, in ⅜ time. A canon at the octave played by the two upper voices. The soprano begins, and the alto joins in two bars later, an octave lower. At exactly the mid-point they exchange roles. The choice of the metre and the consistent use of trochees lend this marvellous piece its 'riding' character.

Variation 25

For two manuals, in ¾ time. The last of the three minor-mode variations, and marked *Adagio* by the composer. It is not only the most profound moment of the work, it also shows Bach in all his greatness. This is the music of the Passions, depicting man's suffering. Wanda Landowska called it the 'black pearl', but even those – or any other – words fall short of doing justice to this miraculous creation.

Variation 26

Is there life after death? 'Yes', says Bach. Listen to Variation 26, for two manuals, in $\frac{3}{4}$ and $\frac{18}{16}$ times. After the darkness there will be light. Two voices play a sarabande (in $\frac{3}{4}$ time) while the third is busy with continual semiquavers ($\frac{18}{16}$ time). The tempo suggests a pleasantly babbling brook, not unlike the one in Schubert's song 'Wohin?' from his song cycle *Die schöne Müllerin*. This may be an over-romantic association, but I find it difficult to understand performers who attack this piece with machine-gun-like aggression. After Variation 25, the music is slowly, gradually, returning to life, and it continues on this course without interruption towards its triumphant climax in Variation 30. But it is premature to divulge this just yet.

Variation 27

We now come to the ingenious Variation 27, for two manuals, in $\frac{6}{8}$ time. It is the last of the canons, this time at the ninth, and unlike its siblings it uses only two voices. The lower of them not only fulfils its canonic duties, it also makes sure that the cornerstones of the ground bass are properly outlined.

Variation 28

We are now at the final stage, and Bach approaches the end with a colossal edifice. Variation 28, for two manuals, is in $\frac{3}{4}$ time. Over the walking bass in quavers, the two upper voices play rapid figures (or written-out trills), which sound like a concert of birds. Beethoven must have taken this as a model for the famous trills in his sonatas opp. 53, 109 and 111.

Variation 29

In Variation 29, for one or two manuals, in $\frac{3}{4}$ time, we are astonished by the richness of the sonority, achieved by the novelty of having chords alternating between the two hands.

Variation 30

This leads inevitably into the grand finale – Variation 30, for a single manual, in $\frac{4}{4}$ time. At this point, we would logically expect a canon at the tenth, but Bach wouldn't be Bach without surprises, and so instead of the canon, he gives us a 'quodlibet'. As the title suggests, it is a humorous piece which incorporates fragments from two light-hearted folk songs. One is *Ich bin so lange nicht bei dir g'west* ('I haven't been with you for so long'), the other *Kraut und Rüben haben mich vertrieben* ('Cabbages and turnips have driven me away'). It is exuberant, boisterous and very funny – and yet profound (the clearly audible ground bass takes care of that). We can imagine the Bach family singing it together with a glass of wine (or was it beer?) in their hands. This is Dionysian music.

Aria de capo

With the final cadence still ringing in our ears, we stop for a moment of silence, and here Bach repeats the Aria unaltered. But we hear it with different ears, as a result of the last 70-odd minutes. We have come back home to our point of departure, a circle has been closed, beginning and end are united. At the moment of homecoming, we feel deep gratitude.

When, in Forkel's story, Count Keyserlingk asks Goldberg to play him one of his variations, we think he must be joking. Today, no one would dare to play bits and pieces of this work: it would be considered a sacrilege. There can be no doubt that Bach wrote it as a monumental whole, but not in his wildest dreams could he have imagined that it would be performed complete. For 150 years, the variations were condemned to virtual oblivion. Musicians knew of their existence, but nobody played them, least of all in public. In ETA Hoffmann's *Kreisleriana*, Kapellmeister Kreisler plays the work to the horror of his snobbish listeners, who either steal out of the room, or fall asleep.

Today we are experiencing the opposite extreme: the work is immensely popular and frequently played. As we have seen on our 'tour', Bach wrote it for a harpsichord with two manuals. There will always be those who think that playing it on a modern piano is an abominable sin. Let us leave them to their opinion – it's just as useless trying to convince them otherwise as it is to make a carnivore out of a vegetarian. Many others prefer the sound of the piano to that of the harpsichord, and let us not forget that we are talking about an hour and a quarter of music – hand on heart, can you listen to the harpsichord for that long?

This length indicates that all the repeats must be observed, for with a design of such perfect symmetry there are only two options. Either you play all the repeats, or none at all. The first solution is preferable: given the complexity of the music, it offers listeners a chance of greater understanding (and the performer of greater success). Of course, a repeat should never be purely mechanical. Variety can be achieved not just by ornamentation, but also through the careful application of different articulation, phrasing and dynamics. But to observe some repeats while omitting others makes no sense at all.

Pianists can play this work without altering a single note. They only have to solve the problem of 'traffic jams' – the frequent collision of the hands caused by the absence of the second manual.

Transcriptions are a further problem. There are modern versions for every conceivable instrument or ensemble, from string trio to string orchestra to brass quintet. The canons work equally well on strings because of their strict polyphony and the special range of the individual voices. The virtuoso variations (nos. 5, 8, 14, 20 and 26) are so unambiguously conceived for the keyboard that it is pointless and stupid to transcribe them for another medium. To alter Bach's voice-leading does the music serious damage.

That every musician would like to play this wonderful work is quite understandable. Its deep humanity, spirituality, optimism and intellectual power speak to us directly in these 'distracted times'. This is one of those few journeys on which we can embark again and again.

Florence 2003

Looking back into the future

Bach's six Partitas*

I made my first recording of Bach's six Partitas a quarter of a century ago, in 1983, in London's Kingsway Hall. Since then, I have continued my intensive study of his great keyboard works and have often performed them in cycles. Conducting the *St. Matthew Passion* and the B minor Mass several times were experiences that have left an indelible mark on my piano performances: we frequently find dance movements in Bach's church music, and his instrumental

---

* Booklet notes to CD recording, 2003 (ECM 2001–12).

works were often inspired by his sacred compositions.

Great music is far greater than its performers. We try our entire lives to unveil its secrets and to convey its unique message. Even if we never quite reach the imaginary goal, our many performances give us experience and knowledge that were hidden from us years ago. We form a better understanding of the music's structure and inner workings; horizons open up before our eyes. This was just as true of my second recording of the 'Goldberg' Variations, from a 'live' concert in Basel in 2003, as it was of the Partitas I recorded during a recital in the historic Riding Hall in Neumarkt – an exquisite little auditorium with superb acoustics.

Admittedly, Bach never imagined that all the Partitas would be performed in a single concert. The object of his *Clavierübung* was, of course, to summarise the forms and genres of his day systematically. The work is designed to be at once encyclopaedic and scholarly, and instructive. Nonetheless, the six Partitas form an ideal, if long, concert programme: Bach's music succeeds over and over again in forging an intimate bond between performer and audience.

It would be simple and logical to play these exemplary suites in their original order, as I used to do in the past. Yet I always had the feeling that something was not quite right. The B flat major Partita calls for great inner tranquillity of a sort that is never quite there at the start of a public recital. Is it really mandatory to place it at the beginning? I think not. If we start with the G major Partita, the keys of the six works form a hexachord: G–A minor–B♭–C minor–D–E minor, with the major and minor modes evenly distributed, and the sunlit, graceful G major work forming an ingratiating and appropriate opening.

This sequence is my personal choice, and it raises no

claims to universal truth. Listeners are invited to put the pieces together in any order they like.

June 2009

Humour is no joke* – hommage à Haydn

It's a well-known situation: at a gathering, someone tells a joke and no one laughs. The person telling the joke feels as though he's taken a cold shower.

As part of the Salzburg *Mozartwoche*, I recently conducted Haydn's D minor Symphony No.80 – an astonishing and completely unknown work full of surprises. Already in the exposition of the *Allegro spiritoso* opening movement the music's *Sturm und Drang* character is suddenly interrupted by a charming and Ländler-like closing theme. In the development section, Haydn introduces unusually long pauses and, with daring modulations, makes unexpected excursions into strange tonalities. The last movement – a Presto – is a *tour de force* of rhythmic ambiguity in which the listener has to guess where the upbeats and downbeats are. Only after 32 bars does the music place its feet firmly on the ground. It's ingenious, and extremely funny. But in Salzburg, no one shared the humour; there was no trace of laughter, not even a smile to be seen. Why? Is it easier, perhaps, to make an audience cry than laugh? It seems that way. There are many music lovers who won't even admit that there's any room for humour in music at all. God protect us from people with no sense of humour!

---

* Quoted from the Hungarian humorist Frigyes Karinthy (1887–1938): '*Humorban nem ismerek tréfát*' ('I see no humour in jokes').

In his essay, 'Must Classical Music Be Entirely Serious',[*] Alfred Brendel shows that failure to understand musical humour can lead to wrong value-judgements and to mis-understandings. A while ago, in a Tokyo bookstore, I came upon a strange book in which the author explained in all seriousness how to understand jokes. Each joke or anecdote was followed by several pages of 'instructions' to help the reader get the point. It has often been my experience in Japan that at a social gathering I have said something I thought was quite trivial or harmless, and my hosts have burst into uproarious laughter. Evidently, we Europeans have a completely different conception of what constitutes humour and the comical.

Haydn was writing for a public that understood his musical language perfectly. In Eisenstadt and at the Ester-házy court, in Vienna and Paris, and first and foremost in London, he was surrounded by a small but knowledgeable circle of professional and amateur musicians who received each new work with interest and appreciation. His audience was familiar with his compositions, they knew his personal style and immediately recognised the unusual features of a new symphony or string quartet. His humour worked only in this circle of music lovers who could listen to the expected and the unexpected, the conventional and the surprising, with perceptive ears, note by note. Audiences today are larger, but all the more uninformed. Sometimes they could do with one of those Japanese books, to explain the point.

Haydn's keyboard works are full of comical elements. An early example is his Capriccio in G major, which takes as its theme the folk song 'Acht Sauschneider Müssen Sein'.

---

[*] Alfred Brendel: *Music, Sense and Nonsense* (London, 2015), pp.85–118.

The song's text is incredibly funny. It describes the castration of a pig – an operation for which no fewer than eight 'experts' were needed. The way Haydn jumps from one key to the next, the manner in which he varies fragments of the theme in wild contrasts of register, is confusing in the extreme. His audiences of 1765 knew the folk song well; the rustic, light-hearted character of the piece hardly needed explaining to them.

Nearly a quarter-century later, in 1785, Haydn wrote his Fantasy (or Capriccio) in C major – a much more mature masterpiece than its predecessor, and a curious mixture of sonata, rondo and variation forms. On two occasions – on a pause over an octave in the bass – the music comes to a standstill. Here, the composer instructs the player: '*Tenuto intanto, finché non si sente più il suono*' – hold until the sound is no longer heard. That can take a painfully long time! The audience might begin to think the poor pianist has had a memory lapse or has somehow 'dropped out'. But suddenly the bass quietly slides a semitone upwards. The effect is extremely funny, as long as those present have got the point.

In his late piano sonata in E flat major Hob.XVI:52 the second movement is in the key of E major. Following, as it does, the majestic, symphonically conceived opening movement, the change of key is extremely surprising – indeed, shocking. According to the conventions of the time, the middle movement ought to have been in the dominant key – B flat major – or in the relative minor, C minor. There is nothing at all self-evident about Haydn's bold innovation: it marks a real break with tradition. The juxtaposition of E flat major and E major was extremely daring. It was not until late Beethoven (the string quartet Op.131, with its first movement in C sharp minor, and second movement in

D major) and Schubert that similar so-called 'Neapolitan' key relationships were exploited. To Schubert, such relationships were of fundamental importance: the F minor piano duet Fantasy D.940 has its slow movement and scherzo in F sharp minor; the slow variations of the C major 'Wanderer' Fantasy D.760 are in C sharp minor; and the scherzo of the C major String Quintet D.956 has a sombre trio in D flat, while the middle section of its E major slow movement unfolds in F minor.

Haydn's chamber music is no less unconventional, and the unjustly neglected piano trios, above all, are remarkable. The E flat minor Trio Hob.XVI:31 – who else would have chosen such an unusual key at that time? – begins with an expressive *Andante cantabile*, written in double variation form. The following Allegro (there are only two movements) carries the subtitle of 'Jacob's dream' – an allusion to his vision of a ladder stretching up to heaven. According to a contemporary anecdote, the violinist who first played the piece was infamously arrogant and vain. How does Haydn extract his revenge on this individual? He writes a comparatively simple violin part to begin with, but when he turns to the second page the player is confronted with hair-raising passages rising to stratospheric heights. And so, Haydn put paid to the cheeky fellow in an inspired fashion.

The wealth of inspiration in Haydn's symphonies is infinite, and it astonishes us time and again. No. 60, 'Il Distratto', is a theatrical masterpiece in six movements. In the last of them, the music comes to a complete standstill, and the violins find they need to retune their instruments! In the second movement of No.93 (the first of the 'London' symphonies) we hear a melody of tender lyricism which is brutally interrupted by a 'rude' note on the two bassoons. They sound like the proverbial bull in the china shop. Even today, such effects still feel extremely funny, and sometimes – as in the above instance – even unfit for polite circles.

In Haydn's minuets we are struck by the asymmetry of the phrasing. A four-bar statement should normally be followed by a four-bar answer, but Haydn loves disrupting the symmetry with units of five, six or seven bars.

To sum up, one could say that the most important characteristics of Haydn's humour are the juxtapositions of expectations and surprises, of the conventional and the unconventional, of symmetry and asymmetry. Added to those are unusual sound effects, playing games with silence and with time, and drastic dynamic contrasts.

Humour is admittedly only a part of Haydn's great art. In every genre and type of music he produced exemplary pieces. The perfection of his craft is unique. He is able to build entire movements, even multi-movement structures, out of a single tiny cell. His taste is elevated, his feeling for proportions unfailing. His church music – the late Masses and the *Seven Last Words* – are masterly and deeply moving. His string quartets, symphonies and piano sonatas reveal new worlds. We need to understand him and to get to know him better, since of all the truly great composers he is still the most underrated.

Let me finish with a joke which Haydn would no doubt have appreciated.

On a psychiatric ward the patients are sitting in a circle, telling jokes. The jokes are numbered. '58,' says one. The others roll about with laughter. Another shouts out: '63.' Deafening laughter. The chief psychiatrist is jealously observing the proceedings and wants to show willing. He summons up his courage and says, '17.' Deathly silence. 'Why aren't you laughing? Isn't there a joke number 17?'

'Of course there is,' a patient answers, 'but you told it so *badly*.'

Florence, March 2009

Mozart's Piano Concertos

Suggestions for students and performers, in the manner of Eusebius and Florestan

1. These works are among the greatest, most beautiful and purest ever written. Look upon them with humility.
2. Study the scores intensively and learn the orchestral parts. Only then can you understand and interpret the works correctly. Mozart's piano concertos are true ensemble pieces, in which the piano functions as *primus inter pares*.
3. Always pay attention to quality of sound. Ugliness and brutality are out of place here. The piano is not a percussion instrument. Even the smallest note-values – semiquavers and demisemiquavers – must be performed *cantabile* (in a singing manner).
4. Always play with clear articulation, never ever lose the large line. Speak and think in whole paragraphs and movements, not just in syllables and individual letters.
5. Use the right pedal carefully and sparingly: it can easily become the foe of clarity. Study the sound and mechanics of the instruments of Mozart's time.
6. Use the *una corda* (soft pedal) seldom or not at all. On most modern instruments it produces a muffled, nasal sound, not at all suited to Mozart. You must learn to be able to play *piano* and *pianissimo* without the help of the left pedal.

7. Devote your attention to Mozart's operas. They are intimately bound up with the piano concertos. In that way you will find a better key to the music's character on the piano, too. Learn from the best singers. Adopt their manner of phrasing and natural breathing on the piano.

8. Embellishments and ornamentation enhance the beauty and refinement of the musical performance. Take the time to study the use and realisation of these elements, which are among the most important requisites of the style. For these and other stylistic questions, turn with confidence to Leopold Mozart's *Versuch einer gründlichen Violinschule* ('Treatise on the Fundamental Principles of Violin Playing'). You cannot find a better source of advice.

9. Take care when it comes to improvisation. It's true that Mozart practised it, but you are no Mozart. With knowledge of the style and good taste (*buon gusto*) you must feel exactly where an added trill, a turn or an appoggiatura is appropriate, and where not. Less is more. Concerning the meaningful filling-in of some of the large intervals in slower movements, think of Fiordiligi in *Così fan tutte* or the Countess in *The Marriage of Figaro* and sing them expressively instead of joining them up with banal chromatic scales.

10. Find the right tempo for each piece. In this regard, he – Wolfgang Amadeus – is merciless. A Bach fugue can be played and enjoyed in very different tempos, but in Mozart the degree of tolerance is extremely small. Follow the harmonic development and the modulations. Andante means at walking pace, not slow. Presto means fast, but not tremendously so. If you are unsure, try singing or dancing the doubtful passages. Dance

and song are known to be man's most natural modes of expression.

11. When you have found the correct tempo, stick to it! Too many fluctuations cause listeners to experience an unpleasant feeling of seasickness. The secret of *tempo rubato* lies in an even accompaniment above which the melody can float freely. Your guide should be not the unyielding metronome, but the pulse of your heart.

12. Be sensitive and expressive in your playing, not sentimental and histrionic. *Viva la semplicità!*

Cadenzas and 'Eingänge' for Mozart's Piano Concertos

It is almost miraculous, and at all events a piece of luck, that Mozart, who was such a brilliant improviser, wrote down so many of his own cadenzas and left them to posterity. There is absolutely no reason – except for arrogant performers who regard concoctions by others as more worthy of being heard – to ignore these wonderful creations, and not to play them. Unfortunately, there are quite a few concertos for which no cadenzas exist. In these cases, the pianist has the choice of either writing his own, or improvising them at the appropriate moment. Both demand a good deal of imagination and initiative. Those who don't possess those qualities, or who don't want to take risks, will probably have to turn to a third party.

The huge number of attempts in this direction paint a varied, but also rather sad, picture – varied, on account of their diversity, sad and even ridiculous in view of their shortcomings in terms of quality. Only Beethoven's cadenzas for the D minor Concerto K.466 can hold their own against Mozart's. It's true that they are very different in style, yet they are nevertheless sympathetic in spirit. Most of the others completely miss their target.

It's true that all piano concertos display a fair amount of extroversion. Particularly at moments where the orchestra pauses, the soloist inevitably becomes the centre of attention. Such moments offer the player the opportunity to shine. Mozart handles this situation in a unique fashion: between a six-four chord and a dominant seventh chord he improvises with absolute naturalness, taste and a feeling for proportions. The whole thing is never over-ornate, never too long or superficially virtuosic. He keeps within the bounds of his self-imposed discipline, and the modulations never lead him too far from the home tonality. In short, he constructs and shapes the cadenzas in his own spirit and carries out a kind of procedure of refinement.

His successors, on the other hand, are poor: the cadenzas spread themselves to form a major part of the movement, like monsters. One has the impression of a dog being wagged by its own tail, for the grand virtuoso rules the roost with his thundering octaves, thirds and sixths, and with meaningless runs up and down the keyboard, awkward modulations into virtually unattainable landscapes. And the whole thing stretches out into a duration that turns 'heavenly lengths' into their opposite and becomes a journey into hell. It's amazing how many pianists these days offer monstrosities of this kind.

Even more curious are those twentieth-century cadenzas that experiment with atonality, as Artur Schnabel – a great and divinely gifted pianist, by the way, and an outstanding musician – did with the cadenzas he contributed to Mozart's C minor Concerto K.491. The arguments for the procedure are well known: by means of a new approach to the cadenza their creator hopes to forge a link between Mozart and his own contemporary world. No, for goodness' sake no! They are worlds that cannot and will not belong together; their two languages are totally different. It is as if a body had acquired a new, artificial organ, and feels unwell as a result, protesting vehemently against the foreign intrusion.

To sum up, it should probably be said that as far as cadenzas or freely formed *Eingänge* (lead-ins) are concerned, there has hardly been any development in the sense of evolution. The whole process could laconically be described as 'From cadence to decadence'.

In the narrow field of cadenzas Mozart remains unequalled. All the same, it ought to be possible to keep within his sphere when devising improvised passages, and to write and play them in his spirit. After all, his models are at our disposal. It is, for instance, a fact that the highest note on Mozart's fortepiano was the F with three ledger lines above the treble stave. Shouldn't the cadenza respect this limit? Why should the modulations not revolve within the leeway he prescribed? Should the concerto's prevailing dynamic range not be valid for the cadenza, too?

These are a few questions which can admittedly be answered in various ways, according to one's taste and conscience. Some will find my own stylistic stance absurd, just as many of us regard the hybrid collages of the past 150 years with a mixture of astonishment and indignation.

And Mozart? In the end, he gently smiles and forgives us all our sins. He knows that nothing can destroy him.

Florence, New Year 2003

Mozart's Piano Concerto in A major K.488[*]

Vollendet ist das große Werk – 'Completed is the mighty work'. Thus we hear at the end of Part II of Haydn's oratorio *The Creation*. How well these words apply to Mozart's piano concertos. They are truly complete, mighty and perfect. This was a genre in which Mozart created unique masterpieces which present a synthesis of opera, symphony and chamber music. Among them, like a resplendent jewel, stands the A major Concerto which now appears for the first time in a facsimile edition. In this work Mozart does without oboes, and turns instead to his beloved clarinets in A. The key of A major is also that of two later masterpieces: the Clarinet Quintet K.581 and the Clarinet Concerto K.622. All three are connected through the inflection of the A major *dolcezza* which is so inimitably conveyed by the clarinets.

Mozart discovered the magical sound of the piano in combination with wind instruments with his E flat Quintet K.452. In his excitement he wrote to his father on 10 April 1784: 'I myself regard it as the best thing I have written in my life.' The six piano concertos of 1784, K.449, 450, 451, 453, 456 & 459, gain a new dimension through their inspired handling of the winds. Two years later, in the *Figaro* year of 1786, Mozart went a few steps further.

Aller guten Dinge sind drei – 'All good things come in threes'. In our concerto, there are three protagonists: the strings, the winds and the solo instrument. This becomes clear at the very beginning of the opening movement. The strings give out the main theme on their own; then in

---

[*] Preface to the facsimile edition of Mozart's manuscript (Henle Verlag, Munich 2005)

bars 9–12 we hear it together with the winds; and once the orchestral exposition has run its course, the solo piano enters (bar 67). The first movement is a cantabile Allegro whose lyrical character has melancholy undertones. Fortunately, Mozart wrote his own cadenza, an object lesson in tasteful invention.

The middle movement is unusual from two points of view: first, it unfolds in the relative minor, F sharp minor – the only occasion on which Mozart used this rare key; and secondly, its tempo marking of *Adagio* indicates that this is a genuine slow movement. It is worth remembering that the headings of most of Mozart's concerto middle movements – 'Andante', 'Larghetto', 'Allegretto', etc. – do not suggest true slowness. This Adagio is one of the most moving, profound and saddest slow movements Mozart ever composed, and its siciliano rhythm recalls the aria 'Erbarme dich' from Bach's *St. Matthew Passion*. In the central section, the clarinets bespeak reconciliation, before the deep sorrow returns. In the coda, from bar 84, the violins play *arco*, the lower strings pizzicato. That can clearly be seen from the manuscript. Earlier editions erroneously marked all the strings pizzicato.

The finale, an 'Allegro assai' in *alla breve* time is an incomparable masterpiece. We hardly know what to admire most: the wonderful themes, the colours of the orchestration, the unique give and take between the instruments, or the impetus of the almost *perpetuum mobile* rhythm, with its irresistible drive. It is a life-affirming apotheosis, comparable to a great operatic finale.

It is to be hoped that this new facsimile will lead to a better and deeper understanding of the piano concertos, and that many professionals and music lovers will find pleasure in it. My heartfelt thanks for this important publication – a valuable contribution to the 250th anniversary of Mozart's birth – go to the owners of the manuscript, the Bibliothèque nationale de France in Paris, and to Henle Edition in Munich.

Florence, Autumn 2005

Reflections of a mountaineer – some superfluous thoughts on Beethoven's piano sonatas[*]

Hans von Bülow's well-known metaphor, that Bach's *Well-Tempered Clavier* is the Old Testament of music, and Beethoven's 32 piano sonatas the New Testament, hits the nail on the head; it has proved to be well founded. With their unity and strictness, the 48 Preludes and Fugues arouse Biblical thoughts in us. And what about Beethoven's sonatas? To me, they stand in splendour like a gigantic chain of mountains, a mighty Himalayan range, so to speak. These mountains – whether gigantic, powerful or smaller – form a logical unity, an extensive whole. For mountaineers climbing towards the heavens there is probably no greater challenge than to scale the peaks. It is like the challenge faced by us pianists who want to learn the Beethoven sonatas and perform them as a cycle. It's true that the questions which arise are not those of athletic achievements (although purely physical difficulties and tough endurance should certainly not be underestimated), but rather of the intellectual, emotional and above all spiritual tasks.

After fifteen complete cycles (others will soon follow),[**]

---

[*] From booklet notes to a recording of the sonatas Opp.109–11 (ECM, 2008).

[**] Meanwhile, a further 10 cycles of the 32 sonatas have been performed. That does not alter the substance of these reflections in any way.

allow me to try and summarise the experiences of these long musical journeys. There are two series of works which afford an insight into Beethoven's development: the string quartets and the piano sonatas. In them, his whole life and being can rigorously be followed, like two red threads. Between the sonatas Op.2 and Op.111 and the quartets Op.18 and Op.135, respectively, we can perceive an unprecedented degree of development, a true evolution. Beethoven was not a *Wunderkind*, or an early developer. During his life, which beside those of Mozart and Schubert was comparatively long, he literally had to struggle with each new work in order to conquer fresh territory. In the genre of the piano sonata he astonishes us with his almost endless diversity. These pieces could hardly be more heterogeneous or different, whereas Bach's Preludes and Fugues impart a remarkably homogeneous effect. The manifold nature of Beethoven's character is a fundamental reason for the interpretative problems that are so difficult to overcome. Each sonata has its own countenance, its own distinctive character. Of course, there are common features and aspects, but the differences are far more significant. The performer's real task is to reveal the uniqueness, the individuality and singularity of each sonata, so that it is truly meaningful.

Like all aspiring pianists, I played Beethoven sonatas after a fashion in the course of my student years and my youth, without taking a tremendous amount of trouble over them. While some works – the 'Pastoral' Op.28, for instance, and the sonata Op.109 – seemed congenial and natural to me, others, such as the 'Appassionata', presented me with huge and almost insuperable hurdles. The richness of sonority which I had in mind in order to lend this music its meaning seemed unrealisable to me. I admired the last two sonatas, Op.110 and Op.111, enormously: I showed my reverence towards them by treating them as sacrosanct. My thinking in those days was that a young whippersnapper shouldn't touch these monuments of art at all. During the early years of my concert career this attitude made it quite self-evident to me that I was to steer clear of Beethoven's works. A curious exception was formed by a single recording: on the Broadwood fortepiano which belonged to Beethoven, housed in the Budapest National Museum, I played the Bagatelles Op.119 and Op.126 together with other short pieces.

All the same, it was some very important listening experiences which provided me with the stimulus and inspiration to return to Beethoven's piano music. Above all, I have to thank Annie Fischer. This wonderful pianist played the complete 32 sonatas in Budapest in the 1970s. By good fortune, I was able to hear the whole cycle twice. Many years later I told her about my difficulties with Beethoven. She just said, 'A pity – it's such divine music . . .'

In 1978, I got to know Rudolf Serkin at the Marlboro Festival in Vermont. I learned a huge amount from him – for instance, the correct way to read the score. For him, faithfulness to the text was a *sine qua non*; he was unbending in his view that Beethoven's indications were to be followed to the letter. His stance, determined by a very high ethos, has remained a shining example to me.

Shortly afterwards, in the early eighties, came my meeting with the consummate musician Sándor Végh. It was a gift, and a privilege, to be able to make music with him. We rehearsed, performed and recorded all ten of Beethoven's violin sonatas. Végh, the superb former leader of the famous string quartet which bore his name, had a profound understanding of Beethoven. His free spirit finally liberated me from my fears and complexes; he gave me the courage I needed for the future.

Sometimes one thinks of oneself as having been born too late, or at the wrong time, and having had the bad luck to miss out on many things. My generation knows the art of Artur Schnabel, Edwin Fischer, Wilhelm Furtwängler, Bruno Walter, Otto Klemperer or the Busch Quartet only through recordings. All the same, it's lucky they at least exist! These legacies are yardsticks for the interpretation of Beethoven.

Over a period of two-and-a-half decades, from 1978 to 2003, I concentrated mainly on the works of Bach, Haydn, Mozart and Schubert. That was very good schooling as a preparation for Beethoven. Only when I was 40 did I begin systematic work on his sonatas. Around half the works were already in my repertoire; the other half had to be worked on step by step. Each year, I prepared two or three sonatas that were new to me. Last of all I learned the 'Waldstein' Sonata, and then Op.110 and Op.111. After ten years, in 2003, I had thoroughly assimilated the complete sonatas and was playing them in concerts. As someone who had reached a 'mature' age, I felt the time had come to plan complete cyclical performances.

This huge project requires careful solutions to various problems, and answers to the inevitable questions it poses. How should I arrange these masterpieces, and why dive into this undertaking at all? So many pianists have played and recorded the sonatas. Given this plenitude, does the world need yet another addition? Am I in a position to offer an individual and essential contribution? These are questions that need to be taken seriously – and answered honestly and self-critically. This music is so endlessly great, timeless and of permanent relevance that it constantly invites new interpretations – indeed, it demands and inspires them. Just as theologians endlessly discuss the Holy Scriptures, so time after time the Beethoven sonatas open the gateway to new readings and interpretative approaches. The answer, then, is an unequivocal 'yes'. In Beethoven's own words, *'Es muss sein!'* ('It must be!')

The next decision concerns the division and arrangement of the individual programmes. Nowadays, a concert normally lasts around two hours, including an interval. (The necessity for concert intervals could, incidentally, be the subject of a long discussion . . .) The Beethoven sonatas vary in duration, and it makes sense, therefore, to spread them out into seven or eight concerts. But in what order? About this, thoughts differ: there are almost as many opinions on the subject as there are pianists. Most of my colleagues prefer mixed programmes in which early, middle and late sonatas rub shoulders. In so doing, they are careful to include at least one well-known work – a 'hit' – each time. The public seems to prefer this procedure, and many concert promoters are not averse to it, as it may well help the box office.

Not long ago, I heard a Beethoven evening given by a well-known pianist. The programme consisted of the sonatas Op.14 No.1, Op.7, Op.54 and Op.111 – a series of works that is incoherent, disjointed, and in the end absolutely nonsensical. The sequence of keys alone – E major, E flat major, F major and C minor – is devoid of all logic, and any internal relationship. For my part, I was quite sure from the beginning that a chronological order was the most convincing. Why? The sonatas fit perfectly into seven or eight individual programmes, like a hand in a glove. Listeners are able to follow the continuity of a logical progress, as when reading a long novel. In addition, the groups of sonatas which the composer published under a single opus number (Opp.2, 10, 14, 27, 31) are not unnecessarily separated from each other – indeed, they belong together.

Needless to say, first of all one needs opportunities to be able to perform the complete cycle. As far as that is concerned, I should like to thank the many concert promoters who invited me to realise the project as I had imagined it. The experience of these 'journeys' proves that the less well-known sonatas are unjustly overshadowed by their more famous companions. Interestingly enough, these old audience favourites for their part acquire a still stronger effect when they are heard together with their immediate neighbours. The public should not be underestimated. They are hopefully not there for cheap entertainment, but should be prepared for a process of learning, and a collective experience. And the ideal listeners – and it is on them that one's attention should be focused – are those who follow the performer through the entire cycle. A person who impulsively buys a ticket five minutes before the concert begins simply because he or she happens to be staying in the area is probably not in the right spiritual frame of mind to listen to Beethoven and to assimilate him. Beethoven demands almost as much from the audience as from the performer.

Playing a sonata for the first time in public is of little consequence. One can study, analyse and practise the work for an eternity, but only repeated performances allow for a true process of maturity. For that reason, it's a blessing for players when they have the opportunity to perform the sonatas not just once, but often, one time after another. With repetition, performers acquire greater courage and self-confidence; they can be empowered to take certain risks. Does such repetition engender the danger of falling into the merely routine? Not at all: the music is too strong, and its depths can never fully be plumbed. It is as inexhaustible as nature: different every day.

After an individual programme had been performed several times, the producer, promoter and I all agreed to set down the entire cycle in Zurich in the form of 'live' concert recordings. The large and beautiful hall of the Zurich Tonhalle has excellent acoustics and is ideally suited to recordings. The audience is not only knowledgeable, but also extremely quiet and disciplined. For those reasons, I decided against working in a studio, and preferred concert recordings. Beethoven's music comes to life through its forward momentum, and risk-taking is one of its main components. In a studio, you can always stop, make corrections and start up again, and you can put a large structure together out of many little pieces without problem. That often produces – and not only with Beethoven – a result that is clinically sterile and artificial. Beethoven's music, in particular, demands big gestures, and moments which only happen in concerts, if you are lucky. But what if the concert goes wrong? There is absolutely no pressing need to perpetuate an unsatisfactory experience, or a complete washout. I willingly admit that my recording of the last three sonatas does not come from a Zurich concert performance. A few months after the concert, I played them again in the empty hall of the Reitstadel in Neumarkt, and this recording appealed to me more. For the remaining 29 sonatas – all taken from the Zurich concerts – only a few very small corrections were made using material from the rehearsals.

For the complete cycle, I used Bösendorfer and Steinway pianos, and even chose more than one of the same make. The works are so multifaceted and many layered that – at least for me – there was no question of playing them all on the same instrument. In addition, Beethoven's sonatas tell us a great deal about the history of the piano's development. As an outstanding keyboard virtuoso, Beethoven took great interest in visiting the workshops of the various Viennese piano manufacturers. He made friends with some of them and carried on a fruitful exchange of ideas with them. The fortepianos of his time all have individual and specific qualities.

The situation now is completely different: almost all pianists play on Steinways. I regard this kind of globalisation as unhealthy, just as it is in the worlds of fashion or gastronomy. In music, however, it is still more detrimental. Most pianists favour an even sound, thereby ironing out any diversity or strong contrasts. Not surprisingly, many interpretations these days sound almost identical. Instead, one should make the effort with each Beethoven sonata to find its own specific tone of voice. Without doubt, a good Steinway is an excellent piano, but not the be all and end all. Why are we not more curious?

Meanwhile, the listening habits of the public have been equally trimmed to a standard, to the extent that nowadays only the Steinway sound is accepted, and other piano timbres are regarded with scepticism and suspicion. That is a great pity! The great pianists of the past played various instruments: Schnabel and Bartók preferred a Bechstein, Cortot a Pleyel, while others favoured Blüthner or Ibach. Since 1828, the Viennese firm of Bösendorfer has been producing pianos which, with their warm, singing tone and their subjectively coloured timbre, best represent the Viennese tradition. As a result, the music of Schubert sounds thoroughly idiomatic on these instruments. Many of Beethoven's sonatas evince similar characteristics to those of Schubert, who worshipped the older composer without wanting in any way to be a slavish follower. Beethoven was his model, the source of his inspiration. And so, I decided to play half the sonatas on a Bösendorfer, and half on a

Steinway. Which work is heard on which piano shall remain a secret. Guessing is absolutely allowed! Please forget your preconceived ideas and listen with open ears and without prejudice. In ideal circumstances I should have liked to have been able to present a third alternative: historical keyboard instruments.

Prejudices can be seen not only in the choice of instrument, but also in the way the works are thought of and perceived. People know the sonatas, or think they do, because they have heard them umpteen times. They achieve the status of comfortable favourites which should preferably not be interfered with. Please do not disturb! These well-worn paths frequently lead us on false journeys; or the apparently trustworthy notion proves to be shallow, because it does not tally with one that is based on a thorough study of the musical text. Particularly with the most popular works, the performer's task must be to fight against the worst inaccuracies. Where does the repeat begin in the first movement of the 'Pathétique'? How should we deal with Beethoven's unconventional pedal markings in the C sharp minor sonata? Which tempo and which rhythm are correct for the first movement of the 'Appassionata'? (You can bet that at least nine out of ten music lovers will sing the main theme wrongly!) Why is it absolutely necessary to take heed of the composer's metronome markings for the 'Hammerklavier' sonata, and to treat them seriously? When will we finally take note of the fact that the nickname of 'Moonlight' doesn't originate with Beethoven – and, which is worse, leads to a misjudgement of the sonata's character?

'Tradition is sloppiness' (or more precisely, 'What you theatre people call tradition is laziness and sloppiness'), said Mahler. Even though traditions can hand down important and useful knowledge, the quote contains a grain of truth. Like a picture restorer, the musician must scrape away the dirt and the hardened layer of dust – in other words, he must eradicate bad conventions in order to present the work in a manner that reflects the intentions of its composer as closely as possible.

Having reached the summit of the mountain, the exhausted climber is filled with joy and gratitude. He cannot scale the entire mountain range, he can only go on climbing further and higher. The higher he reaches, the further he can peer into more and more distant horizons. The experience is one that makes life worth living.

Florence 2008

'Only from the pure source' – questions and answers on Beethoven's 'Diabelli' Variations[*]

Why have you chosen these works?

Firstly, because I love them passionately and dearly. The 'Diabelli' Variations are one of Beethoven's major works, and surely his *opus magnum* for piano. In them he summarises all the different characters of his 32 sonatas. The Op.126 Bagatelles are his last thoughts for his favourite instrument, poetic and profound aphorisms. Listen, for instance, to the fourth Bagatelle – probably his only venture into B minor

---

[*] Booklet notes to a recording of Beethoven's last three piano works – the Piano Sonata Op.111, the 'Diabelli' Variations Op.120, and the Six Bagatelles Op.126 (ECM 2294–95). The Variations were recorded twice, on different instruments: a Viennese fortepiano from Beethoven's own time made in 1820 by Franz Brodmann, and a Bechstein of 1921.

– daemonic music of astonishing modernity. The piano sonata Op.III, the largest and greatest of Beethoven's two-movement works of its kind, presents us with two strongly opposed worlds: a highly-charged, dramatic Allegro in the minor, and a serene set of variations in the major.

The Arietta of Op.III and Diabelli's waltz tune are closely related. They share the same key of C major, both start with an upbeat, and both are in triple time. More importantly, both themes are determined by the same two melodic intervals, the descending fourth (C–G) and the descending fifth (D–G). For this reason, I wanted to play the 'Diabelli' Variations in the context of the works that come immediately before and after them.

Why are you using two instruments?

Why not? For one thing, it's always a joy to be able to play on different and beautiful instruments. For another thing, the listening habits of audiences (and music critics) are as biased as ever. Prejudice rules; there's a lack of curiosity. People are used to hearing the whole piano repertoire from William Byrd to Pierre Boulez played on Steinway concert grands, and they're perfectly happy with that. This only fosters an unfortunate 'globalisation' of piano music, whereby all composers and pianists sound alarmingly similar. Performance traditions strangle the individuality of the works and keep players from rethinking and breathing new life into them.

In the right hands, a good Steinway is certainly a marvellous piano, but not for everything. Haydn, Mozart, Beethoven and Schubert require more than power, brilliance and cool objectivity. The 1921 Bechstein represents a long-forgotten world. Wilhelm Backhaus played it often and recorded on it. And let's remember that Bechstein was Artur Schnabel's preferred make of piano. Schnabel's tone, especially in Beethoven and Schubert, has always been my ideal. This instrument helps me to get closer to it.

With the fortepiano we are right at the source. Vienna, 1820: the place and time of the composition. This instrument is an original, not a modern copy, and it's in perfect condition. On it the music sounds fresher, bolder and infinitely more sensitive.

Many of my listeners will share my enthusiasm and will find the sonorities of the fortepiano magical; others will (at first) find the sound strange and unusual, and will prefer the Bechstein. Finally, those incorrigible Steinway enthusiasts will dislike both versions and will long for another pianist – on a Steinway, as always.

Does your performance differ on a fortepiano as opposed to a modern piano?

The interpretation will not be fundamentally different. Nevertheless the fortepiano opens up a whole new world. Modern pianos sound perfectly even, from top to bottom, and that is seen nowadays as a virtue. However, it is not at all what Beethoven had in mind. The fortepiano is not supposed to sound even; it has distinct upper, middle and lower registers. The upper notes are finely chiselled and clear, the middle ones are naturally resonant, while the basses are lean and transparent. The lower tuning (A=430 Hz, whereas today it is 442 Hz or higher) is much more pleasant to listen to and richer in overtones. Dynamics are much subtler: when reducing the volume, the soft and softest passages – with the help of the *una corda* pedal and the moderator pedal (which interposes a strip of cloth between hammer and strings) – sound magical and mysterious. Needless to say, the qualities of the fortepiano can be fully appreciated only under ideal circumstances – that is, with excellent acoustics and a venue that is not too large, like the Kammermusiksaal HJ Abs at the Beethoven-Haus in Bonn. Many pianists frequently err in their choice of tempi; the lively movements are much too fast, the serene pieces much too slow. The fortepiano immediately corrects these mistakes and sets the appropriate tempo. So this question deserves to be answered the other way round: our playing on modern pianos benefits greatly from our experience with old keyboard instruments.

How do you deal with Beethoven's pedal markings?

In the first movement of Haydn's C major Sonata (Hob. XVI:50) there are two passages which are marked 'open pedal' – his only indications of the kind. Nor in all of Mozart's piano works is the pedal ever mentioned. The first composer to use the pedal consciously and creatively was Beethoven. His pedal usage is highly unusual and revolutionary. Piano teachers tell us the pedal has to be changed with every change of harmony. That is not Beethoven's way; he often wants strange and quite alien harmonies to sound together. His first two piano concertos, Opp.15 & 19, and the sonatas Op.27 no.2, Op.31 no.2 and Op.53 are full of such effects. Incredibly, most pianists completely ignore Beethoven's instructions. They argue that his use of pedal makes sense only on the fortepiano, and that on modern instruments we have to revert to conventional usage. What nonsense! Most of these people have never even seen a fortepiano, yet they want to be cleverer than the composer. (And they are the very people who play Bach with one foot permanently on the 'accelerator'.)

To sum up: Beethoven's pedal markings are important ingredients of his creative genius. They must be strictly observed, on any instrument. To ignore them is the height of arrogance, a falsification of the music. On the modern piano we don't have to put the pedal down completely – half way, or two-thirds of the way is sufficient. Under the final chord of the 'Diabelli' Variations the sign 'ped.' can be seen. There is no release sign anywhere. This could well mean that he wants this C major chord to resonate as long as possible. The piano is a 'diminuendo-instrument', and a note that has been struck will gradually diminish until it vanishes. On the fortepiano it lasts for about ten seconds, on the Bechstein twice as long. Should this difference be eliminated? I don't think so. *'Es muß sein!'*

Do you think Beethoven would have been happy with a new Steinway?

Never. His first question would have been, 'Why is this thing so black? It looks like a coffin!' And then, 'Why is the bass so thick and heavy? Why is there no difference between the registers? Why is the pitch so sharp?' And finally, 'Why is everything so loud? I may be deaf, but are you all hard of hearing, too?' To this one would probably answer today: 'Esteemed Master, nowadays your music is performed in huge auditoriums with 2000 seats and more. And so the piano must be brilliant and powerful.' Here Beethoven would have become angry: 'You fools! Do you really think I wrote my piano music for such gigantic halls? A piano sonata is not a Battle Symphony!'

Did Beethoven know Bach's 'Goldberg' Variations?

Almost certainly, yes, although Bach's music was virtually unknown and unplayed in the Vienna of those days. Beethoven, like Mozart, belonged to the circle of friends of Baron Gottfried von Swieten, whose famous library housed many manuscripts and editions of Bach and Handel.

Bach wrote very few compositions in the form of a theme and variations, and the most important of them is the 'Goldberg' Variations. Beethoven had always been a master of the genre, not least through his studies under Haydn. The variation movements in his sonatas and his various individual sets are glorious manifestations of his improvisatory art. Even so, with the 'Diabelli' Variations Beethoven managed to make a quantum leap. His model was Bach, his challenge the 'Goldberg' Variations. Diabelli's waltz and Bach's aria are light years apart but their structure is identical: twice 16 bars with both halves repeated; and they are both in triple time. Bach's work has a great deal to do with the number 3: there are 30 variations of which every third one is a canon, so that we have ten groups of three pieces each. In the first phase of his composition, in 1819, Beethoven completed 23 variations. When he continued the work in 1823, he increased the number of variations to 33.

Both works are divided into three sections. The first section ends in each case after Variation 10. In the Bach, the second part ends after Variation 22, in the Beethoven after Variation 20. The third part leads both works to their conclusion. Bach marks the mid-point of his cycle after Variation 15 with a French Overture which releases new energies. Beethoven reaches the same point with the brilliantly extroverted twin variations nos. 16–17. The sublime Fughetta (Var. 24) is a pure homage to Bach. The Dionysian fugue

(Var. 32) reminds us more of Handel's oratorios. Finally, the wonderful minor-mode variations (nos. 29–31) correspond with the three in Bach's masterpiece (nos. 15, 21 and 25), and Bach's no. 25 and Beethoven's no. 31 are particularly closely related.

How do you see Beethoven's relationship to Mozart reflected in the 'Diabelli' Variations?

Mozart died in Vienna in 1791 and Beethoven arrived there in the following year. Thus, he missed what could have been the most important encounter of his life. Mozart would remain his unapproachable idol, just as Beethoven was to be for the young Schubert. The 'Diabelli' Variations contain two references to Mozart: the Leporello quotation in Var.22 is a hilarious parody, while the final Minuet (Var.33) is a sublime evocation of Mozart's spirit, and it brings the work to a transfigured close.

Why are the 'Diabelli' Variations regarded as such a problematic, difficult work?

Great art is never easy. The world reveres and venerates Beethoven, especially his best-known works. The sonatas with nicknames ('Moonlight', 'Waldstein', 'Appassionata'), the 'Eroica' and Fifth Symphonies, as well as the Ninth (especially its finale), are understandably popular. They are the clearest manifestation of the generally accepted cliché of Beethoven's heroic struggle. But many people have problems with Beethoven's works that do not fit into that pigeonhole. The 'Hammerklavier' Sonata, the *Missa solemnis* and the late string quartets are among the highest peaks in musical history, and yet they have not been taken to heart by the general public. Respect, yes, but not love. Small wonder with these highly complex works which have nothing to do with light entertainment. Among them, the 'Diabelli' Variations are a particularly hard nut to crack.

How can we characterise them? Some are dramatic, others majestic, lyrical, tender, witty, roguish, philosophical, mysterious. No other work by Beethoven contains so many different facets of his genius. A masterpiece like this needs to be listened to over and over again. As for us performers, we have to spend a lifetime trying to fathom its secrets.

How important is the study of Beethoven's manuscripts and sketches for you?

So important that I can hardly put it into words. Good Urtext editions are undoubtedly invaluable, but they can only complement the manuscript, never replace it. Only the autograph score can reveal the compositional process and its inner significance. Fortunately, several manuscripts are now available in good facsimile editions. The autographs of the 'Diabelli' Variations and the Bagatelles Op.126, as well as that of the first movement of Op.111 are in the archives of the Beethoven-Haus in Bonn. This is a real treasure trove, and I am eternally grateful for the privilege of being able to see and study these priceless items. To play this music in the Beethoven-Haus, in the immediate vicinity of the manuscripts, is a gift and a real honour. As Bartók said, 'Only from the pure source.'

Florence, June 2013

Beethoven's String Quartet Op.132[*]

Beethoven's string quartets are among his most important works. Alongside the piano sonatas, his contributions to this genre allow us to trace his development most clearly. Beethoven's manuscript of the A minor String Quartet Op.132 is published here for the first time in a facsimile edition – reason enough for celebration. For while facsimile publications of the piano sonatas have enormously enriched our knowledge about them, the manuscripts of the string quartets have mostly remained unpublished.

The late quartets constitute the peaks of Beethoven's output; and one of these summits is the work in A minor. Beethoven richly endowed us pianists with sonatas, variations, bagatelles and concertos, for which we are eternally grateful. However, after Op.111 Beethoven wrote no further piano pieces, apart from some bagatelles and the 'Diabelli' Variations. He communicated his last and most important thoughts to us in these string quartets.

But how does a manuscript distinguish itself from the printed edition? The differences are enormous. Good editions are indispensable for performers and students. They reproduce the musical text clearly and legibly in accordance with the latest musicological findings. An autograph, on the other hand, is something very personal. It does not always present the last authentic version, but it affords us an insight into the compositional process, into the history of the work's genesis.

Beethoven's manuscripts are as different as his works. Some radiate inner peace and harmony and are clear and

---

[*] Preface to facsimile edition (Henle Verlag, Munich 2011).

almost without corrections. Others are stormy, dramatic and wild, with endless numbers of changes. Beethoven's writing is always expressive and lively. One is reminded of Bach. The waves and curves of the lines suggest the appropriate interpretative style (always in waves, never in geometrical lines). The autograph of this quartet is a genuine treasure for all Beethoven connoisseurs and admirers. With what forcefulness and decisiveness he wields his pen! How bold are his accents, how turbulent the crescendo-decrescendo hairpins, how endless and full of longing the sweeping slurs! It becomes immediately clear that Beethoven never notated staccatos as dots, but always as energetic dashes:

He only writes dots when they are beneath a slur, and a *portato* is intended (for instance in the first movement, bar 53, violin 1). If we look at bar 131 in the first movement, we can see that Beethoven needs three times the amount of space for it than for the next bars. Only the manuscript can show us how breathtaking the soaring flight of the first violin is. In the printed music, it all looks very harmless and normal.

The quartet's centrepiece is the famous slow movement – the '*Heiliger Dankgesang eines Genesenen an die Gottheit, in der lidischen Tonart*' (Holy Song of Thanksgiving to the Deity from a Convalescent, in the Lydian Mode). Beneath these words is the Italian translation. It is well known that Beethoven was happier with German markings than Italian. 'Mit innigster Empfindung' sounds different from

'Con intimissimo sentimento'. And one should note how the writing changes in bar 31, where the music, gaining 'Neue Kraft' (new strength) from the archaic modality, leads into a dazzling D major! We look upon this manuscript with admiration, humility and love. May it be a source of inspiration for performers and students, for professionals and music lovers.

Florence, Autumn 2011

Confessions of a convert: Schubert on the fortepiano*

It was the beginning of the 1980s, the heyday of the historical performance movement, and vinyl records had been superseded by compact discs. Authenticity had become the byword. Suddenly one wanted to hear everything – at first, just Bach and Handel, but then soon Haydn, Mozart and Beethoven – played on period instruments. We were flooded with recordings of varying merit and quality. In these initial stages the standard of instrumental playing had not yet reached the level we now take for granted.

Public reaction was mixed. The majority took to authenticity enthusiastically; they were curious, delighted by new sonorities, lower tuning, unusual tempi. What joy it was for them to experience well known works anew! Others were more cautious and sceptical, arguing that it was impossible to recreate music of another era in its original sound, since authenticity makes sense only to authentic listeners. In the end, we tend to examine the past as though through a

---

* Booklet notes to CD recording of the sonatas D.780 & 960, the 4 Impromptus D.935 and the 'Moments musicaux' D.780 (ECM, Munich 2015).

looking glass, influenced by layers of more recent listening experiences.

The critics were, almost without exception, euphoric. They praised everything unconditionally as long as it was historically 'correct'. Dilettantism and charlatanism used to be derogatory words; now they had become virtues.

I was living at the time in New York, where the 'fight' between purists and their opponents was often vicious; like a religious war. My own views were ambivalent. On the one hand, I was fascinated by philology and textual fidelity; but on the other hand, the movement's arrogance and dogmatism annoyed me. This dualism is expressed in my various statements, articles and interviews from that time. I once sarcastically wrote, 'The time will come when we will be playing Schubert sonatas on Graf fortepianos.' And now look: scarcely 30 years have gone by, and my prophecy has been fulfilled – by myself.

What has happened? Is this a metamorphosis like that of Saul to Paul? Not at all. It has now become clear to me that I was quite wrong in those days. My knowledge of historical keyboard instruments was incomplete and perfunctory. In the late 1970s, I made a recording on Beethoven's Broadwood piano, housed in the National Museum in Budapest. It was not in prime condition, and so it turned out to be a most moving, but in the end unhappy experience.

My encounter in the mid-1980s with Mozart's fortepiano, made by Anton Walter, was much happier and more satisfactory – a life-changing event, in fact. Playing in the very house where he was born, and on his own piano, was a privilege and an unforgettable experience. On this instrument, his music seemed fresh, bold and new; the great C minor Fantasy K.475 sounded immensely dramatic, like a concentrated version of *Don Giovanni*. Pianists need to be very careful when playing this work (and this composer) on a modern piano. Today's instruments are much heavier, stronger and more brilliant than their eighteenth-century ancestors. Those enormous thick bass strings can be a menace if we want to achieve lightness, transparency and a natural equilibrium. And so we switch back and forth between caution and strength, like Odysseus between Scylla and Charybdis. How different things are on a fortepiano by Anton Walter! There, one can play unrestrained and with abandon. Mozart uses the keyboard to the limits of its range and expressive powers, and so on the right instrument the music's revolutionary nature is shown to full advantage.

My curiosity aroused, I felt I had to delve further. There is an astonishing wealth of old keyboard instruments hidden in museums, foundations and private collections, many of them in prime condition. Getting to know them, and playing on them, is essential for the student, scholar and musician: it is a condition *sine qua non*. Their diversity is amazing. At the time of Beethoven and Schubert in Vienna alone, there were more than a hundred manufacturers. Each maker, each instrument, is different and individual. Each one is capable of something specific, something unique that the others cannot match.

My own fortepiano was built in Vienna in 1820 by Franz Brodmann. It is, for me, ideally suited to Schubert's keyboard works. There is something quintessentially Viennese in its timbre, its tender mellowness, its melancholic cantabile. In the Biedermeier period (and even later) Schubert was often performed in a sentimental, harmless manner. There seemed to be no idea of the dark forces and deep chasms that lie hidden in his music. The dramatic crescendos and shattering climaxes are overwhelming; and yet it is in the quiet and quietest moments that Schubert – like nobody else – touches our hearts. *Piano* and *pianissimo* markings dominate his scores; even triple *piano* (*ppp*) is not uncommon. The Brodmann can realise these huge dynamic contrasts wonderfully well. *Piano* is its basic speaking tone. For *pianissimos* it has the *una corda* (soft pedal) at its disposal, which produces a somewhat willowy sound. Its 'secret weapon' is the moderator pedal, an ingenious device that interposes a thin layer of cloth between the strings and the hammers, so that the softest *ppp* passages can be ideally performed. The keys are narrower, the mechanism is lighter than with a modern piano. Those notorious repeated chords, as, for instance, in the last movement of the G major Sonata D.894, are easy to play.

Finding the right venue for the fortepiano is essential. The room must be not too large, its acoustics, proportions, resonances and atmosphere should be ideally attuned to the needs of the instrument – as they are, for example, in the Kammermusiksaal HJ Abs at the Beethoven-Haus in Bonn.

Does this mean that I'll never play Schubert again on a modern piano in a large concert hall? Not at all: I shall do so often, on Bösendorfers, Bechsteins and even Steinways, but the sweet tone of the Viennese fortepiano will always remain at the back of my mind. How wonderful it is to imagine being able to convey the illusion of intimacy in a large auditorium!

Not everyone will share my enthusiasm. Some music lovers find the fortepiano dull, colourless and monotonous. To them, it cannot match the modern piano in strength, robustness and brilliance. However, for those with sympathetic ears for the sound world of the fortepiano, and who 'listen in secret', as Friedrich Schlegel expressed it in the poem quoted by Schumann at the head of his C major

Fantasy Op.17, a whole new world may open up. Who knows, perhaps some of you will also be converted?

Florence, September 2014

Schubert's Piano Trio in E flat D.929[*]

Schubert's Piano Trio in E flat major is not only one of the peaks of the genre, it is surely one of his most important works altogether. Unlike its sibling, the wonderfully lyrical B flat Trio D.898, this one is a highly dramatic work of enormous, almost symphonic dimensions. The manuscript is in private hands and has been inaccessible until recently. For this reason alone, the present facsimile is a minor sensation.

Good printed editions are essential, but manuscripts are irreplaceable. They are the source; only through them can we feel really close to the creators of the works. That is precisely the case here.

The title page already demands attention: November 1827, Op.100. His hundredth published work, written just a year prior to his death. The handwriting is clean and tidy, with relatively few corrections. In the first movement the crescendo hairpins are marked with tremendous élan, and the huge piano chords in bars 410ff. are so heavily written that one can sense the music's elementary strength. The flowing triplets in bars 116ff. recall the babbling brook in the song-cycle *Die schöne Müllerin*.

To this day, musicologists and performers have not been able to distinguish between Schubert's accents and his decrescendo hairpins. To be fair, he did not make things particularly easy for us. Some wedges are shorter (e.g. fol.

---

[*] Preface to facsimile edition (Henle, Munich 2014).

2 verso, bars 90 f.), others longer (same page, bars 105, 107), and several of them were added later in pencil (same page, bar 83, also bars 56 and 65). The musical character of these passages suggests that these are all accents. Furthermore, Schubert often prefers to write out *decrescendo* or *diminuendo* as words (as in bars 188, 359 and 615). A huge ink stain graces the page at bars 577 f., similar to the one in the fugue in Beethoven's autograph of the 'Diabelli' Variations: Schubert must have been so carried away by this *fff* climax that he could constrain neither his energy, nor the inkwell.

The second movement, *Andante con moto* ('*con moto*' is a later addition marked in pencil), is reminiscent of the 'walking' songs in *Winterreise*. It is one of Schubert's darkest and most tragic pieces. Its frequently turbulent nature is clearly visible in the manuscript – hence the unusual corrections in bars 122–125. In bar 57 we find the direction *pedale appassionato*. What did Schubert mean by this? Could it have been the use of the moderator or *una corda* pedal? *Appassionato* hardly suits the mood of this passage. However, there are other *pianissimo* moments in Schubert that carry the same marking – the opening bars of the so-called 'Notturno' for piano trio D.897, and the crossed-hands episode in the F minor Impromptu D.935 no.1 – suggesting that the composer wanted a particular intensity of expression to be conveyed. The *ritard.* in bar 194, and the *un poco più lento* in bar 196, are pencilled in, as though they had been afterthoughts.

A remarkable moment occurs at bar 200, where the grace notes in the piano part which form part of the main theme in all its other appearances are missing. This could well be an oversight on the part of the composer, because they are precisely notated in the sketch and in the first edition. (To me, the sequence of grace notes here – A natural

– B flat – C, instead of A flat – B flat – C as hitherto – is heart-breaking.)

The following Scherzando could not be more different: it is bucolic, dance-like and merry, and the handwriting is duly clear and harmonious. Only those powerful *fz* accents in the central trio section suggest hidden danger lurking behind the peaceful facade.

And the finale? It is one of the world's miracles. When the E flat major Trio was first performed in public, on 26 March 1828, listeners found it too long. Unfortunately, Schubert paid heed to his critics and made drastic cuts in the last movement. The first edition and almost all subsequent publications present this shortened version. In Schubert's autograph score the last movement stands complete, including the exposition repeat and the missing passages between bars 358–407 and 463–513. The latter section ingeniously combines the slow movement's main theme with two ideas from the last movement. It would be a terrible pity to have to dispense with this. In bar 819 we have a glimpse of heaven, and after 846 bars the work reaches its final destination, a true apotheosis. To quote Schumann, Schubert has achieved 'heavenly length'. Divine, but never too long.

Florence, Autumn 2013

In defence of Mendelssohn

Let me begin with a confession. Since my earliest childhood, I have loved Mendelssohn's music passionately. As was not uncommon in medical circles, my father, a gynaecologist, played the violin in an amateur capacity and had an impressive record collection, consisting largely of recordings of famous violinists. The very first piece of music from this collection that I am conscious of having heard was Mendelssohn's E minor Violin Concerto with Yehudi Menuhin and an orchestra conducted by George Enescu. I was fascinated, charmed and delighted by both the concerto and its interpretation. My spontaneous youthful impressions have in no way become less vivid to this day.

Mendelssohn was born in Hamburg in 1809 – and so this year we celebrate his 200th birthday. The anniversary offers the musical world a good opportunity to reconsider, and if necessary, to revise received ideas and opinions about the composer. I am firmly convinced that our view of him is terribly distorted; and on top of that, it is stamped with misguided and malicious prejudices which often lead to misunderstandings. His life's work, which bears witness to an incredible talent, deserves to be regarded with far greater esteem and affection.

The talent is by no means incidental! Schumann once described Mendelssohn as the Mozart of the nineteenth century, and, truly this God-given, natural musicality which Mendelssohn already showed as a child can only be compared with Mozart's. It might even be possible to come to the controversial conclusion that Felix's adolescent works surpass those of his great predecessor written at a comparable age. His early string symphonies, written between 1821 and 1823, show such stylistic competence, good taste and sheer craftsmanship that many a more experienced composer might have been proud of them. In the last movement of the D major Sinfonia No.8, we can hear echoes of the finale from Mozart's 'Jupiter' Symphony, which the twelve-year-old Mendelssohn had heard for the first time at the Leipzig Gewandhaus. He recognised it immediately as a wonder of the world whose study demanded an entire lifetime. The hugely talented boy penetrates the labyrinths of polyphony and counterpoint with astonishing assurance: he knows all there is to know about the art of Bach and Handel.

While his contemporaries (Schumann, Berlioz and Liszt) and his forerunners (Beethoven and Schubert) wrestled with the art of writing fugues all their lives, the young Mendelssohn, like Mozart, seems like a fish in water. His first string quartets, in E flat major Op.12 (1829) and A minor Op.13 (1827), show his profound knowledge of the quartets of Beethoven. The D major Sextet for piano and strings, of 1824, which I was often to perform, arose under the influence of Mozart's *Don Giovanni*. All these great models do not make Mendelssohn an imitator: they simply inspired his art, and he very soon found his own personal fingerprints. Two shining examples are the Octet of 1825, and the overture to Shakespeare's *A Midsummer Night's Dream* (1826). It is no exaggeration to say that no other composer, before or after him, wrote such perfect, original and inspired music at so early an age.

That Mendelssohn never surpassed these masterly achievements of his youth is something for which posterity never forgave him. Certainly, there are exceptions in his later years which reach the same high level. In the field of chamber music mention must be made of the two piano trios, in D minor Op.49 and C minor Op.66, which are worthy descendants of the trios of Beethoven and Schubert. Of the two string quintets, the first, in A major Op.18, in particular, reaches Mozartian heights. His last string quartet in F minor Op.80, written under the shock of the sudden death of his beloved sister, Fanny, stands out through its unique aura of trauma and despair.

Mendelssohn was a highly gifted pianist: both Robert and Clara Schumann reported enthusiastically on his playing. It goes without saying that his predilection for the instrument led him to write pieces for it which he could make known through his own performances. 'Songs Without Words' – miniature masterpieces which he published in sets of six – are found throughout his life. The genre is his invention; the performer functions simultaneously as imaginary singer, and as accompanist. In one of these wordless songs, the unusually constructed 'Duetto' in A flat Op.38 no.6, the pianist even makes music with two 'singers'. These jewels are altogether proof that the piano is a singing instrument, and only in extremely rare cases a percussive one.

The wonderful songs and duets for voices and piano sometimes suffer from the fact that their texts are based on poetry that is not always of the front rank, but in the settings of Goethe, Heine, Lenau and Eichendorff poetry and music complement each other superbly. Unfortunately, these songs have been, and still are, much neglected and hardly ever performed.

Among his piano works, the *Variations sérieuses* Op.54 stand out – perhaps one of the most beautiful pieces in all early romanticism. The key of D minor, and its minor-major-minor design, make it somewhat reminiscent of Bach's famous Chaconne for unaccompanied violin.

In my opinion the piano concertos, which I have often played and have also recorded, are not among his most important works. They are admirable, brilliantly scored, perfectly balanced between soloist and orchestra, and yet one misses in them that sense of fantasy and poetry which distinguishes, for example, the piano concerto of Schumann. The famous E minor Violin Concerto is another matter altogether! As I did in my childhood, I still find it fresh and new. In my eyes and ears it rightly belongs among the finest of works of the kind, along with the significant contributions to the genre by Mozart, Beethoven, Brahms,

Bartók and Berg. There is such originality in the unity of the three movements, and the through-composed pauses and links between them. With this work Mendelssohn set foot in a new world.

He was probably the first important conductor in musical history. For that reason, the mastery of his orchestral works is scarcely surprising. Among his five symphonies, the 'Scottish' No.3 and the 'Italian' No.4 enjoy great and deserved popularity. The 'Hebrides' Overture is one of the most often performed pieces of our time. These pieces are painterly without resorting to tone-painting in the sense of musical depiction. The music reflects the misty melancholy of the Scottish landscape, the stormy waves of the Atlantic or the sun-flecked splendour of Italy, and thereby hints at another important side of Mendelssohn's talent: he painted and drew excellently. Finally, the two oratorios, *St. Paul* and *Elijah* carry on the tradition of Handel and Haydn.

This range of works, without mentioning the organ pieces and choral music as well as many other compositions, is endlessly rich. Certainly, their artistic quality is uneven, which is hardly surprising. We love Beethoven without doubt, but not necessarily for 'Wellington's Victory' Op.91. Mozart, too, left us comparatively weak pieces, such as a few of the piano sonatas, or the concerto for flute and harp. A composer should be judged not by his lesser works, but by the best of them. With *Carmen*, for instance, Bizet achieved a stroke of genius: it was this opera that made him justly famous, although he wrote a handful of other first-rate pieces. And so, Mendelssohn must take a place of honour in musical history for his many masterpieces.

We should also not forget that in addition to composing, there were other invaluable activities. March 11, 1829 is a red-letter day in the history of music. On that day, Bach's *St.*

Matthew Passion was performed in Berlin under Mendelssohn's baton. This memorable occasion marked no less than the beginning of the Bach revival. The first performance of Schubert's great C major Symphony in 1839 was also given thanks to Mendelssohn. At the same time, he supported and disseminated the works of his most outstanding contemporaries, Schumann, Chopin, Berlioz and Liszt, with committed enthusiasm. And thus he was simultaneously a custodian of old values, and a pointer towards new stylistic directions.

Why, then, do we encounter so much dismissal, disapproval and reluctance whenever Mendelssohn's name is mentioned? What exactly is the problem? There are several. Many people tend wrongly to assume that true art can only be produced on the back of experiences full of worry and suffering. There is no shortage of examples: Mozart died early, and in tragic circumstances; death claimed Schubert even sooner. Beethoven went deaf, Schumann suffered depressions and eventually became mentally deranged, Bartók starved both psychologically and physically in America. Such fates arouse feelings of sympathy and compassion in us 'healthy' people and lead us to believe that tragedy is a precondition of greatness. On the other hand, one cannot feel sorry for Mendelssohn, or pity him: at most, he arouses envy on account of his talent, his success and the wealthy middle-class background of his happiness.

Once in a while a criticism does the rounds that Mendelssohn's music is sentimental in the bad sense of the word. That is simply untrue. In fact, it is only poor and tasteless performances that are sentimental, and harmful to Mendelssohn, just as they are detrimental to Chopin or Liszt.

Finally, the dark chapter of anti-Semitism must be opened. Moses Mendelssohn (1729–1786), Felix's grandfather, was one of the greatest philosophers and thinkers of his time. His friend Gotthold Ephraim Lessing immortalised him in the title role of his play *Nathan der Weise*. Felix's parents, Abraham Mendelssohn and Lea Salomon, converted from the Jewish faith to Protestantism in 1822, and their children had already been baptised in 1816. Grandfather Moses never wanted to take this step. However, the younger generation believed that in the Europe of those days Jews stood at a disadvantage. They wanted to give their children a brighter future through the change in faith. That's why, in 1823, the Mendelssohns were given the 'Christian' title of Bartholdy. The parents' fear was not unfounded: their son was faced with threats and hostility which have continued to this day.

'It would be a strange thing if a real artist could ever emerge from the son of a Jew,' writes Felix's teacher Carl Friedrich Zelter to Goethe about his favourite pupil. It proves that even the more noble spirits of the time were not free from anti-Semitic tendencies. Similarly, malicious remarks about Mendelssohn, in a similar vein, can be found in Chopin's letters or in the marriage diaries of Robert and Clara Schumann.

With the pamphlet 'Das Judentum in der Musik' ('Judaism in Music'), which he published anonymously in the *Neue Zeitschrift für Musik* in 1850, Wagner moves up to a quite different and appalling level. In it, he attacks Mendelssohn in a highly malicious manner, maintaining that even the most gifted Jews can never reach true greatness and profundity in art. This revolting essay is a disgrace, not only for Wagner, but for the entire world of culture. Worse still: Wagner's excommunication was not without its evil consequences. The cultural politics of the Third Reich banned Mendelssohn's music, and with it all Jewish, and in Nazi jargon so-called 'degenerate art', from cultural life.

Carl Orff composed new incidental music to *A Midsummer Night's Dream*. (I don't know if a god will ever forgive this lapse, and that of *Carmina Burana*!) Wagner's unfortunate judgement is still to be felt today. Even some significant musicians of our time think that the important composers are those who determined the course of the evolution of music, and for that reason include, for instance, Wagner, Berlioz, Liszt and Schoenberg. In their eyes, Mendelssohn simply wrote very pretty music, but musical history would not have taken a different course had he not existed.

Again, that is wrong. Mendelssohn's music is immediately recognisable by its own individual tone of voice. The magical world of Shakespeare's fairyland which opens up before us in his incomparable scherzo movements is his own highly original invention. Equally original is the already mentioned genre of the 'Song Without Words'. How can anyone claim that he didn't create anything new? The smart-alecks should also be reminded that neither Bach nor Mozart was revolutionary in spirit, for their genius is founded not on starting out in new directions, but on a summation of previous achievements.

I freely acknowledge that Mendelssohn means more to me than just the great composer that he was: he stands much more as a key figure in the cultural landscape of the nineteenth century. As I think about his status, the painting by Moritz Daniel Oppenheim showing the highly gifted youth playing Beethoven to the aged Goethe appears before my eyes. Yet another image for which Mendelssohn could be envied.

May my gracious readers forgive this small defence. It would have been nice to think it had not been at all necessary. I can hardly expect you to share my enthusiasm for Mendelssohn. The time is not yet ripe to assign him his due place on Parnassus, but I hope with all my heart that things will look different for Mendelssohn in this anniversary year.

Florence, March 2009

Letter from Dresden (with a continuation from Leipzig) to Mr Robert Schumann, Elysium

Dear Robert Schumann,

On the occasion of your 200th birthday, allow me to convey my deeply felt respect from the town of Dresden. May you spend this anniversary day in the right surroundings, where you are honoured and justly celebrated. I have no means of telling whether news about contemporary occasions and events concerning us earthlings reaches you in your world. Allow me, therefore, to tell you something about present-day Schumann reception, so that you may become aware of how our musical world understands and values your art.

I fear you would not feel at home in the musical life of today. It's true that the number of concertgoers has risen dramatically all over the world, but unfortunately the quality and general culture of audiences has diminished in equal measure. The average listener of today has hardly the faintest idea about what he is hearing. He neither knows anything about new music, nor can he differentiate between outstanding, moderately good and poor performances. Two days or so after the concert he reads the opinion of a so-called 'expert' in the local paper and adopts it as his own. And with few exceptions, these reviews have sunk to an alarmingly low level, especially if I take you, esteemed Herr Schumann, as a yardstick. You raised music criticism to an art in the highest degree when, in 1834, you founded the Leipzig *Neue Zeitschrift für Musik* – which is still being successfully published – and actively contributed to it yourself. In comparison with that, we can only be horrified at the depths to which this profession has sunk.

Taking a general view, we have lost sight of good taste, even in your homeland of Germany. Just imagine: for your 200th birthday German television (perhaps you have heard of this modern means of communication) broadcast not, for instance, a celebratory Schumann concert, but instead showed the dreadfully kitschy film *Spring Symphony*, starring the gorgeously pretty Nastassja Kinski. The film doesn't have much to do with your music, or the facts of your life – which did not, however, seem to bother either the programmers or the viewing public. Hopefully you have found the opportunity in Elysium to discuss such feeble efforts with WA Mozart, because *Amadeus* – a highly successful film, by the way – took a similarly distorted view of him. These 'art films' mislead the viewer because their intention is to make him believe that geniuses are quite normal people who eat, drink, sleep and digest their food like everyone else. They don't explore what goes to make up the extraordinary qualities of a genius, the secrets of his soul and spirit – such questions are not touched upon, even in passing. It would surely be more rewarding to have fewer composers' biographies, and to get to know and understand their works instead. As far as that's concerned, your life's work offers a shining example. The number of Schumann biographies is huge. Among them are many romantically poetic and sentimental accounts, but also – although in a clear minority – knowledgeable and insightful portraits. Published editions of your letters, diaries and so-called household books are available in German and other languages. They offer intimate and even indiscreet glimpses into the secrets and details of the Schumann family's private life. You will rightly and indignantly exclaim, 'I did not write those for public consumption!' Posterity has lost all respect for private life. (Just a remark on the side: I am nevertheless pleased that all the towns which played a central role in your life – your home town of Zwickau, the later places of Leipzig, Dresden, Düsseldorf and Endenich – have all gone on to honour you with museums and commemorative plaques.)

All this forms the basis of the picture of Schumann we have today. Or will it change? A few days ago, I read an article in a German medical journal, in which a professor from Cologne maintains, and attempts to prove, that most of what has been known until now about the last years of your life – from the supposed suicide attempt of 1854 to the long months in the asylum in Endenich – does not represent the truth. According to the author, a suicide attempt never took place; you were taken – and this was confirmed, so there is no doubt about it – to Endenich at your own request, yet the principal cause of your alarming condition was neither syphilis nor depression. The true cause was alcohol abuse. When you began to feel better in the nursing home, the Cologne medical expert goes on to say, you wrote to your doctor, Dr Richarz, asking him to discharge you and send you home. Richarz would no doubt have done so, but your wife, Clara, declined to have you released, and prevented it. Those are serious accusations which raise questions to which no satisfactory answers can be given. Was the relationship between you and Clara a fulfilment of ideal romantic love, or is that only an alluring legend? Or does profound love mutate in some inexplicable way in its later years into disharmony? That is something we neither can nor should know. It remains nevertheless a fact that the C major Fantasy or the F sharp minor Sonata are touching declarations of love and affection that are almost unparalleled in musical history.

It is striking that your first works, from Op.1 to Op.23, are exclusively written for the piano. This is no doubt not by chance: you prepared yourself for a career as a pianist, which soon came to an unhappy end because you permanently injured your right hand with an unfortunate 'stretching' device. As a composer, you already found your own style and individual voice with your first works. Who else, apart from you, could magically coax true poetry out of so semi-mechanical an instrument? Doubtless, Beethoven, Schubert, Chopin, Mendelssohn. But your music involves another element that until then did not exist: the short character-piece. Let us look at the *Papillons* cycle Op.2, for instance. If someone were to ask me what romanticism in music is, I would suggest they study this work. It is inspired by the penultimate chapter of the novel *Flegeljahre* ('Fledgling Years') by Jean Paul, though without being programme music. As though at a masked ball, figures appear in the briefest and most diverse of character-pieces, and alternate with each other in a quite unexpected manner. Chameleon-like, the music is constantly changing its colours and gestures; the whole thing has the effect of a spontaneous improvisation but is nevertheless strictly controlled through its ordering and musical logic. The tonal relationships between the sections are by no means arbitrary: the first and last pieces are both in D major, and so they lend a circular form to the work as a whole. Your wonderful song cycles *Frauenliebe und-leben* Op.42, *the Liederkreis* Op.39 and *Dichterliebe* Op.48, all of them written in the happy 'song year' of 1840, have a similar circular design.

Clearly, you concentrated on specific genres at certain times in your life. In addition to the piano works and song cycles that have already been mentioned, we could think of the 'chamber music year' of 1842 that gave rise to the three string quartets, the piano quintet and the piano quartet. The year 1841 saw the composition of the symphonies in B flat major and D minor; 1843, the oratorio *Paradise and the Peri*. The series doesn't end there. Your encyclopaedic spirit and the extraordinary breadth of your creative mind enabled you to compose important works in every genre: concertos for piano, for violin, for cello; an opera (*Genoveva*), choral works, sacred music (a Mass and a Requiem), the *Scenes from Goethe's 'Faust'* and incidental music to Byron's *Manfred*; chamber music for piano with instruments that were seldom used in a solo capacity (oboe, clarinet, horn), fugues and contrapuntal studies. A many-layered life's work of that kind is scarcely found in any other composer.

It would be naive and presumptuous to pretend that all these works enjoyed widespread popularity. A significant proportion of your output has remained virtually unknown to this day. But why? I believe the full implications of your music can hardly be understood unless one is thoroughly versed in the Germanic world – its language, poetry and literature. Just how important this is can be seen from your own writings. The works of your favourite author Jean Paul are unknown outside of Germany and have hardly been translated. It's true that ETA Hoffmann is a little better known, but he still doesn't rank among internationally famous writers. As a result,

Schumann performers who haven't mastered the German language find themselves at a serious disadvantage. That is a great pity, for your pieces, more than almost any others, need outstanding, deeply thought-out performances, or a wrong impression of both the works and the composer will be conveyed. How many prejudicial and false judgements arise out of poor interpretations! I have just been amazed to read – in June 2010, in Dresden! – on the Culture page of the *Sächsische Zeitung* that *Genoveva* is a failed opera, and the *Manfred* Overture is boring and lacks tension. How is it that such stupidities can be published with impunity? Or can judgements like that arise out of poor interpretations? But in that case the composer can hardly be blamed.

Another supposed shortcoming ascribed to you concerns your orchestration. The cliché that, to put it mildly, it is defective is one that seems to die hard. Great conductors, from Mahler to George Szell, have retouched, rewritten and reorchestrated your symphonies, for instance through doubled woodwinds, or have smoothed out, and thus blurred, its contours. Were you of any help to them in this? Quite the opposite: your instrumentation is marvellous, but to achieve the right balance of sound, and to produce equal weight of sonority between the various groups, demands a great deal of rehearsal, which in today's restless world is usually lacking.

The third truism, and one for which your highly esteemed wife Clara and her protégé Brahms carry the greatest burden of guilt, is the claim that your late compositions bear witness to a sick and declining mind and would not represent the great composer in a worthy light. For that reason, the Violin Concerto, for example, was locked away for nearly 100 years. (The lifting of the ban itself was, however, hardly a glorious chapter in musical history. It took place under shameful conditions: the cultural policy of the Nazis championed the piece as a romantic, German violin concerto, having banned performances of the one by Mendelssohn.) Clara and Brahms went so far as to burn your five Romances for cello and piano. Your last work – the E flat Variations, whose theme, you declared, had been dictated to you in a dream by the spirits of Schubert and Mendelssohn – only appeared in print in the 1930s. The manuscript was owned by Brahms, who himself composed a wonderful set of variations on the same theme for piano duet.

This anniversary would offer an ideal opportunity to bid a permanent farewell to nonsensical and baseless prejudices and clichés about you and your oeuvre. May your works resound in performances that are as good as possible and let us leave their appraisal to musical listeners.

With the greatest esteem and deepest respect,
Your grateful and enthusiastic earthly disciple,
András Schiff
Dresden, 8 June 2010

Dvořák's Piano Concerto*

Among Dvořák's three mature compositions in concerto form, the Piano Concerto has always been treated as something of a neglected stepchild by the musical world. The magnificent Cello Concerto in B minor Op.104 is firmly established as a crowning centrepiece of the repertoire.

---

* Preface to the facsimile score (Henle Verlag, Munich 2004).

It's true that the very beautiful Violin Concerto in A minor Op.53 has not achieved similar popularity; and yet, thanks to the devotion and enthusiasm of many important violinists, it too has found its way into all our major concert halls.

With the best will in the world, we cannot say the same of the Piano Concerto in G minor Op.33. Yet it has not lacked true champions – from Rudolf Firkušný to Sviatoslav Richter, among others – who have believed in the work and tried to make it better known. What is the reason for this resistance on the part of the public and many pianists alike? Perhaps pianists are spoiled for choice when it comes to concertos, while the same cannot be said for violinists, and still less cellists. Moreover, Mozart, Beethoven, Mendelssohn, Chopin, Liszt and Brahms were all brilliant pianists who could contribute to the success of their compositions through their own performances. Dvořák was not a virtuoso pianist; he could never have mastered the enormous technical hurdles of his concerto, which Sviatoslav Richter considered the most difficult piece he had ever played. Compared to Chopin and Liszt – who set the standard for demanding and effective pianism – Dvořák's writing for the instrument strikes many performers as forbidding and unidiomatic. In view of this prejudice, the well-known Czech pedagogue Vilém Kurz (1872–1942) reworked the solo part, increasing its virtuosity and at the same time lending it a certain element of extroverted superficiality. Kurz's version appears directly beneath Dvořák's original in all the important printed editions, even the critical complete edition of 1956. Through the intervention of another hand, the piano part is robbed of its distinctive voice: it sounds almost as though it had been written by Liszt.

Let us, therefore, lay the 'Kurz' version aside and return to the original, exactly as Dvořák composed it. It is a wonderful concerto, conceived in the best symphonic tradition of Mozart, Beethoven, Schumann and Brahms. Here the soloist is not the sole centre of attention, as is often the case with Paganini, Chopin and even Liszt, but is *primus inter pares*, first among equals. The orchestra is not restricted to the role of accompanist – and how beautiful it sounds in Dvořák's hands! Already the main theme – soulfully sung by the violas and cellos – is memorable and irresistible. The light-footed and charming second theme dances gracefully and elegantly; in fact, the whole piece seems to be swarming with lovely melodies. Small wonder that Brahms praised the natural melodic gifts of his younger colleague.

The mighty opening Allegro agitato, in an expansive sonata form, is a self-contained piece. Had he wanted, Dvořák could have allowed it to stand alone as an independent *Konzertstück*. Fortunately for us, he added two further movements which, taken together, provide the necessary counterweight to the opening movement. The Andante sostenuto, with its main theme intoned by the horn, evokes images of nature; the concluding Allegro con fuoco is an invigorating rondo incorporating elements of folk song and dance.

The pianistic difficulties are a challenge to the performer, but they are more than offset by the musical delights. Several nineteenth-century piano concertos that are in the repertoire of many a pianist – and are heard far too often – are technically just as difficult, without giving us the emotional warmth and technical mastery that radiate from Dvořák's work.

This beautiful manuscript appears for the first time in print. May this facsimile edition awaken the interest and curiosity of students, performers and music lovers, and lead to the concerto's belated but well-deserved recognition.

Florence, Spring 2004

Bartók at the piano

Like Bach before him, Bartók was an outstanding musical educator of the young. Together with his two- and three-part Inventions, Bach's *Clavierbüchlein* for his son Wilhelm Friedemann and the one for his second wife, Anna Magdalena, are model examples of the best pieces that have ever been written for young musicians. More than 200 years later, this high art of teaching was taken up again by Bartók in his four-volume collection *Gyermekeknek* ('For Children') and the six-part *Mikrokosmos*. When his younger son, Péter, began taking piano lessons, he wanted to give him pieces that were both educationally useful, and demanding and modern.

When I started my piano lessons with Elisabeth Vadász, in 1959, these Bartók pieces were my primary teaching material right from the beginning. One of the few positive features of post-Stalinist Hungary was its excellent and systematically organised musical education, which was free. In it, the music of the recently deceased Bartók played a prominent role. A musical child could absorb its idiom as though it were his mother tongue, and at the same time become acquainted with the composer's peculiar harmonic, melodic and rhythmic elements and modes of expression.

Gyermekeknek is a collection of Hungarian and Slovak folk song arrangements, whose texts are included at the end of each volume. For me to play and sing these little pieces was a real joy and pleasure. (Some of the publisher's comments, such as 'Text is not printable', naturally aroused our curiosity and it's true that they are not always suitable for children, and some of them – to our delectation – verged on the indecent.)

In *Mikrokosmos*, on the other hand, Bartók works with material that is not directly drawn from folk music, which makes the collection a much harder nut to crack. *Mikrokosmos* is a wonderful introduction to Bartók's musical language. The pieces and individual volumes are arranged in progressive order of difficulty, so that students can use them for many years. The last two volumes contain pieces of considerable complexity which can no longer be regarded as being of purely pedagogical intent.

My thorough study of these two cycles gave me insight into Bartók's great piano works. The most significant of them are the Sonata and the *Out of Doors* suite, both written in 1926. Together with the First Piano Concerto, they are his most radical and dissonant works. In the concerto, he experiments for the first time with weaving the solo instrument together with the very individual colours of percussion instruments, above all the various nuances of cymbals and drums. We seem to hear percussion instruments in the solo works, too, although they are not physically present.

At this point, I should like to say something about Bartók as a pianist. No other player, past or present, has impressed and influenced me to such a degree. Unfortunately, I was born too late to have been able to hear him in person, but even on recordings his artistry is breathtaking. Luckily, he left a comparatively large number of recorded documents which allow us to study the authentic Bartók style at close hand. The notion that he treated the piano as a percussion instrument is a well-known cliché, and one that has often been repeated. What an inaccurate and absurd assertion! One only has to hear his playing: his rhythm is firm as a rock, but is paired with a wonderful touch in which the piano is never hammered, and a style of playing that at no point degenerates into ugliness. He can produce unbelievable

lyricism and tenderness, without the slightest trace of sentimentality. His rubato and *parlando* playing are quite unique,
and deserve special notice. They allow the music to speak.
In this sense, Bartók the pianist is a child of the nineteenth
century.

There is no other composer who notates his scores
with greater care and precision: the music is full of remarks, metronome markings, and indications of phrasing,
articulation and dynamics. Listening to him, one notices
how meticulously he keeps to these guidelines. And yet the
notation and the actual sound experience are worlds apart.
Bartók shows that the contemporary system of notation
falls short of being able to convey sensitivity and agogic
subtleties. But does the same not hold true for all the great
composer-performers? In traditional piano teaching, great
emphasis is laid on the fact that four semiquavers have to be
played absolutely evenly. But that is far removed from the
musical truth!

Bartók's unique qualities are always in evidence, even
when he plays Bach, Mozart, Beethoven, Chopin or Brahms.
On top of that, he was a marvellous chamber player, and
his recordings with the violinist Joseph Szigeti and with the
contralto Mária Basilides are legendary.

It is impossible to imitate other artists, and foolish to try.
Imitations can easily turn into caricatures. And yet to me it
seems natural that Bartók's way of playing his own music
is not only 'correct', but also a yardstick. It is obvious to me
that as a performer I have to follow his style and his spirit,
but without losing sight of my own personality in doing so.

Bartók's music is Hungarian – indeed, it could hardly be
more so – but you don't have to be Hungarian in order to be
able to play it well. What is essential is to discern its idiom,
which is as closely related to the language as German is to

Schubert, Czech to Janáček and French to Debussy. In all these cases the performer has to be able to convey the language. And so, to reiterate: Bartók's music is never brutal, and if it seems to be so it must be the result of a misguided approach on the part of the performer.

London, 1996

Pál Kadosa – a short tribute to my teacher

Is there a 'Kadosa School'? If so, what were the master's secrets? The first question must be answered with a firm 'no'. Kadosa Tanár úr (Professor Kadosa) worked individually with each pupil, guiding him or her shrewdly and wisely according to the student's specific character. Dogged, doctrinaire methods were alien to him, and in addition he also renounced any authoritarian mannerisms. Like a good gardener, he tended the plants that were entrusted to him, cutting away wild shoots and eradicating the weeds. His reputation as a distinguished pianist is documented by recordings from the sixties. Unfortunately, he had to give up playing the piano shortly afterwards owing to a hand injury. During my eight years as a student, I heard him play only one time. He sat down at the piano and played – quite beautifully – the first eight bars from the second movement of Beethoven's 'Pastoral' Sonata Op.28. Kadosa was mainly active as a composer – and a very good one, incidentally.

I am firmly convinced that thinking like a composer strongly influences interpretation, which demands a clear understanding and perception of the inner structure of a work. From that point of view, Professor Kadosa had clearly defined ideas about the great works of the repertoire, to which he clung steadfastly. He taught me the sonatas by his favourite composer, Beethoven, with absolute dedication and a deep understanding of the music. Form, harmony, rhythm, style and expression – he was deeply familiar with all these elements, and he didn't tolerate any arbitrary interpretative notions. This middle European, in the best sense of the term, was distinguished by his excellent taste; he was the embodiment of a true *homme de culture*. When teaching, he often illustrated his remarks with metaphors from literature and the pictorial arts. His home, where lessons often took place, was like a small museum, with extremely valuable works of art and a fabulous library.

Kadosa's class was known and envied for its familiar atmosphere. It was like a group of grandchildren sitting in a circle around their beloved grandfather. Every year we celebrated Christmas together. A piano lesson lasted precisely 60 minutes – enough time for a whole *tour d'horizon*: a Bach prelude and fugue, a complete Beethoven sonata, a few Chopin Etudes, and a large-scale work by Schumann. And sometimes it was sufficient for him to tell a story.

Imagine the scene: the master sitting behind the desk in Room VIII of the Franz Liszt Academy of Music in Budapest. When a work had been played through, he said in a quiet voice: 'Please bring the score over here.' 'Here, not so vehement, please' – and he indicated the passage in question. 'Here, a touch hesitant.' 'There, a little more emphatic.' Just small things like that, nothing else. Significantly, he left the hard, long and sometimes relentless work week after week to his assistants, György Kurtág and Ferenc Rados. They carried out the hard labour, so to speak. They were responsible for the analytical part of our studies, while the old master integrated and summed up their lessons.

Among the successors of Bartók and Kodály, Kadosa may be regarded as one of the most significant creative personalities of his generation – one whose reputation ought to extend well beyond Hungary. On the occasion of his centenary it would be nice, as well as opportune, to be able to hear his most significant works occasionally in concerts. They ought to have earned a firm place in the repertoire. During a piano lesson in the seventies, he said almost resignedly, 'One of my very best compositions is, of all things, my Stalin Cantata.' And he sighed, 'It's a real shame that it can't be performed.' A performance ought to be a possibility again these days. What would stand in the way of it?

Florence, 2003

The best piano in the world – reminiscences of György Kurtág

It was in the spring of 1968 – an important year historically speaking, even if for reasons other than those that concerned me personally. I won first prize in the music category of a Hungarian television competition for young people. I was 14 years old and still a pupil at the music school. My piano teacher, Elisabeth Vadász, thought that I should continue my studies by going to Professor Pál Kadosa at the Franz Liszt Academy in Budapest. At the time, that was not so easy. In accordance with the Hungarian educational system, first of all you had to complete four years of conservatoire, that's to say secondary school, before you could be accepted at the academy – the college. But Professor Kadosa heard me play and was prepared to take me on sooner.

First, however, I had to take an exam in front of the entire faculty, and so, in teaching room VIII, I played a few pieces. I no longer remember what they were. All the teachers were seated in the room, and as a concertgoer I knew some of them by sight. It was a rather stern, unfriendly assemblage, which was hardly surprising since this circle regarded my dubious success on television with prejudice and suspicion. But when you are 14, nerves don't affect you; and my youthful innocence and naivety lent me sureness and self-confidence. As a result, while I didn't play particularly well, it was probably promisingly enough. And so, Professor Kadosa kindly accepted me for his preliminary class for a probationary year.

Among the jury, sitting on a radiator, was a very interesting man. He was much younger than his colleagues; with very short hair, and wearing a grey pullover, while all the others were dressed formally. He had a youthful energy, and his eyes shone sympathetically and encouragingly. 'Who was that?' I asked my teacher afterwards. 'György Kurtág', she answered. The name meant little to me. Just one distant memory came to mind: in a junior concert two girls had played a suite for piano duet by him.

Pál Kadosa was the legendary head of the piano department – a very good composer and pianist, though he no longer played owing to a hand injury. Kurtág was his assistant. We had lessons with Kadosa once a week, and twice a week with Kurtág. I shall never forget my first lesson with the latter: it had a decisive influence on my life. We were in Room VIII again, the scene of my entrance exam. There were two pianos there: a Steinway, and one called an Estonia – a dreadful instrument from the former USSR. The first piece I played to him was the E major three-part Invention by Bach. It lasts one minute and sixteen seconds. Yet two-and-a-half hours later, we hadn't even got through the first third of the piece. I realised in a flash that I hadn't the slightest idea about Bach or about music, to say nothing of playing the piano.

Kurtág explained, analysed, sang – and played so beautifully on the appalling Estonia, as though it were the best piano in the world. I was shattered, but not depressed. After me, it was always Zoltán Kocsis's turn for his lesson. He was a bit older, and much more advanced than me – the new star of the Academy. Naturally enough, after my lesson I stayed on to hear him. He played the Prelude and Fugue in B flat minor from the first book of the *Well-Tempered Clavier* superbly, and in a way that I found impressive. When he finished playing, there was complete silence in the room. After what seemed a painfully long time, Kurtág quietly uttered a single word: 'Ugly.' Kocsis was taken aback: 'The piece or the way I play it?' 'The way you play it' was the answer he received. What followed was an extraordinary piano lesson lasting several hours, in which Kurtág opened up new worlds to us.

And so it went on, week after week, with Bach, Haydn, Mozart, Beethoven, Chopin, Brahms, Debussy and Bartók. If you played him a Mozart sonata, he quoted *The Marriage of Figaro*, *Così fan tutte*, *Don Giovanni* and *The Magic Flute*, as though it were the most obvious thing in the world that we knew all those operas by heart. That wasn't so, but Kurtág had awakened our interest, and we immediately rushed off to the library to pore over the scores and vocal scores, and to plug the gaps in our cultural knowledge.

On another occasion, I had to perform Schubert Lieder to him – *Der Zwerg* and the two Suleika songs. I had to sing and accompany myself. Schubert songs play an important role in my life and I owe my first stimulus to György Kurtág. The collaborative work between Kurtág and Kadosa functioned perfectly: one of them took care of analysis, while the other was responsible for teaching musical coherence. Both were composers, and as such they saw unity and hierarchies in music of a kind that remain largely hidden to pianists.

After a year, Ferenc Rados – another legend – took over the position of assistant, and I learned actual piano technique with him. From then on, Kurtág only taught chamber music. Hungary has a great and enviable chamber music tradition which is closely associated with the name of Leo Weiner, who was an excellent composer. He taught at the Academy from 1908 to 1957. If you asked musicians like Reiner, Doráti, Solti, Végh and many others whom they learned most from, the answer was always the same: Leó Weiner. Kurtág felt the same way, and he continued the tradition.

I was lucky enough to be able to be Kurtág's pupil for a further nine years. During that period, we studied a huge number of pieces for various ensembles. Our studies were never finished – they were a kind of 'work in progress'. Kurtág was enormously demanding. No one could play him the beginning of the Brahms G major Violin Sonata Op.78 beautifully enough: he gesticulated and sang it over and over again, for hours. Occasionally, he was satisfied with a note or a phrase, and then he was so happy! We loved him so much that we wanted to play better and more beautifully, to give him pleasure.

To Kurtág, music is not a profession: music is essential, more important than life itself – a privilege for which one has to be ablaze. Anyone who doesn't feel that fire had better do something else. During this long period of study, we were hardly aware of the fact that our teacher was one of the greatest composers of our time. In those days, he had only completed a few of his works and they were seldom performed. Nor did he ever talk about them, which was typical of his modesty. Today, if you play his works to him, he has an absolutely precise idea of how every note has to sound. With living composers, that isn't often so. When, much later, I played his *Sayings of Peter Bornemisza* with the singer Lucy Shelton – a concerto for soprano and piano, and the hardest work I've ever seen – he said laconically to me after the performance: 'When you've managed the other half of the notes, we can have a further discussion.' I'm still working on it.

Neue Zürcher Zeitung, 2008

For Ferenc Rados's 80th birthday

Mrs Amália Fuchs (*née* Baracs) – our beloved Aunt Máli – was, so to speak, one of the core personalities of the Hungarian colony in London. As a teacher at the Jewish school in Budapest she had taught German and Hungarian literature to an entire generation of girls. Next to Goethe, her greatest love was Mozart. To the end of her long life (she died at the advanced age of well over 90), she played his music passionately on the piano every day. 'Mozart is the greatest benefactor of mankind,' she used to say with her angelic expression.

Aunt Amália and her husband lived in the same house in Budapest as the Rados family. The childless Fuchs couple followed the development of their neighbours' child, Ferenc, with great affection as he was growing up. He often liked to stop and chat with them for a while or rummage around in their impressive library. That's how the boy stumbled one day across the then newly published multivolume Révai encyclopaedia and asked for permission to borrow one of the thick volumes. The next day he rang the doorbell again and said, 'I'm returning your book.' 'Why so soon?' asked Aunt Amália. 'I've already read it.' 'Really? Well, we'll see about that.' And Amália opened the book at random and asked him, 'What do you know about the long-toed salamander?' Without hesitation, 'Ferike' (little Ferenc) quoted the relevant article from memory, word for word. The little boy passed further spot checks with no problem and then proceeded to read all the other volumes of the encyclopaedia and familiarise himself with their contents.

I am often asked by young pianists from all over the world if I can recommend a good teacher to them. My answer is always the same: 'Yes – Ferenc Rados.' And other tutors? There are as many of them – both teachers and pianists – as there are grains of sand on the beach. But without doubt, there is only one Rados! All those who have been fortunate enough to have studied with him are fully aware of that, as are those who still make the pilgrimage to Budapest to play for him. It is, alas, symptomatic of present-day circumstances in Hungarian cultural politics that the Budapest Academy of Music chooses to do without his services, while hordes of students from all over the world seek him out and flock to him.

It's true that Rados Tanár úr (Professor Rados) can't be recommended to everyone. Anyone who expects to be encouraged by praise and compliments will be misplaced with him. Candidates of this type won't be able to put up with his strictness for long. Like a good doctor, Rados uncovers the root causes of weaknesses and offers infallible diagnoses. 'I didn't understand a note of what you were playing' is his most frequent criticism. Or, 'Now I understand, but I didn't like it at all.' 'I understood it' is the highest praise one can receive from him.

For all his extraordinary intellect, it would be wrong to describe Rados as an intellectual. He combines intellect, understanding and feeling in ideal equilibrium, and in perfectly attuned proportions. Thanks to both his intellect and his good taste he always avoids the pitfall of cheap sentimentality, and playing the piano never becomes a superficial physical *tour de force*, or an arbitrary act. The meaning and purpose of playing is to implement both the musical imagination's interpretive concepts and their sonic realisation in the best possible way. How endlessly lively Rados's imagination is, and how deep is his knowledge backed up by an unparalleled cultural formation! And he is inspired to impart all these great qualities and pass them on, but not in some stolid or insipid manner. His humour, his jokes and his inimitable Mephistophelean laughter are an important element of his teaching.

In the late sixties – I remember it as though it were yesterday – it was Péter Nagy who had his piano lesson with Rados immediately before mine. To Rados, this enchanting eight-year-old boy with dark eyes as big as saucers wasn't a child at all, but a grown-up on his own level. I had a much harder time with him. He picked on me mercilessly, and sometimes really tormented me. Not infrequently, I was reduced to tears. But I accepted the challenge, and I now think back on those times with gratitude. What could one learn from him? The art of pianism, which is to say refinement of touch, imaginative treatment of tone, unqualified respect towards composers and their works, the necessity of never being satisfied – never to give up, continually to pose new questions. Rados himself was and remains a living question mark.

As a man who is omniscient, there is almost no limit to the extent of Rados's teaching. It makes no difference

whether he is dealing with piano, violin, oboe, horn or singing, or with old, new or the latest music. I often witnessed
him having to study works which he had never heard, or
of which he had absolutely no knowledge. But thanks to
his intuition he immediately understood the composition's
form, harmonic structure and expressive range, and I
was fascinated every time. While I was preparing for the
Moscow Tchaikovsky Competition in 1974, I played him the
obligatory contemporary piece – a scherzo by Alexander
Pirumov. Like an alchemist, Rados immediately changed
the rather mediocre, meaningless piece into pure gold.
After my performance in Moscow, the composer, who
witnessed it, said with astonishment, 'Ah, Comrade Schiff, I
never thought I had written such a good piece!'

'He who can, does; he who cannot, teaches.' George
Bernard Shaw's typically mischievous saying doesn't apply
to Rados at all. Very few people are fortunate enough to be
able to play the piano like him. He performs everything,
demonstrating the music's course in a wonderful way. The
variety of his touch is indescribably beautiful. He knows the
secrets of sound, and the manner in which one can draw
unprecedented sonorities out of what is a semi-mechanical
instrument. Quality and variety of tone together with the
relationship between the individual voices – piano music is,
after all, mostly polyphonic – are the most important criteria
in the art of playing the piano, and not, for instance, speed,
strength and accuracy, as is so often wrongly thought. Some
of Rados's performances – the D minor Concerto of Bach,
for instance, or a few of Mozart's concertos, Schubert's
'Trout' Quintet – are among my unforgettable concert
experiences.

This much-loved teacher abhors clichés: he finds plati-
tudes or eulogistic sentimentality unbearable. For that

reason, I find it difficult to end this little homage without paying compliments. May he not take it amiss if, on the occasion of his 80th birthday, I convey to him a simple expression of admiration, with gratitude not only on my own behalf, but also that of countless pupils.

Berlin, October 2014

Albert Simon

Among the many important musicians who have had a strong influence on me, mention must be made of Albert Simon. In the first half of the twentieth century it was Leó Weiner who defined musical education through his activities as a teacher. In the years between 1960 and 2000, Simon played a comparably important role. He was an extremely sensitive and difficult person who had been deeply affected by the tragic events during the Nazi era, and he had no wish, nor was he able, to accommodate himself to general musical life. In such surroundings he was a stranger. He found his island, his own world, at the Budapest Academy of Music, directing the student orchestra there. Not for nothing was he regarded as a great analyst: his studies were distinguished by minute remarks in which not the slightest detail was neglected. He could talk for hours about a single note, and work on it until after his explanation the beginning, middle and end of the note had been singled out. The orchestra would rehearse a Haydn symphony for an entire year, but it was worth it. I shall never forget the performance of the G major Symphony No.88. Simon was a musical prophet, a fanatical obsessive in the best sense of the term.

After he left the college he dedicated himself completely to musicology, and above all to the analysis of Bartók. He was convinced that his discoveries would make Bartók's harmonic world comprehensible for the first time. Sadly, his great work in progress was not published during his lifetime. It is all the more welcome, then, that thanks to Bernhard Haas, Simon's analytical methods have posthumously been made available. It is a belated but well merited tribute to a great musician.*

London, April 2004

Annie Fischer

With the death of Annie Fischer an era has irrevocably come to an end. As someone who was probably not a typical representative of her age, her wonderful artistry and her unique charisma outshone her run-of-the-mill contemporaries. I owe my very first musical experiences to her. As a six-year-old child sitting on my mother's lap I was able to hear her concerts in the large hall of Budapest Academy of Music, or the Erkel Theatre. It was immediately apparent, even without being able to make any comparisons, that we were witnessing extraordinary events with both our ears and eyes. Every single seat in the hall and on the stage was taken, and there was a feeling of anticipatory tension in the air. In the charged atmosphere one could sense that a special event was about to take place. Then the door to the stage was opened and, like in a fairy tale, a queen entered. But the six-year-old boy could not have known what a queen looked like – Hungary hadn't been a monarchy for

---

* See Bernhard Haas, *Die neue Tonalität von Schubert bis Webern. Hören und Analysieren nach Albert Simon*, (Florian Noetzel Verlag, Wilhelmshaven: Noetzel 2004).

decades . . . Well, he couldn't know, but he felt it intuitively, because that was exactly how he had imagined the entry of a noble lady from the fairy tales he had heard and read himself. Her appearance was completely natural, and in no way studied or artificial. She appeared on the stage neither in the posed manner of a diva, nor as the ritual sacrifice of a lay priestess celebrating in the temple of the arts. On the contrary, what impressed us was her simplicity and unpretentiousness. The tasteful elegance of the evening clothes she had chosen captivated us; I never saw her appear twice in the same dress. She hurried over to the piano with the lightest of steps and acknowledged the audience's applause and warm reception with a little smile and a meek bow. And then a miracle happened, and we became witnesses of a metamorphosis, as, in a manner of speaking, the performer disappeared, and in her place the spirits of Mozart, Beethoven and Schumann arose. They spoke to us through the medium of this wonderful woman. It seemed as though we who were listening almost drank the music, and – not exactly used to such fortune – we were filled with gratitude and love. At the time I was struck by how wonderful a piano recital like that could be, and for 35 years it was always the same with her concerts. All the more bitter, and even devastating, was it for me to have to experience afterwards that this kind of magic was missing in most other pianists.

Already at her early concerts I was struck by the presence of an imposing old man with grey and white hair. Many of the people there greeted him with utmost politeness, calling him Aladár. My mother explained to me that this man was Aladár Tóth (1898–1968), a marvellous music historian and the leading, and best, music critic in Hungary. From 1946 to 1956, he was director of the Budapest Opera House, and during that time he invited Otto Klemperer to Budapest, where, as principal conductor from 1947 to 1950 he directed wonderful and epoch-making performances. Tóth married Annie Fischer in 1937, and thenceforth played an extremely important role in his wife's artistic activities and her development. Of course, as a child I had not the slightest idea about these circumstances. Perhaps one day someone will be in a position to give an authentic and adequate account of this unusual artistic relationship. To me, it seems as though to a certain extent Aladár Tóth made music through his wife. He had a decisive influence on her taste, which he refined, at the same time broadening her cultural horizons. After each concert, and even after his death, Annie secretly asked herself, 'What would Aladár have thought of it?'

For approximately three-and-a-half decades, I was able to follow her career and could experience many of her unforgettable concerts. There is no other pianist whom I heard in person so often. Her repertoire encompassed two-and-a-half centuries of Western musical history, from Bach and Handel to Bartók and Kodály. Like all significant artists, she was extremely self-critical and selective in putting her programmes together. She didn't play everything, but only those works which she passionately loved, and for which she felt a natural affinity. The list of pieces which have lived on in my memory through Annie's interpretations is a long one.

The great Mozart piano concertos were particularly close to her heart. As a little girl she had already made a great impression with the D minor Concerto K.466 conducted by Willem Mengelberg. This was a work in which she could portray the rich variety of Mozart's imagination brilliantly: the interplay of dramatic and lyrical elements, the alternation between smiles and tears. Her performances of the C major Concerto K.467, the E flat K.482, A major K.488, C minor K.491, C major K.503 and B flat K.595 are among my most profound experiences, even if the overall impression was occasionally marred, or even ruined, by the conductor and orchestra. (Anyone who has been lucky enough to hear the 'live' Amsterdam concert performance of the Concerto K.482 conducted by Klemperer will understand the meaning of an equal musical partnership on the highest level.) With Aladár Tóth, she got to know and value the world of Mozart's operas. Without this knowledge her idiomatic understanding of the piano concertos would have been unimaginable.

Beethoven's works played a central role in Annie Fischer's life. In this, she was influenced, formed and inspired by great models – above all her teacher Ernö (Ernst von) Dohnányi, and the profound playing of Bartók. To her husband, Eugen d'Albert was the most distinguished of Beethoven performers. Annie knew him only through Tóth's descriptions. Alongside these ideals, she could develop her own independent style of performance, and find her own sound. In this context, her own feminine nature played a role that should not be underestimated. How should a woman pianist approach Beethoven, that Promethean being with his dramatic and at the same time unsentimentally lyrical expressive personality – that's to say, perhaps the most 'masculine' of composers? Annie succeeded in finding the golden mean with the instinct of genius. When necessary, she could produce enormous sounds out of the instrument which never threatened to overwhelm one in a powerful or even thunderous manner: they had the effect of being created out of an innermost strength. At the same time, she was capable of playing that was extremely sensitive and soulful, in a way that threw new light on Beethoven's poetry. When she struck the first chords of the 'Pathétique' Op.13, they already embodied the work's entire events in a nutshell:

they were weighty and powerful, but in no way crude. And this woman played the F sharp major Sonata Op.78 with moving tenderness and flexibility. True Beethovenian sound is extraordinarily varied: the performer has to be endowed with a palette of innumerable characters and shadings of tone-colours for each work, and even for each individual movement of a sonata. Annie knew her way through these labyrinths perfectly, so that the listener had the impression that it was exactly right: this was the way it has to be – the piece cannot be played in any other way. She played these masterpieces throughout her life, yet only at the height of her career, when she was in her mid-seventies, did she feel ready to play all 32 sonatas in a cycle, in two concert series at the Budapest Academy – one in the afternoons, for young people; the other in the evenings, for 'grown-ups'. It was from this time, too, that the recordings were produced in the studios of the Hungarian company Hungaroton.

Of the Beethoven piano concertos, the only one she didn't have in her repertoire was the B flat major, No.2. I heard her do the remaining four often. A performance of the C minor Concerto under the sensitive baton of Antál Dorati has remained one of my vivid and indelible memories.

She played the Schubert B flat Sonata and the second Book of Impromptus indescribably beautifully. I should like to single out her performance of the first F minor Impromptu, which was undoubtedly one of her great achievements. The piece is actually a sonata movement whose secondary theme is like a dialogue between two imaginary voices (soprano and baritone), accompanied by semiquaver figuration evoking flowing water. To conjure up this 'Duet Without Words' is an artistic task of the utmost difficulty, and one which nobody but Annie could manage to achieve in so poetic a manner. It was only at a late stage that she included the great A major Sonata D.959 in her recital programmes: she played it in public for the first time at the first concert she gave following the death of her husband. Also on the programme were Chopin's B minor Sonata and the C major Fantasy of Schumann. The loss of her beloved husband hit her hard: for a long time she kept away from the concert platform. The Schubert sonata was the sign that marked the end of her silence and soul-searching. The 'new' work signalled, perhaps, a fresh start to her life.

If there was one composer of whose works Annie Fischer was a consummate performer, it was Schumann. His piano music, so full of colours and characters of a kind not to be found in his predecessors and contemporaries, make him a master of romanticism *par excellence*, feeding his endlessly rich imagination on literary models. For those not familiar with the worlds of Jean Paul and ETA Hoffmann, Schumann's music will be a closed book. Annie was the ideal interpreter of Schumann's duality, his split personality swaying back and forth between Eusebius and Florestan – the feminine and masculine sides, respectively, of his creative persona. The short, chameleon-like scenes of *Carnaval*, the wild madness of *Kreisleriana*, the moving poetry of the F sharp minor Sonata and the C major Fantasy – I shall never again hear these works more beautifully and convincingly played.

She performed Chopin, Mendelssohn, Liszt and Brahms in an equally exemplary fashion, as well as Debussy, whose music she treasured, associating it with the French Impressionist painters. Last but not least, she was devoted to Bartók's Third Piano Concerto, and made an important contribution to the international dissemination and recognition of the work and its composer.

For the younger generations, it was unfortunate that she didn't want to pass on her experience through teaching. (She made an exception during her exile in the war years in Sweden, where, as a Jew, she had fled with her non-Jewish husband in order to survive. Immediately after the end of the war the couple hurried back to Hungary, because she had felt rather bored in Sweden.) It's true that as a student at the Academy of Music I could hear all her concerts, but it seemed impossible to get to know her personally. At that time there was an unbridgeable chasm between the great artistic personalities and the younger generation. In itself, a seemly distance is no bad thing . . . It is even possible that patient respect helped me to make contact with her later, and to form friendly bonds.

Our friendship developed during the eighties, when I was no longer living in Hungary. We often met in London, Paris, Copenhagen, Edinburgh, New York and Boston. I was very pleased that she was received abroad with the same enthusiasm as at home. When, after 1968, I visited Hungary regularly again, my first port of call after my parents' house was her residence in Szent István Park. We had long sessions, not ending until the early hours of the morning, which gave us wonderful opportunities for deep conversation. One of the great moments in my life was when, at a late hour, and lifting her glass of vodka, she suggested we should address ourselves in the familiar 'Du' form.

Annie indulged in three passions: cigarettes, coffee and beer. As a chain smoker, she lit one cigarette after another. On top of this, she was an excellent cook, and her fried chicken was legendary. At four o'clock in the morning, you literally had to cut your way through the heavy smoke that hung thickly in the air of her living room: we could just about make each other out through the fog. Visitors could hardly keep awake, but she was always bright and cheerful. She finally went to bed around six o'clock and slept through until the afternoon. This was her normal pattern of life – a way of living that went against all doctors' advice. But apart from a cataract operation, she never needed any medical help.

As I have said, I never studied with her, or even played to her at all. On the other hand, she often came to my concerts, and we discussed them in critical detail afterwards. She was strict in her judgement, but honest and uncompromising. She could be genuinely pleased when things went well. Then she would talk about Aladár Tóth again, which was always fascinating to me, and about the musical experiences of her youth: the way Bronisław Huberman played Chopin's C sharp minor Waltz, how Toscanini conducted *Falstaff* in Salzburg. Or she would talk about the literature that was close to her, such as the great Tolstoy novels *Anna Karenina* and *War and Peace*.

Annie hated studio recordings, as the following anecdote shows:

'In EMI's Abbey Road studios in London we had arranged a recording of Brahms's F minor Sonata Op.5,' she told me. 'The red light goes on, I begin playing, and I soon realise that everything is going really well, and that it's going to be an unusually inspired performance. In the middle of the second movement a voice comes out of the loudspeaker, as if out of the blue: "Tea break." I quickly packed my things together and went home.'

All the same, her recordings are of huge importance, especially for those who never heard her in concert. Of course, recordings can't reproduce her unique concerts, but they are true documents of her art and her indescribably beautiful piano sound.

If you wanted to attempt to describe Annie's art in a nutshell, you would probably have to say it was a combination of instinct and intelligence. Philology was alien to her; she didn't worry much about which edition of the music she used. I once asked her if she had studied with Leó Weiner. (Weiner was widely acknowledged as the most important teaching authority for chamber music in Budapest; he taught nearly all the good musicians.) 'No,' she said, 'Dohnányi wouldn't let me. He felt Weiner was too much of a nit-picker.' It's true that she wasn't obsessed with analytical details; she didn't go in for hair-splitting.

Her critics – and unfortunately they were many – took this liberal attitude as sloppiness. One can only feel pity for those Beckmessers, particularly since they also thought that good piano playing is marked above all by speed, pure strength, and accuracy. They failed to understand the difference between technique and mechanics. A pianist with good technique is someone who enjoys a lively imagination and has the means to convey it in his performance. Sound production, the graduation of colours and matters of touch, all fall under the banner of 'technique'. From this aspect, Annie – like Cortot or Edwin Fischer before her – was extraordinary. The way in which she and the piano were knitted together reminded one of the figure of a centaur. In this connection, a word about the beauty of piano tone would be in order. We live in a time – and not only in Hungary – of ugly, brutal and percussive piano playing. Annie's sound was diametrically opposed to this way of thinking and was even more than beautiful. She could not only make the instrument sing, but also speak. Her tone was varied – different for every piece, every composer – and always artistic, never ugly and caricatured.

She died, in Rilke's meaning of the term, her 'own death'.

She was listening to a live transmission of Bach's *St. John Passion* on the radio and passed away during the broadcast. A beautiful way to go.

Florence and Freiburg, February 2002

George Malcolm

Perhaps it was just a stroke of luck that brought us together. My meeting with George Malcolm proved to be one of the great and far-reaching fortunes of my life. How did it come about? In the sixties I received a letter from Lady Margaret Lamington. As a great music lover, she was a patron of the arts and a sponsor of young talent, and she regularly held house concerts in her beautiful home in Cadogan Square, in London. That was where I was to appear for the first time in the city, as an eleven-year-old boy. Not long after that, Lady Lamington wrote to tell me that George Malcolm would soon be giving a harpsichord recital in my home town of Budapest, and since he never played from memory he would need a reliable page-turner. She thought I would be suitable. (The 'art' of turning pages is, incidentally, not as easy as is generally assumed. We musicians could write amusing books about fiascos, goofs and bad luck involving page-turners.) I was glad to accept this kind invitation, and I wasn't at all nervous during the concert. As one of his encores, Malcolm chose a short piece called 'For Two to Play' by Thomas Tomkins. To my great pleasure, I had to play one of the parts together with Malcolm. My performance as a page-turner had met with his complete satisfaction, and it marked the beginning of a friendship which lasted for many years.

Unfortunately, in those days Budapest was a very long

way from London – not so much geographically, as inevitably through the frosty East–West relations of the Cold War. For that reason, we met only sporadically, when I was staying with my relatives in England during the summer months. On these rare occasions I could visit George – he insisted I should call him by his first name – and play to him. These auditions – they were not conventional lessons – opened up my horizons in a new and decisive way, and they were unbelievably inspiring. George criticised my playing mercilessly, but never destructively and never impolitely: he remained always a gentleman. He treated me as a grown-up would in giving advice to a somewhat younger fellow-spirit.

What did I learn from him? In the first place, stylistic awareness in old and less old music. In Hungary, Bach was played in the post-romantic nineteenth-century manner, *sempre legato* and with little dynamic shading. George showed me the varied kinds of articulation, the colouristic possibilities and the boundless imagination of this music. No one could introduce and execute ornaments and decorations as brilliantly and inventively as him. He taught me the art of improvisation and continuo playing. He made me familiarise myself with period keyboard instruments, the harpsichord and clavichord. But he never forced me to play Bach, Handel, Scarlatti or the English virginalists on the harpsichord.

Among the many pieces of advice he gave me, and which I still follow to this day, were: 'By all means play this music on a modern concert grand, but do it in the right style!'; 'Read and study the most important textbooks of the time: CPE Bach (*Essay on the True Art of Playing Keyboard Instruments*), Johann Joachim Quantz (*On Playing the Flute*), Leopold Mozart (*Treatise on the Fundamental Principles of*

Violin Playing), and use the information on the instruments of today.' And, 'Use the sustaining pedal sparingly, or not at all: legato playing must be achieved through the fingers, not the feet.'

The rewarding hours we spent together always ended with us playing music for four hands – above all Mozart and Schubert, but also Mendelssohn, Schumann, Brahms, Dvořák, Bizet and Debussy. (This repertoire is wonderful, but very tricky to play. Aside from well-established duos, pianists seldom fit well together on account of their individual characters and their manner of sound and attack.) Making music together with George afforded pure pleasure and a wonderful feeling of happiness. Our playing was beautifully documented in a recording of pieces by Mozart made on the composer's own Walter fortepiano in his birth-house in Salzburg.

I also gained valuable insight from George as an orchestral director. He always arrived at the first rehearsal with impeccably prepared musical material. All the parts were very precisely marked up in their bowings, phrasing, articulation and dynamics. This was especially helpful and time-saving with English orchestras, because in Britain there is usually less rehearsal time available than elsewhere, but the level of sight-reading is incomparably high. Thanks to precisely marked-up parts a good orchestra can concentrate on the essentials of making music right from the start. Time-wasting and laborious discussions about such matters as bowing become unnecessary. In my work as a conductor, I always use this method.

George enjoyed worldwide fame for his wonderful harpsichord playing. Not that it was his favourite instrument: there wasn't a single one to be found at his home! For concerts he preferred the English harpsichords by Thomas

Goff or Robert Goble, with their many pedals. Thanks to these devices, he could introduce unbelievable colours into his playing, changing registers often and obtaining crescendo and diminuendo effects which were not necessarily 'authentic', but which were all the more musical for that. He was continually being criticised for this by dogmatic, self-righteous purists, who maintained that the instruments of the baroque era had fewer registers, and that modern performance practice should reflect that. As far as I'm concerned, the result of doing that is as monotonous as a sewing-machine. George was opposed to this sectarian credo: he wanted to avoid setting limits on his lively imagination. He was entirely guided by the human voice, by singing, which for him was the be-all and end-all of music. It's not surprising that he was a very experienced choral director. Under his direction the Westminster Cathedral boys' choir achieved worldwide fame. Benjamin Britten composed his *Missa brevis* for it in 1959. He handled the organ – he had been an organ scholar of Balliol College, Oxford – in no less masterly a fashion.

In Bach's time, a musician had to have very wide-ranging abilities if he wanted to apply for an important position. Candidates were expected to excel on all keyboard instruments, to be able to play some stringed instruments, to conduct an orchestra and choir, to play continuo parts and to show some skill in composing and improvising. George Malcolm fulfilled those Baroque requirements to the highest degree some two hundred and fifty years later, with modesty and humility.

Berlin, October 2014

Sándor Végh

In the summer of 1970, I was due to take part in George Malcolm's masterclass at the Dartington Summer School of Music in Devon. At the same time, it was announced that a violin class would be taken by Sándor Végh, whom I very much wanted to get to know. In my student years in Budapest we only knew about him through hearsay, since he had left Hungary in 1946 and hadn't been back for a long time, being out of sympathy with the communist regime. Occasionally, recordings of his string quartet were broadcast by Hungarian Radio; that was the limit of our knowledge about him. In Dartington, Végh gave two concerts with the pianist Peter Pettinger which were revelations to me. The violinist's very presence on the stage immediately left deep marks on me – the beginning of Bartók's Second Sonata, for instance, where Végh appropriately 'spoke' with his violin, or the equally unforgettable scherzo of Beethoven's C minor Sonata Op.30 no.2 and the gigue from the Bach D minor Partita: one wanted to leap up, or even dance along with the music. His teaching was unbelievably inspiring and instructive for his students, and at the same time delightfully amusing for the audience. Végh was a born actor, and his comedic imitations, parodies and banter came naturally to him.

Our next meeting took place in 1979. In the ravishingly beautiful surroundings of Prussia Cove in Cornwall – the ideal setting for Wagner's *Tristan und Isolde* – Végh, following the example of Rudolf Serkin's Marlboro Festival, founded the International Musicians' Seminar (IMS), where established players studied and performed chamber music together with talented young musicians. In this environment, and to my great joy and honour, I was to play Brahms's F minor Piano Quintet Op.34. The success of this partnership gave me the courage to ask him if he would be prepared to rehearse the Beethoven sonatas for piano and violin with me. To my delight, he agreed. Over the next four years, we worked on the ten masterpieces and tried them out intensively, introduced them into concert programmes and played them for a studio recording. These years of apprenticeship meant more to me than all my piano lessons: from his experiences as a quartet leader Végh knew Beethoven's music inside out. Thanks to him, my panic-stricken fear of this giant among composers was dispelled and I lost my Beethoven inhibitions.

I played with him in one of his last concerts as a violinist, in the large hall of the Budapest Academy of Music, in 1986. It was Végh's first appearance in Hungary since he had emigrated 40 years before. The audience was thrilled with his playing; the applause lasted so long that it seemed as if people didn't want to go home. It was an extremely moving evening. Unfortunately, shortly afterwards he had to give up playing the violin owing to rheumatism in his arms and shoulders. Anyone who never heard him in concert absolutely must get to know the 'live' recording taken from a concert at the Prades Festival, with the Végh Quartet and Pablo Casals giving the most beautiful of all performances of the Schubert C major Quintet.

Because Végh was such a wonderful and inspiring teacher, it was a natural step for him to concentrate his musical activities on conducting. He had already founded his own ensembles in the fifties, in Freiburg and Basel, though in those days the string quartet was still his main activity. In 1978, he took over the directorship of the Camerata Academica in Salzburg, marking the beginning of a new era in his life. He developed this chamber orchestra into an outstanding ensemble: it became his own instrument – the continuation, in a way, of his quartet. The violins, consisting entirely of Végh pupils, sounded magical and homogeneous.

When I was asked by Decca to record the Mozart piano concertos, I absolutely wanted to do them with Végh and the Camerata. What we needed for this project, of course, was first-class wind players to supplement the ensemble, since it was regarded above all as a string group. In this, I was greatly helped by my close friend Heinz Holliger. He not only played an active role in this undertaking, he brought such fellow-players with him as the flautist Aurèle Nicolet, the clarinettist Elmar Schmid, the bassoonist Klaus Thunemann and the horn player Radovan Vlatković. We could not have wished for a better wind group. Between 1982 and 1990 we recorded the complete Mozart concertos, from K.175 to K.595, in a long and fulfilling project to which we dedicated ourselves with much love. We rehearsed each time in a shabby hotel called 'Hartlwirt' in Liefering near Salzburg, not far from Végh's home – first, just the winds with piano, then the strings and piano, and finally the full ensemble. After rehearsing for three or four days we gave a public concert, and only then did we undertake the recordings. Maestro Végh, who was never tired out even after the most strenuous sessions, always surprised us with new ideas and deep insights into the music.

What was the secret of his music-making and his communication? They were things that could never be learned. He played and conducted with complete naturalness and with no fuss, which perhaps had something to do with his origins. Végh came from Kolozsvár (Cluj) in Transylvania, where the roots of folk culture have remained particularly deep and lively. They speak a much more beautiful and locally inflected Hungarian there than in Budapest, for instance. As far as speaking is concerned, Végh was able to let the music speak for itself.

There's a good story about that, which he often told me. In his solo evenings, the famous bass Feodor Chaliapin, who was already a legend in his lifetime, performed various songs and arias. Between his star turns, as sort of 'fillers', young up-and-coming talents were engaged, to give the main attraction a rest and to entertain the audience before the next group of songs. That's how, when he was young, Sándor Végh was given the opportunity to appear. One evening, while he was playing a violin piece, he glanced up at the manager's box, where, to his horror, he saw the great singer. 'What is he going to say about my violin playing?' he wondered. 'Look here, young man,' Chaliapin said afterwards, 'you sing very well. Now you'll have to learn how to speak.' Sándor carried that advice with him throughout his life. On top of that, from this great singer Végh learned the art of breathing, in itself something quite obvious, but an indispensable necessity for music-making, and one which all too many instrumentalists completely ignore.

Végh evolved and developed his rhythmic and dance-like character out of folk music. His intuition was infallible, and his perceptiveness was unbelievable. His imagination and insight were incomparably lively, and he always found images or a metaphor to illustrate what he wanted to convey. The colours he brought to his playing were limitless, too. In short, the gods obviously loved Sándor Bácsi (Uncle Sándor), and he was downright 'shamelessly' gifted. It's true that gift and talent are the most important prerequisites, but genius requires more. On top of that, hard work is needed, together with a pinch of luck. Sándor Bácsi was very hard-working and had the necessary pieces of luck in his life – above all in his meetings with Bartók and Casals. Végh baptised Bartók's Fifth Quartet and captured the idiom of the Hungarian composer's music brilliantly and in a unique manner, because he could approach it with loving devotion and affinity. Fortunately, his collaboration with Casals is well-documented. From him, Sándor obtained fresh ideas and inspirations, because Casals was a kindred spirit: a tremendously strong and natural musician with both feet on the ground.

In an age of mediocrity and musical commercialism, Sándor stood out as an exceptional case – a huge personality like a 'last of the Mohicans'. He is deeply missed.

Salzburg 1991 – Berlin 2014

Recollections of Rudolf Serkin

While it would be an exaggeration to say I knew him well, Rudolf Serkin had a considerable influence on my life. Some of his concerts are indelibly engraved on my memory, especially the sonatas and concertos of Beethoven. Among his interpretations, Reger's Variations and Fugue on a Theme of Bach was a real revelation. At his request, I learned this grandiose piece. We got to know each other in Marlboro, Vermont, at the famous chamber music festival which he founded together with his father-in-law, Adolf Busch.

As a great admirer of the recordings made by Busch and Serkin, it had always been a dream of mine to come into his presence. In 1978, my wish was fulfilled. Serkin's influence in Marlboro was tremendously strong, but it wasn't easy to establish contact with him. When we students asked him musical questions, we never got a direct answer. Serkin shrugged his shoulders and said to us with a smile, 'Ah, you know, that's so difficult, it can't be answered easily, it needs time.' He wasn't in any way being unfriendly or negative. He was just a wise man who knew that there were no easy answers or quick fixes to musical questions, that we each had a long and strenuous journey ahead of us if we wanted to reach our desired goal.

If I wanted to find a single word that characterised Rudolf Serkin, I would choose 'integrity'. Almost all performers claim to be simply faithful servants of the composer, but very few of them practise what they preach. Serkin was one of the few who did – a man for whom fidelity to the text was an obsession. His library was full of manuscripts and first editions; his researching mind needed proximity to the sources.

Serkin never looked for easy solutions: he never steered clear of difficulties. To take an example: the beginning of Beethoven's 'Hammerklavier' Sonata Op.106 presents a fearsome challenge. Beethoven instructs the pianist to take a huge leap using the left hand alone, in order to reflect the notion of a spiritual and physical struggle. It would be far more comfortable to use both hands (the right hand, after all, is not otherwise occupied), but that would go against both the composer's intentions and the sense of the music: the entire tension would be lost. Many pianists fall down here, because the music's speed and their desire for accuracy (not to mention comfort) leads them to choose the easy option. Not Serkin. For him the handicap presented a challenge which he had to overcome at all costs, just as did the similar example at the start of the Sonata Op.111. That is the true moral of music-making.

Serkin was an artist without compromises, and he dedicated his long life exclusively to the greatest among composers – he had no interest in second-rate music. He gave interviews only very seldom. He appeared neither on dull television programmes and mind-numbing talk shows, nor as a figurehead in commercials. Nevertheless – or perhaps precisely because of that – he was widely respected and esteemed by a whole host of music lovers. He was a mentor and a role model for entire generations of musicians. I remember this man of exalted ethics with gratitude and admiration.

Florence, January 2003

Why do we need musical manuscripts?
In memoriam Stefan Zweig

In our age of digitisation and the internet, this question is especially relevant. Cynics can easily lay the matter aside: musical manuscripts are just old pieces of paper, they are extremely difficult to decipher and therefore belong in museums and libraries; they are hardly of any value and are more or less useless. The many editions of masterpieces, scrupulously edited by the best musicologists, form an adequate and solid basis for performers and music historians alike. Is that really true? Or is there something missing in even the most scientific of editions?

I admit that it's difficult to convince the sceptics – the most one can do is to pity their woeful wretchedness. Let's leave them to their point of view and try to approach the question constructively and logically. In his day, the great Austrian writer Stefan Zweig was one of the most important collectors of autographs. His famous collection encompassed around a thousand precious manuscripts of world literature and musical history.

He will always remain a pathfinder and a yardstick, and it would be difficult to imagine a better counsellor. 'The world of autographs is no immediately visible and material world: it can be felt through the imagination alone, is perceptible only through culture, and benign only to those who bring to it their positive understanding, and the all too infrequent gift of reverence.' So writes Zweig in 1923, in his essay 'The World of Autographs'.

In a later essay ('The Meaning and Beauty of Autographs', 1935), he writes the following: 'This secret realm is not open to all. He who wants to enter it must possess the key that opens understanding, he must be moved by an emotional spirit – the most beautiful and powerful on earth: reverence. In order to love manuscripts with understanding, to admire them, to be stirred and moved by them, we must first of all have learned to love the people whose lifework is perpetuated in them.'

And also, 'Only when we poets, musicians and other heroes of the spirit and the deed already apprehend with a kind of religious feeling – only then can the trails of their handwriting reveal their meaning and beauty to us.'

The manuscript is the original source. Through it we find ourselves in immediate proximity to the work and its creator. It is not necessarily the ultimate version – there are manuscripts of early versions, sketches and corrections which are equally fascinating. Aside from their graphological aspect, manuscripts show us the various stages of the compositional process, and the composer's states of mind at the moments in question.

The manuscript of Beethoven's 'Diabelli' Variations, which has been owned by the Beethoven-Haus in Bonn since 2009, shows these character traits in exemplary fashion. Beethoven struggled with the piece: he worked on it for five years, the birth pangs lasting from 1819 to 1824. In the first year he wrote 22 variations, before he laid the work aside and until 1823 was occupied with completing the last three piano sonatas and the *Missa solemnis*. Only after that did he compose a further 11 variations. Last of all, he wrote the very first variation – a tongue-in-cheek march. The music's character can clearly be seen in the handwriting: the extended bar-lines and the sweeping stems of the notes bear witness to self-confidence – the pictorial transference of decisiveness and conviction.

Beethoven's manuscripts are multifaceted. Sometimes his writing is wonderfully flowing and clear, at other times it is teeming with corrections, marginal comments and alterations. Real painstaking and finicky work is needed to decipher such pages. In the 'Diabelli' Variations, both types can be seen. Beethoven begins the work in a fair copy, but then he obviously runs out of patience, and corrections inserted in red and blue pencil appear more and more frequently. Right at the end, before the entry of the second fugal subject in Variation 32, Beethoven 'embellishes' the paper with a huge black splodge: right at the climax of the composition, out of pure creative fervour, he spilled the contents of his inkwell. The inkblot so exuberantly flung down onto the paper is an important hint for the performer. It's as if Beethoven were saying, to paraphrase Goethe, 'Only he who knows my handwriting knows what I write.' Not for nothing did Goethe write in a letter of 10 May 1812, addressed to Friedrich Heinrich Jacobi (quoted from the above-mentioned essay by Zweig), 'Since the sensual experience is so vitally essential to me, preeminent people come alive for me in a magical way through their handwriting.'

Bach's manuscripts are among the most beautiful

documents of his great art. How fortunate it is that many of them are relatively well preserved and readily accessible! His writing is strong and sweeping, the voice-leading clear and purposeful. The notation of these scores is almost incredibly clean, with hardly any corrections. Very probably, Bach also made sketches and wrote in corrections, but the fair copies are astoundingly immaculate, and they afford great aesthetic pleasure. The note stems and beams are always wave shaped. Unfortunately, in the printed editions these waves are necessarily lost, and everything is reproduced in straight lines. If Bach performers were acquainted with his handwriting, they would accordingly play his semiquaver and demisemiquaver passages in wave-like formations, and not in dry 'geometric' fashion.

Thanks to autographs, some prejudices and clichés can be done away with. Take, for instance, Mozart's compositional procedure: in contrast to Beethoven, who struggled and literally agonised over every bar, composing seems to have come comparatively easily to Mozart. For him, it wasn't heavy work: the music, in a manner of speaking, flowed easily and spontaneously out of him. Instilled with that impression, that's how posterity regards this genius: whole hordes of music lovers admiringly think of him in this way, which turns out in truth to be merely stereotypical.

A few glances at Mozart manuscripts are enough to prove how unfounded and misleading such clichés are. The C minor Piano Concerto K.491 is one of his most important works of its kind, and perhaps, indeed, of his whole output. In none of his other piano concertos is the instrumentation so rich: apart from the solo part and the strings, it requires eleven winds (a flute and two each of oboes, clarinets, bassoons, horns and trumpets), as well as timpani. The unusually large scoring and the dark mood (even darker than the D minor Concerto K.466, the only other minor-key work among the concertos) confronted him with a task whose difficulty left its mark on the autograph. The hand-writing reveals the compositional process quite clearly: first, Mozart wrote the orchestral part in minute detail, having at times to draw additional staves when the manuscript paper became too crowded, in order to accommodate all the instruments on the page. Moreover, Mozart – as so often – was in a great hurry, probably on account of the work he still had to do on *Le nozze di Figaro*, whose premiere in Vienna's Burgtheater on 7 April 1786 was drawing ever closer, and no longer allowed for any delay.

As a wonderful pianist and brilliant improviser, Mozart could permit himself – and this was not the only occasion on which he did so – to notate his own piano part only in outline. As composer and performer rolled into one, the shorthand notation enabled him to reconstruct and round out the text with no problem. All the more surprising, then, to find innumerable corrections in all three movements. For a few passages in the finale there are no fewer than three different versions. And in all likelihood, when it came to the concert he would play a fourth!

In the Larghetto second movement there is even one of the composer's rare, but all the more serious, mistakes in notation. It occurs in bar 40, at the third return of the theme. The piece is a rondo, whose form can be designated as A–B–A^1–C–A^1–Coda. The movement begins with the theme (A) played by the soloist alone. In the two variants, the winds are added. In bar 40 (A^1), Mozart rounds the theme out with wonderful new harmonic parts, but in his hurry, he notates the solo part exactly as it was at the beginning of the piece. If the player faithfully follows the notation as found in the autograph, the result is a terrible cacophony which makes one's hair stand on end. The leading editions, like Bärenreiter's Neue Mozart Ausgabe, reproduce the (wrong) autograph score exactly, without any commentary or footnote indications, and thus most performers play the bar in question without the necessary harmonic adjustment. It goes without saying that the slip of the pen has to be corrected; the left hand of the piano part needs to follow the harmony of the wind section. This example shows that even manuscripts have to be critically examined and intelligently read. The conventional truism is sometimes thrown out of kilter: not all Mozart autographs are free from mistakes, while those of the 'illegible' Beethoven again and again show not a single defect.

The three last sonatas which Schubert wrote in the year of his death, 1828, are among the most beautiful and exalted works of the entire repertoire. The manuscripts are in private ownership in Basel. On the occasion of a guest appearance in the city, I was lucky enough to have the honour of looking through these treasures. The distinguished owner asked me to wash my hands first, and then left me alone with Schubert. His sketches for the sonatas are well known, and it is fascinating to follow the developmental history of these works. In these manuscripts, too, I discovered nuances and differences which you would not be able to find in the so-called Urtext editions. It is hard for me to put into words what I felt in this quiet hour: humility, gratitude and profound emotion.

In 1975, during the Leeds International Piano Competition, I got to know the pianist and musicologist Charles Rosen. He said to me: 'You live in Budapest. In the Széchényi Library there is apparently a copy of the Schumann C major Fantasy with a completely different ending from the one we know. Would you be able to have a photocopy of it made for me?' No sooner said than done, although it wasn't actually that easy in the Hungary of those days.

The Fantasy, one of the most beautiful of romantic love poems, pays tribute to Beethoven, in that in its first movement Schumann quotes the last song from Beethoven's cycle *An die ferne Geliebte*: 'Nimm sie hin, denn, diese Lieder' ('Accept, then, these songs'). In the Budapest version, this theme appears again, newly harmonised, at the end of the finale. Schumann, who was a highly self-critical composer, reworked his pieces frequently, and in doing so often sacrificed his most brilliant and original ideas in favour of more conventional and harmonious solutions. Such was the case here, too: Schumann struck out the wonderfully poetic Budapest ending, and in its place he composed what I feel to be a less inspired and somewhat 'harmless' alternative. To this day, it is still a mystery to me how Charles Rosen knew about the existence of this 'original' ending. Even in Budapest music historians have no idea that a real treasure lies hidden in their library. I play this ending with enthusiasm and conviction, to the annoyance of a few musicologists for whom only the ultimate version is valid – in other words, the usual ending. All the same, in view of its originality and beauty, I should like to enter a plea for the Budapest version.

Manuscripts are the original source, but not the only one. First editions and early reprints were often read through and corrected by the composer. They contain extremely valuable hints towards performance – for example, for Schumann's *Davidsbündlertänze* Op.6 and *Kreisleriana* Op.16, or for Beethoven's piano sonatas. Out of the latter's 32 sonatas only thirteen autographs – a few of them incomplete – are extant (Opp.26, 27 no.2, 28, 53, 57, 78, 79,

81a, 90, 101, 109, 110 and 111); all the others have unfortunately not survived. If by some miracle the autograph of the 'Hammerklavier' Sonata were to resurface we would at last reliably know if in bars 224–6 of the first movement we should play A or A sharp. The heated arguments between pianists and musicologists, who all come up with endless arguments one way or the other, would finally be laid to rest. Will, by any similar miracle, the autograph scores of Beethoven's Fourth Piano Concerto or Schubert's C major String Quintet ever be found? Let us wait for the Messiah.

The collecting of manuscripts is not only a true and praiseworthy passion, but also an expensive one today, just as it was in Stefan Zweig's time. Fortunately, we don't necessarily have to own these treasures in order to admire them at first hand. Most musical manuscripts are housed in museums, libraries and archives which are open to the public. The British Library, where Stefan Zweig's bequest is housed, or the Library of Congress in Washington DC, are public-friendly institutions where one can handle the manuscripts without too much difficulty. In other places, the procedure may be somewhat more complicated, as the curators are understandably concerned about the preservation of their treasures. Unfortunately, they are not immune to environmental or accidental damage, or even vandalism. Ink corrosion has damaged some Bach manuscripts to the extent that they could be further harmed by any contact.

Facsimile editions of precious manuscripts often provide an inexpensive alternative or substitute for the unaffordable or inaccessible originals. These editions are excellently and painstakingly reproduced and contain essays by experts that make for rewarding reading. All the same, the manuscript itself contains secrets that even the best of facsimiles cannot reveal. To quote Stefan Zweig again, this time from *The*

World of Autographs: 'It is not its content that lends the auto-graph its intrinsic spirit, nor is it the pure strokes of the pen, however significant, characteristic and revealing their effect may be, for otherwise a facsimile, one of those remarkably accurate reproductions of the kind our technology can so effortlessly and successfully produce, would convey the secret magic of these original pages. Admittedly, some of these replicas, for instance that of the *St. Matthew Passion*, emit a strong sense of the creative presence – stronger than the conventionally engraved score – yet one last, incommen-surable quality is reserved for the original handwritten copy alone: around it, and it alone, hovers that spiritual breath that penetrates our innermost being. Only in the handwrit-ing itself does one live in awe in the overshadowing feeling of the proximity of the mighty.'

The idea of digitisation is equally welcome. The most important collections, such as those of the Berlin State Library, the Austrian National Library, the Leipzig Bach Archive, the Mozarteum in Salzburg or the Beethoven-Haus in Bonn, offer their treasures on the internet, so that they are accessible to everyone, whether specialist or music lover.

A marginal comment in that connection: the internet is a wonderful invention, but it is only a means, not an end. A brilliant digital substitute cannot adequately convey the secrets of a manuscript or a rare first edition. The use of the internet remains a pragmatic, down-to-earth matter. We take it as a foregone conclusion that we can look at the manuscript of the *St. Matthew Passion* or the *Well-Tempered Clavier* on the screen, and we feel nothing, absolutely nothing, not even a 'sacred' shudder. To experience master-pieces, whether of music, literature or the pictorial arts, in the depths of one's soul, one has to be involved and moved, to feel humility, reverence and gratitude. Hopefully, the chill world of technology will not cause our cultural heritage, 'the world of yesteryear', to freeze over or die out altogether.

Berlin, November 2014

Music competitions: art or sport?

The satyr Marsyas was a mythological virtuoso on the *aulos* (double flute). He was so carried away by his art that he challenged the god Apollo to a contest. It was agreed that the winner could do whatever he wanted with the loser. The god won the combat, because he could play the lyre upside-down, and he sang as well, and the satyr couldn't match his achievements with his flute. Apollo bound Marsyas to a fir tree and flayed him alive. The myth of Marsyas was perpetuated and varied by the most prominent authors of the ancient world, including Herodotus, and Ovid in his *Metamorphoses*. The satyr was so gruesomely punished not on account of his lesser ability, but because of his arrogance. Clearly, mortals should not pit themselves against the gods.

And so, what was probably the first ever musical competition took place in the mists of antiquity and resulted in terrible consequences for the loser. Musical contests between instrumentalists, singers and choruses took place in ancient Greece as early as the seventh century BC, fortunately without the losers having to suffer the same fate as Marsyas.

The thirst for contests and tournaments – that's to say for competition and rivalry – is one of mankind's most fundamental characteristics. Obviously, it isn't enough to achieve something exceptional within a particular discipline: man would far rather surpass or vanquish his competitors – an ambition that is, however, not without its dangers. The basic idea behind sport is the intensive training of the human body, the cultivation of health: *mens sana in corpore sano*. That is undoubtedly welcome inasmuch as physical activity promotes general welfare. In this sense, people have always happily engaged in gymnastics and movement exercises of all kinds, have willingly gone walking and running, without being persecuted. All these activities are carried out without any ulterior motive other than well-being and physical stamina.

Ambition is another of man's important driving forces. Without it, there would be no evolution, no development. It is not enough to be able to run fast, to jump high or long, to throw the discus or javelin far: one strives for still greater speed, height, length or distance. Man is a presumptuous being – he would like to be able to swim like the fish, fly like the birds, and if possible better than them. We interpret myths like those of Apollo and Marsyas, Daedalus and Icarus, or Prometheus, as moral lessons in modesty and humility. Some sporting achievements can easily be measured or appraised: with running or swimming the result is decided by stopwatch, while a tape measure determines the length or height of a jump, the distance of a throw. The result is clear-cut. Even the cerebral game of chess produces a result that brooks no argument – checkmate is checkmate.

With other kinds of sport, such as wrestling or boxing, members of a jury decide the result. As long as it's not rigged, they are competent, best equipped to know the rules, and can judge the action accordingly. Less clear-cut situations can arise in tennis, when at critical moments the umpire or an electronic sensor has to decide if the ball is in or out. Similar, or even more contentious decisions arise with football, where up to now the validity of a disputed goal is dependent entirely on the endorsement of the referee and linesmen. In such cases, human error or purely subjective judgement plays an increasingly important part.

In the women's figure skating at the 2014 Winter Olympics in Sochi, the jury awarded the gold medal to the 17-year-old Russian Adelina Sotnikova, while the 23-year-old South Korean Yuna Kim came second. There was a huge scandal: without doubt, Sotnikova's performance was technically brilliant, yet Kim's display was artistically and aesthetically much more graceful. Questions were raised as to whether the jury had made the right decision, or whether other, perhaps political, aspects had been a factor. In sports of this kind, one is often rewarded merely for a lack of mistakes, because judging them in this way is easier. Imagination, elegance and beauty are harder to define, as is shown by the example in Sochi.

The outstanding Swiss tennis player Roger Federer has won all the tournaments in the world. His playing, full of refinement and grace, is a sight for sore eyes. And on the rare occasions when he loses, he remains a true gentleman – stylish and distinguished. As an artist, Federer is a pleasant exception among his rigid and merely athletic colleagues. He shows that sport is ultimately a game, and not a battle. In this sense, a special prize should be established for Federer, honouring the aesthetic beauty of his performance.

Wagner's opera *The Mastersingers of Nuremberg* takes place during the time of the Reformation, and its action deals, among other things, with a song competition which happens on stage. The story is fictional, and arose out of the composer's imagination, yet Wagner has people appear who actually lived, such as the cobbler and great poet Hans

Sachs. The rules and regulations of the traditional contest are documented in the appendix of Johann Christoph Wagenseil's chronicle of Nuremberg published in 1697, under the title of *Buch von der Meister-Singer holdseligen Kunst* ('Book of the Mastersingers' Fair Art'). This is the source of Wagner's libretto. He weaves a song contest into the action, in which the participants compete for the rank of mastersinger and for the hand of the beautiful Eva, whose father, the goldsmith Veit Pogner, has pledged her as wife for the winner. With his noble, fresh and original singing, the young knight Walther von Stolzing embodies the ideal type of artist. His adversary and competitor is the town clerk, Sixtus Beckmesser. On top of his role as participant in the competition, he is a so-called 'marker' – that is, he judges and records the performance of his fellow contestant, noting down each mistake with chalk on a board and making a lot of noise in so doing. His figure stands for artistic philistines and conservatives, for envious and malicious colleagues opposed to the avant-garde. Beckmesser has ever since served as a model, a metonym for the unfortunately numerous bean-counters and nit-pickers of our musical world. Despite all the 'Beckmessering' and intrigues, at the end of the opera Walther wins the prize, and with it the hand of his beloved Eva, because it is the competition judge, Hans Sachs, who, with his wisdom and understanding of art, decides.

The judging of musical performance involves both objectively unbiased and subjectively personal criteria. With sport it is different. The objective components can be measured: the winner is the person who runs fastest, jumps highest, throws furthest. Music is, thank goodness, not a sport, or it too would be easily measured: whoever plays loudest and fastest and gets through the rounds without any wrong notes – those would be the criteria for the Beckmessers, who would have no difficulty in observing them and entering them in red pencil in their notebook. Yet when it comes to art, acrobatics and faultlessness are not exactly the most admirable virtues, and as intrinsic values they don't move our souls. Much harder to judge, however, are other, subjective, elements in the art of performance – among them intonation, tone quality and rhythm. Opinions already differ regarding those – that's to say, every jury member interprets such parameters differently. And that's precisely where the experts' judgements should be consistent. The interpretation of a work, the choice of tempi, the mood and character of the piece – as far as those are concerned there is such a vast difference of opinion that one can no longer speak of general judgements and criteria. Prejudice and personal taste prevail, which for the most part makes a fair procedure an impossibility.

Why, then, are competitions organised when the evaluation of performers and interpretations is so unsure and subjective? Are they absolutely necessary? The question is a legitimate one, and can be answered with a definite 'no'. In music, and in the arts altogether, there are no winners. One makes music for, and not against, others. Concerts are the occasions where musical works are performed for an audience. The artist agrees the programme together with the promoter. He is best placed to know what he would like to perform. The programme for a competition generally goes randomly through the whole repertoire. The candidate has to present himself in the guise of a soloist, chamber musician and with an orchestra in every conceivable genre and style. As a theoretical idea that's all well and good, but in practice it will never work.

Artur Schnabel was a divinely gifted musician and pianist

(he placed value on that order), whose legendary interpretations of Beethoven and Schubert remain yardsticks to this day. On one occasion in Berlin when he was at the height of his career, he suddenly felt the urge to give an all-Chopin recital, which was unusual for him since the music of the great Polish composer was not part of his core repertoire. The concert was something of a disaster, and there were a good many mishaps. In the green room afterwards he saw, to his horror, the famous virtuoso and Liszt pupil Moritz Rosenthal among those waiting to congratulate him. The embarrassing meeting caused Schnabel to remark, 'Ah, you know, Rosenthal, to tell the truth I was trying to throw light on the philosophical side of Chopin's art.' To which Rosenthal replied, 'Indeed, Schnabel, you are a real Chopinhauer!'*

Alfred Cortot was a highly distinguished interpreter of Chopin and Schumann, among other composers, but he had no special affinity with the music of Mozart, as is shown by a rare recording of the C minor Fantasy K.475, which he taught and played in a masterclass. We admire the pianism of Rachmaninov and Horowitz, but not necessarily for their performances of Bach and Mozart. On the other hand, Schnabel and Edwin Fischer by no means owe their fame to their Chopin and Liszt. The piano repertoire is vast and almost limitless, and it goes without saying that no one can play everything equally well. Every performer has to accept his limitations and be self-critical about his strengths and weaknesses, so that he can choose his programme to his advantage.

In the realm of competitions, freedom and imagination are alien words. The jury, whose members are more closely

---

* The pun is a double one, involving not only the famous philosopher, but also the verb 'hauen', meaning to thump. (Translator's note.)

related to Beckmesser than Hans Sachs, does not like to be irritated or provoked. Whenever possible, it chooses a candidate who doesn't unsettle anyone – a 'Jack of all trades, master of none'. The audience derives great enjoyment from it all, and the atmosphere is extremely tense, almost electrifying – rather like the Roman gladiatorial fights. (Who gives a thought as to what the gladiators themselves felt?)

In such a heated and stage-managed atmosphere, it is the most self-effacing and mediocre performances that meet with the greatest success. In 'normal' circumstances the same audience would grant them only subdued or polite applause. Obviously, competitions and concerts have entirely different sets of values and criteria. The real purpose of a competition ought to be the discovery of young talent and the development of its further progress (let us avoid the misleading word 'career'!). With a few exceptions, such is unfortunately not the case. The number of competitions has risen to such an extent that they have become almost worthless. It is true that the general level of young musicians is extremely high, but there are as few exceptionally gifted players as ever. There are simply not enough outstanding talents to satisfy the insatiable thirst and hunger for contests.

The age limit for music competitions is usually set at 30 to 32. After that, candidates have to stand on their own feet, and must make a living, as well as they can, out of concert engagements. It is well-nigh tragic that most prizewinners – some of them have won dozens of trophies – have never been able to carve themselves a niche in musical life. After their competition success, they drop out of sight without leaving a trace. No doubt they have had their opportunities, because according to some unwritten law prizewinners receive invitations to give public appearances, but only once. If a prizewinner makes a success of it, or even causes a sensation, he receives a further engagement, and his reputation will spread and grow. But in most cases the invitation is a one-time opportunity, and the young performer sinks into oblivion.

Good musicians are like good wines: they improve with age. Arthur Rubinstein gave his last concert in 1976, when he was nearly 90. Mieczysław Horszowski played his last recital at the advanced age of 99, in 1991. Throughout their lives these two great pianists managed their time and their strengths in the best possible way, so that their art was always developing through their rich experience. Neither Rubinstein nor Horszowski ever won a piano competition.

Fighting against music competitions is like Don Quixote tilting at windmills – a vain enterprise: they will not be stopped. They are too firmly anchored in our musical culture. Whole hordes of teachers, who go from one competition to the next, from one jury to another, benefit from them. Young pianists take part in masterclasses not because they want to acquire greater knowledge or better musicianship, but in order to ask the maestro for a recommendation for the next competition. All this has nothing to do with music and art. Merely criticising this system of bringing art and sport into line is not enough: rather, better alternatives for discovering and encouraging young talents must be found. My thoughts tend towards an international forum where talented performers can present themselves to an invited audience of professionals, music lovers and amateurs in a short, freely chosen programme. On this platform there would be no winners and no losers. By means of their own choice of works and their own programme ideas, each musician would thus be able convincingly to demonstrate their own tastes and own self-critically assessed talents. The individually tailored programmes – without the necessity for an obligatory set piece – would produce a more revealing picture of the performer. The audience would soon know whether or not the candidate is able to convey something significant, or a personal touch, from the platform. Outstanding gifts cannot be confined within a system, because they do not fit in with the prevailing order. Such rare talents must be nurtured and helped, so that they may have the time and space to develop and realise their potential. New structures which are designed to promote highly gifted artists in a more meaningful and careful way than the competition industry are urgently needed – fully in keeping with the ethos of Hans Sachs.

Berlin and Basel, Autumn 2014

What on earth is wrong with German theatre? An attempt at defending the authors

Berlin is a wonderful city. Its cultural offerings are breathtaking: opera and theatre, cinemas and ballet, galleries and museums, symphonic and chamber music concerts – art lovers are faced with agonising choices day after day.

During our two months' stay in the city, my wife and I seized the opportunity and were able to enjoy several events. We heard wonderful concerts, experienced opera performances, visited beautiful museums and saw some good and impressive films. Our visits to the theatre, on the other hand, left us with some extremely mixed or even disturbingly negative experiences. The artistic quality of the five evenings varied: the staged version of *The Lime Works*, based on the novel by Thomas Bernhard, was not only extremely interesting as an experiment, but also outstanding from the point of view of the acting; and Ödön von Horváth's *Tales from the Vienna Woods* in the Deutsches Theater also turned out to be very appealing, and well worth the visit. Friedrich Dürrenmatt's great tragi-comedy *The Visit of the Old Lady* (again in the Deutsches Theater), on the other hand, developed into a ludicrous and vulgar pseudo-musical with – I shudder to say it – songs by Lady Gaga.

Still more unacceptable to us were two productions at the famous Berliner Ensemble. Schiller's *Kabale und Liebe* – or, to put it more precisely, an amputated version of the tragedy – was staged in such an absurd way as to be unrecognisable, and thus completely unenjoyable. The interference with the text and the cuts made in it verged on the impertinent. As for trying to describe the dreadful production of Büchner's great *Woyzeck*, words fail me. Normally, one does not leave the theatre until the final curtain comes down, but on this evening we fled the auditorium in panic after suffering through twenty minutes. Since there was no interval, we had to disturb our neighbours, who followed our departure with uncomprehending and furious glances. If looks could kill . . .

To experience three dreadful theatrical experiences in one week in a cultural centre as important as Berlin is alarming. For all their differences, some common denominators and tendencies between the relevant productions emerge which are symptomatic of present-day German language theatre. In New York, this trend is rightly called 'Eurotrash'. In the strange world of today's theatre the producer rules as an enthroned king. Actors, stage designers and costumiers, dramaturges and technicians have to subordinate themselves to this almighty lord of the theatrical world. He can afford to be treated thus, because like some magical magnet he attracts many theatregoers to come on his account. The graphic designers play along with it: it's true that on their posters you can read the name of the author and the title of the play, but no less prominently displayed on the poster column is the producer's name. What theatregoers experience has woefully little to do with the original production. The producer now seems to know everything better than the author. The know-all gets his red pencil out and makes alterations without consideration for the loss of words, sentences, entire paragraphs; he deletes whole scenes from the text, or preferably changes their original order. He plays with the text like a cat with a mouse. And the author? As a rule, he is dead and thus cannot defend himself. So who should care about his allegedly outmoded text? He needn't worry, because the interest is to be shifted to the production, which is meant to provoke and tickle the theatregoer.

What would Shakespeare, Goethe, Büchner, Kleist and other immortals say to the reigning producers were they to rise up again and see their plays in present-day stagings? The question is a relevant one. With the help of a little imagination, it can be adequately answered. Presumably the great writers would react to the German producers' theatre in a very similar way to their colleague Samuel Beckett. In 1973, the latter received a polite letter from the Cologne dramaturge Peter Kleinschmidt. At the time, Schauspiel Köln was preparing Beckett's play *Endgame*, and didn't want to bother themselves too much with the author's directions. Kleinschmidt wrote to him that they were intending to locate the play in a realistic setting, to wit an old people's home, and therefore wanted to replace his dustbins with hospital beds. Beckett's answer was clear and unambiguous:

Dear Dr Kleinschmidt,

Thank you for your letter.

I am totally opposed to your idea of bringing *Endgame* up to date in an Altersheim or other fashionable hell. This play can only function if performed strictly as written and in accordance with its stage instructions, nothing added and nothing removed. The director's job is to ensure this, not to invent improvements. If and where such an approach is deemed incompatible with prevailing needs the play should be left in peace. There is no lack of others to fit the bill.

Yours sincerely
Samuel Beckett

Dr Kleinschmidt expressed his thanks for Beckett's un-equivocal letter. The Cologne performance nevertheless took place in the old people's home. According to an article in the *Frankfurter Allgemeine Zeitung* of 25 February 2014, the premiere was a disaster.

There is nothing to add. Exponents of all kinds – producers, dramaturges, conductors and instrumentalists – are re-creative or reproductive artists in the service of actively creative authors and composers. That is nothing less than the *sine qua non* of art. To want to breathe new life into old masterpieces is an inner necessity and a praiseworthy endeavour. But the interpreter should not overshoot the mark: he should always keep within the work's frame of reference

---

* Samuel Beckett's letter dated 24 August 1973 to Dr Peter Kleinschmidt reproduced by kind permission of the Estate of Samuel Beckett c/o Rosica Colin Limited, London.

and acknowledge and respect its parameters. That is by no means a purely subjective process, as some theatre professionals maintain. One must agree with Samuel Beckett – he is right. As essential and distinctive components the author and his text are much more important than the producer and the actors.

On the poster for the premiere of *Don Giovanni*, on 29 October 1787 in Prague, next to the composer and conductor, Mozart, and the librettist, Lorenzo da Ponte, the names of the complete cast are given. But one would look in vain for the name of the producer: in those days, the work and its interpretation were the centre of attention, and not the scenic representation. Nowadays, if one reads a newspaper review of a performance of *Don Giovanni*, one sees a topsy-turvy world. The reviewer is mainly concerned with the staging and the production; the conductor, singers and orchestra are reduced to a mere marginal mention, while the 'poor' composer is even more shabbily treated.

Why do most producers find it so difficult to retreat into the background and place themselves in the shadow of the plays and their authors, where they belong? Where does this mania for self-promotion, pomposity and irreverence come from? Why is there such a lack of humility and modesty? Why this panicky fear of boredom? Apropos boredom: it is a subjective phenomenon. What some people regard as monotonous and wearisome, others may find exciting and extremely interesting – and vice-versa. How many times over did Cézanne paint the Mont Sainte-Victoire, in summer and winter, morning and evening, in rain and sunshine? Is Cézanne somehow boring?

It's true that some plays are extremely long, and require the audience to sit still. An unabridged performance of *Kabale und Liebe* lasts around five or six hours. Is that a problem? Do we no longer have the time in our hectic daily lives, or do we run out of patience too soon? Wagner's *Tristan und Isolde* is not a short opera, either, and in view of its length performances generally begin in the late afternoon. But the nature of opera is different to that of the theatre: a play consists only of speech, whereas opera is dominated by its music. That forms the main contrast between the two genres. The principal virtues of musicology and of the art of musical interpretation are the closest possible adherence to the score, and philological exactitude. The musicians go to extreme lengths to comply with the composer's directions in minute detail, to observe his dynamic markings, accents and articulation signs very closely. Meanwhile, what does the producer do? He thinks he has to impose himself – he knows nothing about music in any case, he can't even read a note (yes, I know there are a few laudable exceptions) – and goes to town on the staging all the more unrestrainedly. He changes things like mad: the action, the setting, the period, and 'regales' us on top of all that with sex, violence and tastelessness ad nauseam. If he could, he would probably even like to rewrite, shorten and shuffle Mozart's, Verdi's and Wagner's music around. But fortunately, he can't do that. Music and the stage give rise to discrepancies and contradictions which unfortunately lead to the multitude of atrocious productions which infest the contemporary world of opera.

Music can acquire a role to play in the spoken theatre, too – in a highly topical way like this, for instance: between the scenes in the Berlin *Woyzeck* performance our ears were regaled with sung, or rather shouted, songs by Apples in Space, The Doors, Canned Heat, Dion & The Belmonts, Melanie, Dolly Parton and other celebrities. Dürrenmatt's old lady found herself forced to sing songs by Lady Gaga

– in not very good English, of course, which is best suited to a German-language play . . . Once again, it's a contradiction to infect great literature with miserable music. The majority of the public, of course, finds this pop intervention great and cool. The theatre is sold out, full of schoolchildren who have no idea about the play, and consequently behave badly, but can happily identify with Lady Gaga and co.

Producers don't necessarily have to be musical. But if they happen not to be, they need to enlist the help of an expert adviser, because music and words can complement each other perfectly: just think, for instance, of Berg's *Wozzeck*. In the theatre (and, alas, also in films), one is literally bombarded with bad music – and the high level of the loudspeakers is enough to shatter one's eardrums. Why doesn't it work if it's quieter, or even silent? Silence is the most beautiful music.

The new aesthetics of musicals have also penetrated the actors' art and have had a negative influence on it. Actors sing and speak with lapel microphones, and everything is unbearably amplified. Are most people these days hard of hearing? (That would hardly be surprising given the level of noise we have to put up with on a daily basis.) In a theatre which is not too large, like the Berliner Ensemble or the Deutsches Theater, the actors should have no difficulty in making themselves heard without any artificial amplification. No such help was needed in the same auditoriums in the days of Max Reinhardt and Bertolt Brecht. The prerequisite is that the text should be articulated and declaimed in such a way that the entire audience, including those in the back row, can understand it. Acting and speaking of that kind used to be known as an art.

Much too much has been written, for and against, about *Regietheater*, or director's theatre. The phenomenon is by no means limited to Berlin: it rules the entire world of German-language theatre, from Zurich to Vienna. One can complain about its excess as vehemently as one likes – the triumphant progress of this passing fashion will hardly be affected. All the same, the fight against it should be kept up, in the name of the great authors. They may be immortal, but unfortunately they can still be wounded.

Berlin, November 2014

Andrea Barca – his life

A thick veil lies over the life of Andrea Barca. The diligent efforts of modern musicological research have so far failed to unearth any reliable clues, let alone any written reports about his existence. In all likelihood he was born between 1730 and 1735 in Marignolle (on the outskirts of Florence), and his parents and forefathers were *contadini*, or peasants.

He clearly cultivated a connection with Wolfgang Amadeus Mozart, and at the latter's private concert on 2 April 1770 at the Villa Poggio Imperiale in Florence he functioned as page-turner. Thenceforth, he decided to devote his life principally to the interpretation of Mozart's piano works. His enthusiasm and dedication also led him to Salzburg, where the dreaded local press greeted his appearance with no more than lukewarm praise.

Disillusioned, the musician returned to his homeland, where he presumably went on working as a composer and pianist. Among the numerous works that can be attributed to him, mention must be made of his masterpiece *La ribollita bruciata*, a *dramma giocoso* in two acts which may be regarded as a high-point in the history of Tuscan music.

The death of Andrea Barca – where, when and in what

circumstances he departed this life (if, indeed, he did . . .) – remains a mysterious, dark enigma.

Florence, 1998

The Ten Commandments for concertgoers

Performers are expected to give of their best under any circumstances. They owe it to the composer, to the public and – last but not least – to themselves. But what about the behaviour and responsibility of the audience, that almost invisible thousand-headed Caesar? Is it right to assume that a person can do as they please just because he or she has purchased a ticket? Unfortunately, very little has been done or said to educate people constructively on how they should listen to music. Most of the offenders have not the slightest idea of how a careless cough can destroy a crucial pause in a Schubert sonata, or can throw the performer off the rails when he is playing complex works like a Bach fugue or Beethoven's 'Hammerklavier' sonata from memory.

A live performance is a unique, unrepeatable event. Even the best recording of the same performance will not reproduce the true experience, since it lacks the visual aspect and the sensation of communal participation. Each member of the audience is an active partner in a process of re-creation. A sensitive performer immediately senses the attention level in the auditorium, and these vibrations – positive or negative – will influence the music-making. Since silence is the beginning and end of all music, it is absolutely imperative that listeners must be silent too.

The great composers have been thinking about a remedy and have come up with the following Ten Commandments:

1. Thou shalt not cough, sneeze or make other horrible noises with thy rhino-laryngeal organs. (There are people who seem to want to transform the concert hall into a hospital for lung diseases at a time of an acute epidemic. Those suffering from respiratory complaints would do better to stay at home in bed. Why infect your fellow human beings?)

2. Thou shalt hold thy tongue – in other words, not chatter to anyone.

3. Thou shalt not read the programme notes during the performance. (It precludes proper listening, and is most distracting to others. Luckily, in a darkened auditorium or theatre these sinners don't have much of a chance. The notes should preferably be read before or after the concert.)

4. Thou shalt not unwrap sweets, pastilles or other sugary items. (They may be intended to suppress coughing, but they are just as noisy and even more annoying.)

5. Thou shalt not leave the auditorium and bang the door. (A sudden attack of sickness, an irrepressible urge to visit the toilet, a fear of missing the last bus, train or tram are convincing necessities, but the exodus manifested by certain American audiences of Symphony Orchestra subscription series during the second half of the concert is difficult to justify.)

6. Thou shalt not sing or conduct – with either hands or feet. It's not your job!

7. Thou shalt not turn the pages loudly when following the performance from the score. (It is a most admirable virtue to follow the music, but not when it distracts one's neighbours. In the worst of all possible scenarios, the performers are panic-stricken at the thought of being surrounded by pure Beckmessers. At Lieder recitals the

singer and pianist have to put up with the excruciating noise of several hundred people turning the page in unison, as they try to follow the words.)

8. Thou shalt not take photographs – especially not with flash. (This is almost as bad as shooting the pianist – so let's not shoot him, please.)

9. Thou shalt not make unauthorised recordings – that is, without the consent of all the authorities involved. In addition, thou shalt switch off thy mobile phone and thy ticking, beeping digital watch. (Better still, do not take these high-tech objects along to the concert. Even better, do not own them in the first place.)

10. Thou shalt not applaud too soon. (This is of the utmost importance. Some pieces obviously invite an immediate spontaneous reaction of enthusiasm: a few of the Beethoven symphonies, Tchaikovsky's Fourth and Fifth, Brahms's G minor piano quartet. Many others, however, end quietly and require further silence after the last note has sounded. These moments of reflection and total repose are cruelly destroyed by the intrusion of premature applause. Bach's 'Goldberg' Variations, Beethoven's sonatas Op.109 and Op.111, Schubert's *Die Schöne Müllerin*, and *Winterreise*, Schumann's *Dichterliebe*, Wagner's *Die Walküre*, Mahler's Ninth Symphony – the list could go on for ever – are all works desperately in need of this 'sacred' self-communion. Certain people simply like showing off their education and cleverness, by knowing exactly when and how the piece ends. With their immature reaction they prove that they have understood absolutely nothing of the music's spiritual message. Some other works – Bach's Passions, Mozart's Requiem or Shostakovich's 15th string quartet – rule out applause altogether. Wouldn't it be wonderful if after

music like that the audience would simply stand up and remain silent for a few seconds? What is there to applaud?)

With the warmest recommendation for the observance of the above,

Bach, Haydn, Mozart, Beethoven, Schubert, Schumann, Chopin, Mendelssohn, Wagner, Brahms, Debussy, Janáček, Bartók

Postscript

The authors are fully aware of the sad reality that – as with the other more famous Ten Commandments – audiences will continue to cough, talk, read, unwrap sweets, leave and bang the door, sing and conduct, turn pages, take flash photographs, make pirate recordings, bring mobile phones and digital watches and applaud too soon . . .

Florence, October 1998

Encores[*]

It was 1977, my debut in the Golden Hall of the Musikverein in Vienna. I was to play Bartók's Third Piano Concerto with the Hungarian State Orchestra conducted by János Ferencsik – a great honour for a 23-year-old from Budapest. The performance went quite well, the audience seemed happy, there was plenty of applause. We were called back to the stage and took our bows, thanking the Viennese for their kind appreciation. The applause continued, and by the next

---

[*] Booklet notes to CD 'Encores After Beethoven', 2016 (ECM 1950).

curtain-call I felt a burning urge to play something to express my joy and gratitude. So I sat down at the piano and played a fast movement from a Haydn sonata. The response was enthusiastic, I was in Seventh Heaven. On approaching the stage entrance I suddenly noticed Ferencsik – he was the doyen of Hungarian conductors, and a real old maestro – standing at the door. 'Young man,' he said, 'mark my words. There is nothing worse than a prematurely given encore.' That left me feeling as though I'd taken a cold shower, but at the same time it was golden advice that I've never forgotten.

Encore, meaning 'more' or 'again', is a French word that has found its place in the English language. The French also like to use the Latin 'bis', which stands for 'twice'. With these calls of 'encore' or 'bis' the public shows its appreciation of the performance and expresses its desire to hear and see more.

In earlier times, polite applause was by no means a foregone conclusion. Booing and scandals were not unusual, and sometimes artists were showered with rotten eggs and fruit (according to the season). Audiences were more demanding, but also more knowledgeable. When Mozart premiered his piano concertos in the 1780s in Vienna, he often had to play slow movements again. Not the brilliant finales, but the most intimate and introspective pieces.

Today it has become customary to applaud politely even after mediocre or poor performances. In the Netherlands people habitually stand up at the end of a concert – not as a sign of particular recognition but as part of a local tradition. (On the other hand, in the US, a standing ovation signifies exceptional appreciation of the artist.)

Can we speak of success and failure at all? By what criteria are they measured? Luckily, there are very fine and subtle differences. One feels them the moment one steps onto the stage: the invisible tension and absolute attention in the hall, or their absence. We musicians are not machines or mechanical instruments. Each one of us has better or worse days. A good performer on a favourable day can encourage an unattentive audience to listen better, like Tamino taming the wild beasts with his flute.

The audience is not a passive, but a vitally active participant in the proceedings; it can help and inspire the performer to higher achievements, or can be hugely disturbing to him. Unlike studio recordings, live performances are unique and unrepeatable; they depend on the lively discourse between musicians and their listeners. For my part, I feel an inner need to share wonderful music with others, but this requires an audience that listens to it attentively and sensitively.

Encores, too, arise out of the same sense of communication. Ferencsik was right that it is better not to play them too early, and not to play too much. Some pianists reach the end of their official programme, come back onto the stage once, and immediately play a half-dozen encores, without anyone having invited them to do so. What leads them to think they have earned this success?

Concert programmes differ in character and content. A recital by Horowitz or Rubinstein was usually planned so that the first half contained weightier pieces, while the second was devoted to compositions of a lighter kind – these artists didn't want to overtax their audience. Then came the 'bonbons' – as many as possible – which is what the audience really came to hear. This, too, is great art, albeit of a kind that places the emphasis on the artist rather than the music. Entertainment on the highest level. Things were very different with Artur Schnabel: two or three Beethoven sonatas before the interval, and another two or three after it. Or an entire evening of Schubert. 'In my recitals the first half is just as boring as the second,' he used to say. But joking aside: demanding music draws a better class of audience.

This was the case with my cycle of the 32 Beethoven sonatas in the large hall of the Zurich Tonhalle. The recordings of the encores are documents of a long journey on which I was joined by the wonderful Zurich audience. What can one play after five Beethoven sonatas? For me it's essential not to think of mere entertainment, but rather to look for pieces that are closely related to the sonatas. Thus, Schubert's *Klavierstück* in E flat minor is a close relative of the trio from the third movement (in the same key) of Beethoven's Sonata Op 7. Or Schubert's C minor Allegretto which is a 'sister' of the second movement of Beethoven's Sonata Op.10 no.2 (dark shadows moving in octaves). With Mozart's *Eine kleine Gigue* K.574 I wanted to point out its kinship with the finale of that same sonata: they are both humorous fugal studies in sonata form. The 'Andante Favori' was originally intended as the second movement of the 'Waldstein' Sonata, so it is not such a bad idea to play it after the sonata.

Throughout his life, Beethoven studied the works of Bach and struggled with the art of writing fugues. The last movement of the 'Hammerklavier' Sonata is a towering example of this never-ending battle – a fugue *con alcune licenze* (with certain liberties). How an exemplary fugue *senza alcune licenze* must sound can be best observed and admired in Bach – hence my choice of his Prelude and Fugue in B flat minor from Book 1 of the *Well-Tempered Clavier*.

And how about the last three sonatas? In Thomas Mann's novel *Doktor Faustus* Professor Wendell Kretzschmar convincingly explains why, following the Arietta, Beethoven composed no further movement for the Sonata Op.III. With this movement he bade farewell to the piano sonata: *'Consummatum est'* – It is fulfilled. In this case, further movements or encores are out of place.

Only silence remains.

Index